The Perceived Role of the Military

Studies presented at the
Social Science Conference on
The Perceived Role of the
Military, France, 1970

Contributions to Military Sociology
Vol. 1

The Perceived Role
of the Military

Edited by
M.R. VAN GILS

1971
Rotterdam University Press

ISBN 90 237 62169

The chapters of this volume resulted from papers presented at a conference on 'The Perceived Role of the Military' held in France, September 21–25. The conference was sponsored by the Science Committee of the North Atlantic Treaty Organization.

Acknowledgements

The editor is most grateful to Drs. Jan Mans and Max van de Sandt for their assistance in preparing this volume and to Mrs. Anneke Horsman for the work she accomplished so well. Also his appreciation goes to Colonel René Vial, Centre d'Etudes de Sociologie Militaire, Paris and his Staff in managing the conference at which these papers were read.

Introduction

M.R. VAN GILS*

* Psychological Department, Dutch Steelworks Ltd. IJmuiden (Netherlands).

Introduction

This book contains a number of contributions to a social-scientific conference on 'The Perceived Role of the Military', held in France in September 1970. The topics dealt with are divergent, the most important vein throughout being the social-scientific analysis of the military organization and profession, and the relation of these to society as a whole. Particular attention is given to the influence of strategic, technological and social developments in the last three decades. The book has an interdisciplinary character: sociologists, political scientists, physicians, psychologists and military professionals have contributed to it.

The numerous spontaneous contributions to the afore-mentioned conference reflect the greatly increased interest for defence problems and for the institutions concerned. The necessity for this interest need scarcely be stressed, considering the present international tension. The twentieth century is already known as a period of extreme bloodshed, dominated by violence. There is still little prospect of improvement. When war and peace take so much of our attention the importance of augmenting our insight into the institutions which play a considerable role in such situations must be considered necessary. This certainly applies to the military forces themselves, which have been allocated the function of 'management of violence' and which play such an important role in the shaping of the foreign policy of so many countries.

There is a second reason, apart from this more general consideration, why it is relevant to analyse military institutions: the increasing deterioration in civil-military relations, of which there are various indications.

Smith[1], for instance, establishes that public opinion trends and selected service records show that in the United States the limited Korean and Vietnam wars engendered more disaffection and delegitimation than World War II. Further indications for this trend are the growing criticism (especially from the younger generations) of the structure and ideology of the defence establishment, the discussions on the military-industrial complex, the problems connected with military services, etc. These trends do not apply to the United States alone, but for almost all West European countries too. Efforts are made to gloss over the poor relations between the Military and Society, by maintaining that the forces are never popular in peace time and are always exposed to criticism at such times. These arguments, however, ignore the problems and fail to understand the entirely different situation into which both the forces and society as a whole have arrived. The contradiction now arises that the forces have indeed progressed, as Janowitz says, 'from a relatively self-contained organization to a complex and civilian interrelated agency', but that at the same time society has become more critical of the defence establishment and is less willing to accept what the military always considered as essential. The 'civilianization' of the military organization has made her 'task environments' – i.e. those parts of the environment which are relevant or potentially relevant to military goal setting and goal attainment[2] – more important and also more numerous. It is an environment over which the military organization has unsufficient control and it therefore has to deal with an increased number of uncertainty factors.

Schössler in his contribution to this volume deals with this question in which the institutional level of responsibility of the military organization has become more problematic than its pure technical and organizational function. An inadequate understanding of the problems arising at the institutional level, of the elements of the environment over which the military organization has no formal control, can lead to an increased tension between these two. A tension with possibly a number of unanticipated consequences, such as a further alienation of the Armed Forces from society or an increased political orientation and formation of the military elite in order to obtain their goals all the same. There can also be consequences in society, in the form of greater violence in the attempt to achieve certain objectives, and, at the same time, strong polarization of opinions and attitudes.

Anti-military sentiments as found among the youth in particular, and apparent too in other groups, cannot be made light of nor offset by a silent majority. They must be seen as an outcome of a new, but growing view of society. A view in which traditional military ideology and the related system of values and norms are questioned. This questioning is reinforced by events like My Lai, the publication of the secret Pentagon papers by the New York Times in June 1970, by the lack of clarity these days for non-military people as regards what military duty and function actually are and what a concept like military success still entails.

The current trend in civil-military relations is not favourable, for either the forces or society. And this trend may well continue, as long as the defence establishment has problems in adapting itself to the new requirements and conditions of the present-day world, as long as the professional military ideology has no new meaning. As Sarkesian says '... the military will have to develop a much more sophisticated and understanding approach in its relationships with society. The social causes of domestic ills, the motivations behind the psychedelic culture and its youth appeal, the impact of the mass media, the increasing participation of heretofore non-participatory groups in the political process, the influences these have on military culture; all of these factors (and more) will have to be studied and analysed, and become part of the educated military. This, in turn, will require a political propaganda campaign, judiciously intermingling the virtues and necessities of military service to the relevancies of the current culture'.[3] Like so many other groups in society the military must develop a certain political intuition and in its policy it should anticipate the consequences of this policy for society. This is all the more relevant for the military as society will test military decision making in a more critical way. This criticism is not directed at the military alone. Society has become more critical of the policy of all large scale organizations.

Bobrow's article in part IV of this book can be considered as an example of a more sophisticated approach to civil-military relations. Bobrow stresses the 'social learning perspective for the military'. The 'total institution' aspects of the military should allow for the trying out and the evaluation of social inventions in ways which are less feasible in civilian arenas. Use of the military for social learning can secure public satisfaction pay offs from resources allocated to the military.

Many of the contributions in this book are related to the changed role of the forces after 1945. They try to establish the consequences of these changes for the structure of the military organization, the characteristics of the military profession itself and civil-military relations.

The change in the role of the forces is the result of strategic, technological and social developments. Is one in fact correct in referring to a changed role? The new situation is characterised not so much by a fundamental change in make up as by the addition of new dimensions to the more traditional role and by a shift in emphasis between the roles. Changes which no doubt have made the military profession much more complex. Riddleberger[4] differentiates between six different military roles, which he calls 'marks of sovereignty (symbols of a national prestige), internal and external security, economic and social (as nation-building activities), and political (direct involvement in government) roles'. Each of these major roles is in turn sub-divided into two to four 'behaviors or actions'. For example, under 'internal security' Riddleberger considered patrol of the country-side, riot control, secret police actions and counter-insurgency operations. Under 'economic' he lists civil action, civil defence and disaster work, use of bureaucratic and managerial skills in the country's economy and the technical training of recruits etc.

In the Western world especially the array of functions of the forces has grown considerably. A multiplicity of goals and missions has come about, distinctly altering the traditional, rather uniform picture of the forces. Moreover, there are also decided differences from one culture to another as far as emphasis on the above-mentioned roles is concerned. Kurt Lang in his contribution (part II) deals with the consequences of these role changes on the occupational structure of the military. Also Dean Havron's article (part IV) on 'non-conventional educational requirements for the military' goes into these problems in more detail.

The resultant adaptation problems for the military are far from slight. There is an insistant necessity to find a new focus as regards integration of the military profession. A focus aimed not only at achieving technical expertise but seeking also a renewal of traditional ideologies, whereby propensities toward militarism (Vagts[5], 1959) are avoided and a balance with social developments is adequately reached.

The analysis of these adaptation processes forms a substantial part of sections I and II of this book. Section I enters into the Structural and Cultural Changes in Military Education. In the articles of Radway, Hartman, Preston, and Fauchois an analysis is given of the problems in military education resulting from a further diversification of and change in educational goals. Goals that to a certain extent conflict with each other. In particular Fauchois' article is a good illustration of problems that arise when the introduction of new technologies contradict traditional professional conceptions.

The research study of Mans and Van de Sandt underscores the impressions of the above mentioned authors.

In section II more attention is given to the structural changes in the military organization itself. The contributions of Schössler and Lang we already mentioned. Interesting is also Jackson's article in which he questions the justification of the military career as a distinctive professional career. His topic, which deals with aspects of a second military career is certainly one which deserves, especially in Western Europe, more attention.

In section III several more micro-sociological and social-psychological problems are discussed, whilst section IV deals with a number of aspects of the military and the political order.

NOTES

1. R. SMITH, Department of Sociology, University of California, Santa Barbara; *Disaffection, Delegitimation and Consequences, Aggregate Trends of World War II, Korea and Vietnam*, 24 pp.
2. J.D. THOMPSON, *Organizations in action.* McGraw-Hill 1967, pp. 27.
3. S.C. SARKESIAN, *The military image: myths and realities. A political perspective.* Paper delivered at the 66th Annual Meeting of the American Political Science Association, 1970.
4. P.B. RIDDLEBERGER, Military Roles in developing countries: an inventory of part research and analysis. In R.W. LITTLE (ed.), *A survey of military institutions,* 1969. Inter University Seminar on Armed Forces and Society.
5. A. VAGTS, *History of Militarism.* New York 1959.

Contents

STRUCTURAL AND CULTURAL CHANGES IN MILITARY EDUCATION

R.A. Preston/Military Academies in a Changing World: Possible
  Consequences of the Student Protest Movement   3
L.I. Radway/Recent Trends at American Service Academies   19
C.M.A. Hartman/The Service Academies as a Social System   39
J.H. Mans, M.A. van de Sandt/A Military Academy in
  Transition: A Survey Investigation   49
B. Fauchois/The Adaptation of Professional Soldiers to New
  Training Methods   71

SOCIAL AND TECHNOLOGICAL INFLUENCES ON MILITARY ORGANIZATION

J.A. Jackson/Military Training and Civilian Employment   81
H. Benninghaus, H. Renn, A. Rosner/Some Sociological Aspects
  of Recruitment, Vocational Training, and 'Second Career' of
  Long-Term Soldiers   93
K. Lang/Military Technology and Expertise: Some Chinks in the
  Armor   119
D. Schössler/The Functional Significance of the Military
  Socialization Process for the Internal Stability of the Military
  Organization   139
J.P. Thomas/The Mobility of Non-Commissioned Officers   149
M. Gatineaud/Evolution of the Military Community. 'Associate'
  Groups – Reference Groups   171
J. Garcette/Consequences of Specialization of Non-Commissioned
  Officers   181

LEADERSHIP, MORALE, MANAGEMENT

F. E. Fiedler/Do Leaders Really Learn Leadership?   191
M. J. M. Daniëls/Some Remarks on the Construction of an
   Instrument for the Assessment of Cadet Behavior   211
J. Brémond/The Collective Measure of Morale: Practical and
   Methodological Aspects of Periodic Evaluation in Military
   Surroundings   221
J. P. Moreigne/Military Management: A Fantasm or a Necessity?   235

THE MILITARY AND THE POLITICAL ORDER: AN EVALUATION FROM
A CIVIL-MILITARY RELATIONS POINT OF VIEW

R. D. McKinlay/Professionalization, Politicization and
   Civil-Military Relations   245
M. D. Feld/Professionalism and Politicalization: Notes on the
   Military and Civilian Control   267
D. R. Segal, M. W. Segal/Models of Civil-Military Relationships
   at the Elite Level   277
D. B. Bobrow/Adaptive Politics, Social Learning, and Military
   Institutions   293
M. D. Havron/Non-Conventional Educational Requirements for
   the Military   309
M. Lissak/The Israel Defence Forces as an Agent of Socialization
   and Education: A Research in Role-Expansion in a
   Democratic Society   325
C. C. Moskos jr./Structured Strain in a United Nations
   Constabulary Force   341
H. W. Tromp/The Assessment of the Military Mind: a Critical
   Comment on Methodology   359
R. Nauta/Armed Forces and Ideology   379

Structural and cultural changes in military education

Military Academies in a Changing World: Possible Consequences of the Student Protest Movement

R. A. PRESTON*

* Professor of History, Duke University, North Carolina, USA.

Since the Second World War, because of the compelling need to adapt to social and technical change, military academies have moved closer to the universities in curricula, teaching methods, academic standards, nature of faculty, and other respects.[1] But the universities have now come under pressure from student protest movements to make radical changes, including some that would be revolutionary. Some of these changes would conflict with the functions and purposes of a military academy. Have military academies reluctantly and belatedly modelled themselves on the universities only to find their model moving towards an unacceptable transformation? Does this mean that they will give up the policy of assimilation to the universities? That trend has always had strong opponents within the military hierarchy, and its reversal would find powerful support. Secondly what implications do these developments have for the preparation and production of officers for the armed forces and also for the relation of the forces to society?

The answer to some of these questions is inevitably highly speculative. But they must not be brushed on one side as not yet worthy of consideration because the danger seems slight. Six years ago it would have been regarded as fantasy that by 1970 many American universities would be in a virtual state of rebellion possibly with incalculable consequences not only for the future of the universities but also for American policy and the American system of government. It is therefore a policy of wisdom to enquire whether the production of officers, one of the props on which modern national states have been built, faces unforeseen difficulties in the near future. It is possible that the effects of the student protest movement on the academies may have results that are far greater and much more important than any change we have seen so far.

I. Before attempting to analyse the student protest movement for the purpose of assessing its consequences for the academies, we must first note some relevant features of the development of the academies and also some of the important features of the universities towards which they have recently been moving.

In Europe, from the Middle Ages until comparatively recent times, officers were always drawn from an upper social and economic class. Increasing specialization in the profession of armies in early modern times stressed and added what has been called since Janowitz the 'heroic tradition'. But formal institutional training in military academies did not become regular until the technological revolution of the eighteenth century, and even then at first only for technical officers[2]. Permanent establishment of academies for non-technical officers was a later development[3]; and because of the continuance of the aristocratic and heroic traditions these often had difficulty in maintaining adequate academic standards and even in giving effective military training[4]. In 1856 Sydney Herbert told the British House of Commons that it was believed that if a man was instructed in his duty 'he was likely to become a pedant and a bookworm, and no longer to be an active, zealous, handy officer'.[5]

In North America, where there was no traditional upper class to provide officers, and where West Point (founded 1802) and the Royal Military College of Canada (founded 1876) had therefore to attempt to draw recruits from the whole nation by some form of academic selection, the training of officers for all arms in a single institution[6] had the incidental effect of reinforcing the academic education of non-technical officers in order to supplement and match the technical standards of the academies. Social and technical factors thus co-operated to give greater emphasis to the general academic side of an officer's training. This was a first step towards the assimilation of the academies to the universities.

Increasing demand for technical proficiency even for non-technical officers, and the rapid democratization of society since 1945, has hastened these trends in America and has also introduced them in some parts of Europe where the aristocratic and heroic tradition has lingered. Some degree of general, as well as technical, education has come to be widely accepted as an essential part of every officer's training. It vies with selection on the basis of fighting qualities and with stress on combat training. It is generally believed that the modern officer must be an educated man; and it is even sometimes claimed that he has professional status like that of other 'learned professions'[7]. Technology has become at least as important as generalship in the winning of wars[8]. Multiplication of technical specialisation in the armed forces, and the decline of the value of a common-to-all-arms combat training (the infantry or line officer is now just one of many specialists), has further increased the proportion of general and scientific education which has become the most important common element in a military academy's curriculum.

These various trends, which have assimilated the military academy to the university, have had the effect of decreasing the proportion of time available in the curriculum for professional military training. The means by which the cadet is now best trained, in a way which still differentiates him from the university student, is by having him live a regimented life in barracks. The cadet wing, regiment, or battalion formation inculcates responsibility and discipline and provides experience in command. It has

6

become more important than formal class-room, barrack-square, or field military instruction for both military training and indoctrination[9].

The universities, to which military academies are thus tending to assimilate themselves, are very much older than the academies. Their foundation in the Middle Ages was one of the most important formative developments in the growth of Western Society. Their early achievements were due to successful claims for independence to protect free enquiry in theology, philosophy, and humane studies[10]. Formal civil technical education developed much later than the military technical education in the academies. Not until the late nineteenth and even the twentieth century did it manage to become entrenched in the universities[11], chiefly in order to enjoy advantages of freedom and independence and of association with other scholarly fields of endeavour.

It might seem that military academies cannot accept the university ideal of independence and full enquiry because they aim to indoctrinate as well as to educate. There will, in fact, always be areas of friction arising from the clash between these two functions. But this problem can be seen to be less serious when it is remembered that the ideal of academic freedom in the universities was rarely if ever attained in an absolute sense. The medieval university accepted Christian dogma as a basis of its scholarly effort. In later times rationalism has been the premise upon which intellectual effort is founded. In both cases these were qualifying conditions which in effect established guide lines within which freedom of enquiry operated. Without such guide lines academic life, teaching, and enquiry would have become chaotic and anarchic. Within these guide lines freedom was able to foster initiative. Similarly military academies can benefit from freedom of enquiry and teaching even though they accept some assumptions about the nature of society which establish guide lines for their teaching. Such assumptions conform loosely with the rationalist assumptions hitherto accepted by the western universities.

The student protest movement which we are to consider kicks against the rationalist guide lines within which the universities have hitherto operated[12]. Student protest is an old story in Continental Europe, Asia, and Latin America. What is different about it today is its world-wide incidence, and even more its remarkable outburst in English-speaking countries where it is a new phenomenon. While the student protest movement is too close to our time for definitive analysis, some things about it are clear. It is the work of a relatively small group of activists, what Seymour Lipset called the 'powerful two percent'[13]; but it can evoke support from a large minority or even a majority of the student body by playing on naïve youthful moralism and creating a violent confrontation. It aims to force the university to take a stand on controversial issues. It aims also to use the university as a hostage for political objectives. It presses for the introduction of 'relevant' matters into the curriculum. And it strives to gain control of the administration, the faculty and the curriculum in order to attain these ends. Success for the student protest movement would thus mean the abandonment of rationality, adherence to a new dogmatism, the politicisation of the universities, and the destruction of the tradition of freedom of enquiry[14].

At this point it should be noted that student control of universities is not an entirely new phenomenon. One of the two great medieval prototype universities, Bologna, was student controlled. The other, Paris, was a 'master' university. Paris proved to be, in the long run, much more effective[15]. Since the 1920's Central and South American universities have been largely under student control with serious consequences for the nature and quality of their achievement and progress. Far from becoming 'relevant' to society (which modern student protesters say they want) the Latin American universities have failed to adjust to the modern world, especially to meet technical needs[16]. These historic parallels have not attracted as much attention as they should in our present plight.

The threat posed by the student protest movement to academic development in military academies may seem limited to North America and therefore not a cause for serious concern in Europe. This is so partly because student protest has recently reached more extreme dimensions in the United States. Another consideration is that the North American academies, as suggested earlier, have moved further towards a very high concentration upon academic education as opposed to formal professional military training and are therefore more immediately threatened. But academies elsewhere will probably have to adapt themselves, like the North American academies, to the needs of wider military education to meet social and technical change. Some are in fact already planning to do this by stressing the 'managerial', rather than the 'heroic', side of officer preparation. In these circumstances, and as student protest is even more deeply rooted in other parts of the world than it is in North America, military academies everywhere may also have to face the consequences of student unrest in the not too distant future.

II. Student activism like that seen recently on American university campuses is obviously completely unacceptable in military academies

8

and it has not yet appeared there. Quite apart from the fact that its objectives are often opposed to the military purposes for which the academies exist, its methods of agitation, demonstration, confrontation with authority, strikes, personal violence, and destruction have no place in a disciplined community. Its attempts to introduce politics into the curriculum, and to use the university as a political hostage or weapon, run directly counter to the principle that soldiers must not engage in activity of a political nature. Furthermore, proposals for student control of the decision-making process governing the content of the curriculum, and in the appointment and promotion of faculty, could not be tolerated in a military system especially in one in which education and training is designed to provide the state with reliable officers with certain specific qualifications and qualities. It is just as necessary in the academies, as it is in the universities, to learn student reaction to academy courses and teachers; but any attempt to formalize the means of obtaining information on these points would tend to make the feed-back rigid and sterile and would tend to politicize both student and faculty.

The threat to the academies is not yet of immediate concern. Nevertheless, it is probably wise to argue on the assumption that, even if immediate problems like the Viet Nam war are settled, campus political demonstrations, attempts to change the structure of the university, and perhaps even violence, will continue for a long time in the United States unless severe repression is instituted. As student activism has a longer history elsewhere, it seems even less likely to cool down in many other places. The incoming class of freshmen in the United States in 1970 is said to be as much alienated from the class now graduating from the universities as the latter is from preceding generations. Consideration of the possible consequences of student unrest for military academies must therefore be based on the premise that it will not soon decline and in fact that it may increase. It may also be assumed that, even if the war in the Far East were to cease to be an issue, the student movement would still probably include opposition to all forms of military institutions and activity. In fact it might switch its emphasis from attacking American involvement in the Far East to attacking all other forms of American involvement overseas on the grounds that it is 'imperialist', or that domestic needs are more urgent. NATO might then become the chief target[17].

So far pacifist and anti-war activity in student campaigns in the United States has been directed against recruiting by companies manufacturing certain kinds of weapons, against recruiting for the armed services and war-associated government organizations and industrial firms, and against the presence on the campus of military research projects and of officer training units. In so far as the latter is concerned, a decisive student victory would affect the academies by cutting down the supply of officers with a university-type education that enter the armed forces. It would leave the academies, short courses, and promotion from the ranks, as the only sources of supply. It would make the preservation of academic standards in the academies all the more necessary.

It is obvious that military academies, because of certain built-in factors, have a considerable degree of immunity against student unrest. They are much smaller than the great universities where much of the trouble has occurred. Their students and faculty are hand-picked and are conditioned against political activism by the circumstances of their selection, admission, and appointment. Cadet leaders are appointed and not elected. A cadet, and possibly also faculty member, could probably be summarily dismissed merely for suspected undesirable political activity without his having recourse to appeal. Another factor is that military academies are located far from, or more clearly distinct from, urban communities. For this reason, and because of the wearing of uniforms, the presence of intruders and strangers is quickly noticed. Cadets therefore are less exposed than university students to external influences. Furthermore, as many are engineering students, they have little time for, and also possibly less interest in, social problems; and as all cadets live under supervision it would be difficult for individuals to devote as much time as do university radicals to political agitation, secret or otherwise, instead of to their academic work and military duties.

On the other hand, almost all young people sympathise with certain aspects of the youth protest movement, with some of its ideals if not with all of its objectives and methods. Youth has a natural attraction for youth when there is a conflict with older people and the establishment. While campus conservatives, at present a small minority, seem to be exceptions to this rule, many of them are noticeably as rabid and psychopathic as their rivals on the extreme student left. Almost all young people are more emotional than their elders, more idealistic, and more prone to see thing in harsh black and white. Furthermore cadets now come from all classes in society. They can be as concerned about contemporary society as their civilian counterparts. They straddle a broad range of the political spectrum. They include wide differences of political opinion, though they are admittedly a little more conservative than the mass of university students. Although the vast majority of cadets are nevertheless moderates in the middle of the road politically, or are even apolitical, and although indoctrination brings a considerable degree of uniformity to a cadet's outlook on political and social questions, academy education

10

does not eliminate shades of opinion and certain forms of dissent. Cadets are educated so that they can think for themselves and discussion about current problems is encouraged. But it is unlikely that they will think the way their seniors and elders do.

It has been seen that on the campuses many of the 'silent majority' may turn out in sympathy with radical student activists in certain circumstances. The implications of this for military academies may not be great but should not be entirely overlooked. The military establishment as a whole is not as die-hard conservative as it once was. Expansion has brought in various shades of political opinion. Circumstances might swing the military silent majority one way or another overnight. And cadets might move with it or act independently.

An indirect consequence of the student protest movement must be noted at this point. If youth continues to be alienated, the number of suitable young men willing to apply for entry to the academies could decline. As admission is based on merit, the quality of entry might then decrease. Furthermore, if the spirit of youthful individualism and of student opposition to the establishment continues to rage, rigorous indoctrination of recruits will become even more necessary, but on the other hand fewer young men will be prepared to accept it. The next classes of recruits have been raised by parents who are even more permissive than those of their predecessors. It is not surprising that in some places wastage rates among recruits have already risen sharply. However, since the University Reserve Officer Training unit may become less attractive to students, many able applicants for a military career who would have normally chosen that route to a commission might fall back on the academies. As a result of all these various things the cadet population of the future will probably tend to be more dedicated, more military, more patriotic, more conservative, and probably also more reactionary. Furthermore as a military career is often still a path to higher social status, military academies will increasingly recruit from lower economic strata. These inputs, as in the universities, are potentially recruits for rightist resistance to any radical movements that might oppose their upward social mobility[18].

Student protest movements have, as yet, had no significant repercussions in the academies. But, although much that has been said so far would seem to indicate that cadets are unlikely to participate significantly in any form of protest or agitation for change, and certainly not in line with radical thought, several things should be noted. As everyone who has ever had anything to do with a cadet college knows, cadets are not passive beings. They are continually pressing for concessions and changes and are not necessarily scrupulous about sticking to proper channels of communication or to legal methods of persuasion. They will try to 'get away' with everything they can. Not all are law-abiding citizens. Thus drugs have already appeared in at least one of the academies where drug takers had to be expelled. There have also already been many cadet requests for change in traditional policies and practices, and some of these are in accordance with trends in modern youth's life-styles. Many of these requests date back before the time when student protest became vigorous; and these tend to be less idealistic in substance and more self interested than the demands of university students. However it is noticeable that in all the American academies some cadets are now beginning to question the wisdom of American military policy in Viet Nam; and some are beginning to reject the official stance on many other issues. Cadets are also becoming aware that they are in danger of getting out of step with their peers; and some are not prepared to accept that situation.

Although authorities do not always advertise it, the academies are already moving in a direction that conforms with changes elsewhere. And in many cases concessions have been made partly as a result of the belief that it was wise to meet requests half-way before they became confrontations. Minority groups are being admitted in larger numbers. There has been experimentation with curricula and with regulations, not as much as on university campuses, but perhaps in ways that even more significant since the academies have been more conservative in the past. There are greater concentrations in courses, and more electives. There is a tendency to do away with the school-type of instruction that has often prevailed. Furthermore in some places cadets are getting longer leaves, permission to keep cars, to drink alcohol on the base or off it, to wear civilian clothes more freely, and to marry before graduation. Cadet requests for a modification of the regulation close haircut has been harder to concede, but the close skinhead crop for RMC recruits was modified in 1970 and u.s. Air Force sideburns have been officially lengthened. Perhaps some cadets everywhere, like some American military personnel, have used wigs when off-duty! The Plebe system in the American academies has been modified. In RMC cadet representatives have been added to an important faculty board with voting privileges. While the attempt of one cadet journal to claim the freedom of the press for criticism of the administration of the academy was not tolerated, cadet journalists often try to go as far as they can; but cadet papers are still very different from the irresponsible journalism that appears on every American university campus. These are clear indications that cadet attitudes

12

are being watched carefully by the authorities and that attempts are being made to forestall the intrusion of student activism into the academies.

Remembering this evidence of change in the academies, one important point must be noticed. It has been shown above that the basic method of professional military training in a cadet college is now through the exercise or responsibility and power by cadet officers. This is, however, a form of 'cadet power' that is potentially more efficient and more effective than any 'student power' ever seen on a campus. Cadets have a capacity for organisation and planning that cannot be equalled in universities where habits and practices of discipline do not exist on the same scale. Furthermore, as traditions are handed on from class to class, a most extraordinary spirit of corporate responsibility for the maintenance of what the cadets regard as the essential virtues of the academy is often developed. These include the Honor Codes in the United States, 'Truth, Duty, Valour' in Canada, and also the traditional methods of recruit indoctrination. It is significant that at times in the history of the Royal Military College of Canada the cadets came to believe that they, and not the Commandant and his staff, who were thought too subservient to politicians and bureaucrats in Ottawa and to 'fond mammas', were the bearers and guardians of the College's great traditions. They therefore on these occasions attempted to ensure the preservation of valued traditions in their own ways despite specific orders to the contrary. An incident which brought the most notorious of these cases to public notice was connected with recruit indoctrination that had degenerated into hazing[19]. A similar situation has recently arisen at Duntroon where what the Australian cadets call 'bastardization' got out of hand, possibly because seniors were resentful of juniors who, as a result of an academic change, would receive a university degree on graduation that had been withheld from them[20]; but probably also because they felt that these innovations would weaken the military virtues of the college. The cheating scandals in two of the American military academies in connection with college athletic teams are also evidence of the great strength of 'cadet power' when cadet interests seem to be at stake.

The expression of 'cadet power' would not necessarily react in sympathy with 'student power' in the universities. It might, however, react violently against student radicalism or against a serious decline in social order. History shows that cadet-activism can develop a long way before the academy staff is aware of it, or, more probably, before it is willing to admit its existence. Of course we are still very far from seeing the cadet battalions of military colleges in the West plotting revolt, as

Nasser and his class-mates did in Egypt long before they seized power: in the United States, and also in many other Western countries the whole ethos of the military establishment stands against it. But the subordination of the military to civil control is more uncertain now than it was when Huntington questioned that it was an effective bulwark of American democracy in his *The Soldier and the State* in 1957. Without subscribing to current radical charges about power of the American military-industrial complex, it is possible for some people to suspect that in the United States the higher direction of military policy has become less susceptible to civil control than it is in some other democracies. If social order in the United States continues to deteriorate alarmingly, a demand for the assertion of law and order might create a situation in which 'cadet power' in the academies might assume new significance. Academy authorities are inclined to say, 'it can't happen here'. But that is exactly what was said in the Ivy League colleges a year or so ago; and the explosions which eventually came in them were bigger than anywhere else.

Even though these forebodings may not merit any present action, it is important that we take notice of one other possible consequence of the student revolt. Disorder in the Universities, some of it encouraged by value-laden social science, might lead military authorities to reverse the trend towards assimilation to the university pattern. In view of the increasing importance of technology they would be unlikely to reduce the engineering and scientific content of the academy curriculum. But they might restrict the teaching of humane and social studies. However, more emphasis on military subjects would affect all academic studies, including science and engineering.

But what the cadet needs to enable him to understand and face the difficult social and political problems of present-day society is not less, but more, history, political science, psychology, sociology, moral philosophy, and ethics, even though these are the very disciplines, when infused with radical values camouflaged as science, that have spawned many of the student radicals and activists in the universities. Properly studied, under instructors who are not governed by dogmas and who insist upon academic discipline, these subjects can continue to be advantageous and not dangerous. Western liberalism has nothing to fear but its own fears. Social studies in the military academies can become one of its bulwarks. It would be a tragedy for the academies if the reaction against student activism led to a restriction of their use for the education of potential officers.

A Persian scholar, Alberuni, reporting on India in the eleventh century, talked of the conditions necessary for the advancement of learning. He

14

said, 'To do this [foster science] is, in the first instance, the duty of those who rule..., of kings and princes. For they alone can free the minds of scholars from the daily anxieties.... The present times, however, are not of this kind. They are the very opposite...'[21]. It might thus come to be the case in the future that only in military academies will one get stability and freedom from pressures to pursue scholarly activity. It is thus even possible that, if conditions decline seriously in the universities and free thought is eliminated as the radicals desire, it might be preserved in what some might now think are the most unlikely of places, the military academies of the West. Stranger things have happened.

However it must also be remembered that student rebels are violently critical of the technological approach to 'the manipulation of peoples' lives' by social science techniques. It is not unlikely that the military and the military academies might stress these aspects of social studies even more than they do at present. But in fact behaviourist studies can fail to develop a real understanding of human problems and of the complexity of society. Social studies might thus be maintained in the academies as the tools of military technology in a fashion not unlike their use for propaganda and indoctrination in Marxist states. They would be window-dressing rather than an offering of quality goods in a world in which scholarship was in decline. The military academies would be repositories of debased conservative scholarly traditions by means of which a military-industrial complex could delude itself that it was preserving vital elements of civilization from decay wherever military virtues and defence were still not ignored or decried.

Two elements can be said to be essential for the attainment of the goals of a military academy apart from the indisputable need for maintaining emphasis on quality education in science and technology. The first is the continued fostering of cadet responsibility; and the second is the encouragement of free thought and social studies. But both of these two elements are capable of leading to dangerous forms of cadet power and activism if they are not adequately directed and controlled. In these circumstances it is clear that the quality of the administration of cadet academies is likely to be even more important in the future than it has been in the past.

15

NOTES

1. For a discussion of trends in this direction in the United States and Britain see P. H. PARTRIDGE, *Educating for the Profession of Arms* (Canberra: Canberra Papers on Strategy and Defence, No. 5, 1969). Proposals for further academic development at Sandhurst recommended by the Howard-English Committee in Britain were held up because of financial stringency. See also W. R. SAWYER, 'The Present Four-Year Course at the Royal Military College of Canada', *R.M.C. Review* 33 (1951), pp. 123–6.

2. See Louis ROUSSELET, *Nos grandes écoles militaires* (Paris: Libraire Hachette, 1888); *La Grande Encyclopédie* (Paris: Larousse, n.d.), 15: 410.

3. Alfred VAGTS, *A History of Militarism* (New York: Norton, 1937) pp. 53–55; for West Point see Sydney FORMAN, 'Why the U.S. Military Academy was established in 1802', *Military Affairs*, XXIX (1965), p. 18.

4. *E.g.*, Great Britain, *Sessional Papers*, C. 3818 (1883), C. 5793 (1889), Cmd. 2031 (1924).

5. Sydney HERBERT, *Military Education: Speech in the House of Commons on the Education and Instruction of the Officers in the Army* (London: J. Ridgway, 1856), pp. 13–14.

6. FORMAN, pp. 16, 26; Richard A. PRESTON, *Canada's RMC: A History of the Royal Military College* (Toronto: University of Toronto Press, 1969), pp. 16–19.

7. Samuel P. HUNTINGTON, *The Soldier and the State: The Theory and Politics of Civil-Military Relations* (Cambridge, Mass.: Harvard University Press, 1957), p. 256. The limitations of this professionalism are shown in Thomas C. SCHELLING, *The Strategy of Conflict* (Cambridge, Mass., Harvard University Press 1966), p. 9.

8. Eugene M. ERMINE, 'Technological changes and western military thought', *Military Affairs*, 24 (Spring, 1960), pp. 7–8.

9. PRESTON, pp. 131–7, 193–7, 246–8, 269–73, 333–34. As a result of a recent outcry 'bastardization', as recruit indoctrination is called at Duntroon, has been abolished. Complete elimination of recruit indoctrination by seniors would destroy much of the value of the Australian military college.

10. F. M. POWICKE and A. B. EMDEN (eds.), *The Universities of Europe in the Middle Ages by the Late Hastings Rashdall* (Oxford, Oxford University Press, 1936), I, 204, *et passim*.

11. Lord BOWDEN, 'Science, society, and the university', in Murray ROSS (ed.), *Science and the University* (Toronto: Macmillan, 1967), pp. 8–11.

12. There are many books about the new student protest. Among them are, Daniel BELL and Irving KRISTOL (eds.), *Confrontation: the Student Rebellion and the Universities* (New York: Basic Books, 1968); Gerald F. McGUIGAN, *Student Protest* (Toronto: Methuen, 1968); Barbara and John EHRENREICH, *Long March, Short Spring: The Student Uprising at Home and Abroad* (New York: *Monthly Review*, 1969); Stephen SPENDER, *The Year of the Young Rebels* (New York: Random House, 1968); Lewis S. FEUER, *The Conflict of Generations: The Character and Significance of Student Movements* (New York: Basic Books, 1969); The Embattled University, *Daedalus*, V, 99 (Winter, 1970). An issue of *Horizons* (Spring 1970) is devoted to the idea that the philosophy of the New Left is a negation of rationalism. Geoffrey ELTON, a Cambridge historian, in a B.B.C. talk suggested that the universities may be destroyed (*Listener*, March 27, 1969).

13. In 'The Activists: A Profile', in BELL and KRISTOL, *Confrontation;* see also Stephen SPENDER, p. 22.
14. See especially FEUER, *Conflict of Generations*, and Richard E. PETERSON, 'The Student Left in American Higher Education', *Daedalus*, 97 (Winter, 1968), pp. 294–317; David ZIRNKELT, 'A Student Manifesto: In Search of a Real and Human Educational Alternative', in McGUIGAN, *Student Protest*, p. 53; Steven J. HELMAN, 'Youth and Foreign Policy', *Foreign Affairs*, 48 (April, 1970), pp. 414–427, says that campus Liberals have only the vague desire that the United States should 'cease being bad' and that the New Left seeks a revolution to seize control and therefore opposes all aspects of American foreign policy, even those which are in conformity with its professed goals. See also Alexander COCHRANE and Robert BLACKBURN, *Student Power: Problems, Diagnosis, Action* (Harmondsworth: Penguin, 1969) which describes student objectives as a mass of contradictions.
15. Jacques BARZUN, 'Tomorrow's university back to the Middle Ages: Student Power at Bologna and Paris', *Saturday Review*, 52 (November 15, 1969), pp. 23–25. V. R. CARDOZIN, 'Student Power in the Medieval Universities', *Personnel and Guidance Journal*, 46 (June, 1968), pp. 944–948. For a discussion of student power in the medieval universities see RASHDALL, II, pp. 58–60, and also D. VICENTE DE LA FUENTE, *Historia de las universidades en España* (Madrid, 1884) II, p. 37 where it is said that the effect of student power was to block all attempts at reform. See also George M. ADDY, *The Enlightenment in the University of Salamanca* (Durham, Duke University Press, 1966), pp. 15–18.
16. Michael Edmund BURKE, *The National University of Mexico, 1910–1914* (M.A. Thesis, Duke University, 1966), pp. 81, 86–7, 103.
17. An article in *Economist*, entitled 'Students: N.A.T.O. Here We Come', said that N.A.T.O. was the target of student radicals in 1969 (v. 227, May 4, 1968, p. 31); but the attack did not amount to much in that year.
18. On the middle class origins of student protest and the potential lash-back from students of working class and immigrant origins see John SCHAAR and Sheldon WOLIN, 'Education and the Technological Society', in *New York Review of Books* 13:6 (Oct. 9, 1969) pp. 3–4 and Christopher LASCH and Eugene GENOVESE, 'The Education and the University we now need', *Ibid.*, pp. 25–26.
19. PRESTON, *Canada's RMC*, pp. 238–46.
20. S. BENNETT, 'Changes in Academic Courses of the Royal Military College', *Australian Quarterly*, 4 (December 1969), pp. 49–58.
21. Edward C. SACHAU (ed.), *Alberuni's India* (London: Kegan, Paul, Trench, and Trueben, 1910), I, p. 152.

17

Recent Trends at American Service Academies

L.I. RADWAY*

* Professor of Government, Dartmouth College, New Hampshire, USA.

Although the Air Force, Military, and Naval Academies produce only a small fraction of all newly commissioned officers (3% in 1969)[1], they are of great importance in the recruitment and socialization of the American military elite; for this minority of officers sets standards for the entire profession of arms; its members are far more likely to devote a lifetime of service to a military career[2]; and they will eventually hold a lion's share of rank and responsibility in the armed forces.

The impact of these service academies on state and society depends, among other things, on the kind of students they attract and the kind of experience these students subsequently undergo. In the United States the first of these variables appears to count for more than the second, i.e. self-selection into an academy seems to be a more important determinant of future attitudes than anything that goes on there[3]. For this reason the analysis that follows will begin with an examination of the raw material drawn to these institutions.

The following is based largely on West Point, since the writer has more information on that institution than on the other two.

West Point tends to attract upward-mobile youngsters from medium-sized cities who have to depend on their merits to achieve success and who, in Lovell's words, have already met the challenge of academic work, peer-group relations, and athletic competition[4]. They are more ambitious, forceful, hard-driving and dominant than civilian undergraduates, and admission into an academy promises them a good education and leadership status in a historic profession. Members of West Point's Class of 1973 were more likely than their civilian peers to want to keep up with public affairs, assume administrative responsibility, become community leaders, and obtain recognition from others[5]. Only a distinct minority of cadets can be described as moody, arty, or shy. More tend to see themselves as outgoing friendly people who 'do the work but are not that serious as students'.[6]

It is also clear that West Point entrants are less libertarian than civilian students. Lovell concludes that they are less likely to be 'turned off' by an emphasis on authority, conformity, tradition, or patriotism. The differences are not great but they are consistent. The Class of 1973, compared to civilian undergraduates, was less likely to argue with teachers and less likely to think students should participate in designing curricula or evaluating faculty. It was more likely to support the regulation of student publications, guest speakers, and off-campus behavior. It was

21

more likely to attend religious services. The expressed political preferences of cadets were also distinctive. On a five-point scale, they were more likely than civilian students to describe themselves as 'strongly conservative' (5,4%) or 'moderately conservative' (33,8%), and less likely to describe themselves as 'liberal' (20,4%) or 'left' (0,9%). And while civilians expected to get more liberal during four years of college, cadets expected to become less so! Cadets were less inclined to want to liberalize divorce, legalize marijuana, coddle criminals, abolish capital punishment, or concede the right to publish all scientific findings. They were less interested in Federal protection of consumers or aid for the disadvantaged; they were more interested in Federal control of student activists. During their high school years significantly fewer had protested against racial discrimination or against American military policy.[7]

With the reservation that the data are about ten years old, material is also available to indicate that cadets hold moderately 'hardnosed' views on foreign affairs. When West Pointers were compared with a group of Dartmouth undergraduates heavily weighted by the inclusion of ROTC students, more of them felt total war likely in the next fifteen years. Although the differences were less, cadets led in attributing neutralism to lack of moral fibre or to communist influence in neutral nations. More felt that the Korean War illustrated the desire of communists to conquer the world and that American forces were unnecessarily denied victory in that conflict.[8]

To be sure, none of the foregoing means that cadets are out of the mainstream of American opinion. As Lovell noted shrewdly, a comparison with Gallup poll figures on the likehood of major war suggests that it was the Dartmouth students who were deviant and the West Point cadets who were closer to adult opinion. Nevertheless, the comparisons made above become significant when it is recalled that graduates of institutions like Dartmouth often hold in the national security establishment. For the same reason it is important to note other differences between senior civilian officials and the cadets who are destined to become senior military officials.

Civilian Federal executives are far more likely to come from urban or suburban upper-middle class families. More than 50% of the under secretaries and assistant secretaries appointed by President Kennedy were born in metropolitan areas.[9] In a larger group of political executives who served between 1933 and 1965, over 20% had attended one of eighteen famous residential preparatory schools in the East; if the analysis is confined to national security agencies, the proportion rises to 30–40%.[10] The civilian appointee is less likely to be Catholic, twice as likely to belong to a high-status Protestant denomination, and twice as likely to be a Jew.[11] Since many political appointees are lawyers – 44% in the survey just cited – they tend to rank high in verbal skill, and this is one attribute in which West Point entrants score below students in university-related colleges.

Finally, modest but suggestive data are available on differences between entering cadets and new Foreign Service Officers.

While there is little difference in economic status, FSO's are more than twice as likely to come from urban areas, six times as likely to come from New England, and far less likely to come from the South.[12] They are half as likely to be Catholic. In describing themselves they employ such phrases as 'cultured', 'intellectual', 'sophisticated', 'less likely to be middle-brow', 'rebellious', and 'less likely to be cooperative'.[13] This is not the image which West Point cadets have of themselves; and while the latter are much younger, it is unlikely that the passage of four or five years would increase significantly their tendency to resort to such language. Finally, Harr notes that 75% of all mature FSO's describe themselves as 'somewhat liberal' or 'liberal' in political orientation.[14]

THE CHALLENGE TO COMBAT VIRTUES

No one really knows what effect the service academies have on entering students.[15] My hunch is that before World War II they were more likely to exaggerate the differences noted above, and, more generally, to widen the gap between military and civilian undergraduate experience; and that the converse has been true in more recent years. The argument here is speculative and complex. It begins with an analysis of professional and institutional aims, and especially of their growing complexity.

Armed forces leaders have always required two sets of virtues. One consists of skills and attitudes useful in battle, the other of skills and attitudes useful in coping with the larger social and technological environment.

Combat leadership requires an ability to inspire a special category of men under special conditions. Particularly in the army, combat units draw personnel of little education and low social status. Even if few will ever hear a shot fired in anger, all must be taught to persevere in the face of

23

confusion and danger; for the influence exerted by the prospect or memory of battle is not greatly diminished by the rarity of the contingency itself. And human beings must be *trained* to overcome egoism and fear; it does not come naturally. Hence adamant insistence on loyalty, unity, courage, obedience, hardiness, and zeal. In no man are such qualities much enhanced by long study or reasoned argument, least of all in the underclasses who loom so large in combat outfits. They are enhanced instead by discipline, by symbol and, above all, by personnel example. Moreover, in a nation where Spartan attributes are in short supply, any institution which feels a need for them must seek some protection by isolating itself from civilian society.

The converse is true of ability to cope with the larger environment. In Janowitz's terms, this rests on 'managerial' rather than 'heroic' qualities.[16] But it illuminates some issues of military education to introduce a further distinction between what is required to deal with the scientific and technological environment, and what is required to deal with the socio-political environment. In both cases the civilian world is likely to value the necessary skills more highly than it values combat virtues, and it more often tries to develop them by education. Accordingly, military institutions which also want to develop them are more likely to try to stay in touch with civilian society.

The relative emphasis given to combat skills, and to what I shall call techno-social skills, depends on several factors, among them rank[17], echelon, and type of unit. The pressure for intrepid conduct is felt more strongly by paratroopers than by members of a sterilization and bath company, and more by Marine fighter pilots and platoon leaders than by flag officers at higher headquarters. Less obviously, it has varied with social class. The aristocrats, who led European armies gloried in 'a hard gallop, a gallant fight, and a full jug'.[18] They preferred brawn to brain, and character to intellect, especially because they judged character to be an elusive virtue which they alone shared – like ignorance, a mark of birth! Education, on the other hand, was a weapon of the rising middle class, an accomplishment to be scorned, or a threat to be fought. Thus in England the staff-college graduate was not favored so much as 'that splendid chap, the regimental officer'; and until well into the 19th century naval officers were trained by taking youngsters between the ages of 12 and 14 and putting them on ships. The history of military education, Barnett notes, has been a tug-of-war between two images: one conceives of the soldier as a fighting man, the other as a manager. The claims of the

24

manager are now pressed vigorously. Given more highly educated enlisted personnel, given the nature of modern conflict with its sophisticated and costly weapons and inexorable political constraints, it is hard to preserve the priority accorded to combat virtues in an earlier age. Yet it is just as obvious that those virtues are not obsolete. So the tug-of-war continues. Within the services academies it is reflected in competing codes of behavior. As an Air Force Academy statement put it:

'The Academy must fuse two potentially conflicting values: on the one hand the spirit of intellectual integrity and inquiry, which may downgrade deference to authority unless rationally supported, and on the other hand, the spirit of military loyalty and discipline, which sometimes accents deference to authority without rational justification'.[19]

In recent years, many forces have tended to increase the emphasis on intellectual pursuits at the expense of military training, athletics and, to some extent, traditional character-building activities. Entering students are more demanding, partly because high schools are improving, partly because service academy admissions procedures are more rigorous. The Superintendent of the Air Force Academy stated that the most important reason for the introduction of academic majors and M.A. programs was to provide an incentive for better students. Faculty members are also increasingly demanding. In the case of military faculty, inadequate educational standards lead more quickly to low morale; in the case of civilian faculty, to resignation.

A third potent force is service rivalry. The intensely competitive staffs of the academies are highly sensitive to each other's standing. Information is exchanged at many levels and innovations can pass from one institution to another at stunning speed.

Also important is the growing trend to graduate study. Most of today's service academy students eventually will earn an advanced degree; and while in the past graduate work was rarely started until mid-career, beginning with the Air Force Academy in 1963 each institution now places top students in Master's programs shortly after graduation[20]. Of the midshipmen who completed Annapolis in 1968, about one hundred proceed directly to such universities as Berkeley, Cal. Tech, Colombia, MIT, Michigan, North Carolina, Princeton, and Stanford. Of the Air Force Academy Class of 1969, one hundred and twenty – including 90% of the top tenth of the class – went to graduate school. The career plan for Army officers is such that fewer West Pointers begin advanced study immediately, but 75% will eventually proceed to the Master's level or higher.

Curricular developments at each academy reflect the growing emphasis on intellectual activity. To be sure, the service academies continue outrageously to overschedule the time of their students. They require from 15 to 20% more credit hours than civilian universities, and they pile time-consuming administrative chores on top of athletics, professional training, and their mixed engineering – liberal arts curricula. Since World War II they have added to already heavy programs such new subjects as: orbital mechanics, systems analysis, modern Africa, mathematical logic, oceanography, family relations, communications theory, ethnology, computer science, international organization, space vehicle design, music, microbiology, advanced Chinese, industrial psychology and unconventional war.

In desperation, finally, each academy was finally forced to modify its tradition/policy of a largely common course of study. To be sure, each continues to prescribe certain subjects. But it now permits students to choose among individual electives and 'major' fields of study or 'areas' of concentration. This departure from the lock-step system has been dictated by a need to come to grips with the new techno-social environment without demoralizing the young.

It is unwise to attempt to be precise at this point because detailed arrangements change almost annually. The Naval Academy now offers majors in about two dozen fields, e.g. marine engineering, economics, chemistry, and Far Eastern studies. It also offers the option of two degrees – the Bachelor of Science in Engineering or the straight Bachelor of Science. The Air Force Academy offers a slightly larger number of majors, each requiring a somewhat larger number of courses. The Military Academy has been a trifle more circumspect. Its alumni continue to favor a generalized program with stress on mathematics, science, and engineering. It is also possible, though less certain, that the prospects of curricular specialization reactivates fear of a divided army.[21] West Point now offers four areas of concentration – applied science and engineering, basic science, humanities, and national security and public affairs. These are divided into 22 'fields'. Students who prefer not to choose any area or field may forego a concentration and select any elective courses whatsoever. A quota system is used to ensure that no more than 10% of the cadets will concentrate in the humanities, and no more than 35% in any other area.

26

These changes have been accompanied by a great increase in the number of courses offered. The result is that curricula resemble those of civilian colleges more than before. So do instructional methods. Of course, each academy still emphasizes small sections rather than large lectures. Moreover, prepackaged materials, textbooks, recitations and tests are still more in evidence than at the strongest civilian institutions. But the use of paperback books is growing, and there is a trend to fewer and more comprehensive examinations, seminar work, independent research and honors programs. The Trident Program, adopted by Annapolis in 1963, enables a few midshipmen to be excused from most senior year courses in order to undertake a major research project, usually in science or engineering.

Finally, the departmental structure of the academies, which has implications for the distribution of power and therefore for the direction of change, is coming to resemble that of civilian institutions more closely. It is true that West Point and Annapolis, as recently as 1969, tucked away work in philosophy, music and art among their offerings in literature.[22] But West Point has now divorced chemistry from physics, and history from the other social sciences. Even that giant conglomerate, the Department of History, English and Government at Annapolis, has now been divided into two departments.[23] The existence of more highly differentiated departments offering more varied and advanced courses has led to so-called cooperative M.A. programs, first at the Air Force Academy, then at the Naval Academy. Selected civilian universities are asked to grant credit toward their Masters' degrees for advanced work taken at an academy. This can enable some students to complete the requirements for an M.A. with less than one year in residence at the civilian institution, especially if it has no thesis requirement.

The liberalization of curricula was an understandable response to problems shared by all three institutions. It evolved from longstanding practices, such as conducting honors sections in which abler students passed quickly to topics not examined in standard sections, thereby acquiring *de facto* or covert electives. And once the lockstep system was broken, incentives for curricular innovation grew rapidly, because departments began to compete for customers. At the same time resistance to innovation diminished because a free market of student choice began to supplement the grimly contested allocation of a finite quantity of time by committees of zealous department heads. At the Air Force Academy, where program flexibility is greatest, one official stated: 'It is not much harder to get a

27

new major approved today than it was to get a new course approved
yesterday'. This surely is an exaggeration, but it makes the point.

PROFESSIONALIZATION OF THE FACULTY

The premium placed on ability to cope with the larger techno-social
environment is also reflected in the professionalization of teaching staffs.
Here, too, it is possible to see a growing convergence between military and
civilian education at the undergraduate level. Generalists are being
replaced by specialists better equipped to deal with the new curricula.
Although the process is incomplete its direction is clear; greater insistence
on graduate work prior to appointment; more opportunity to enhance
competence while on the job; and a demand for prerogatives enjoyed by
faculty members at civilian institutions.

The proportion of doctorates at the Air Force Academy is now 28%,
and while it is only 11% at West Point, it has risen rapidly in the last
decade and is likely to keep rising. Officer instructors are now more
frequently assigned for longer tours of duty than in the past. Moreover,
in addition to the one or two 'permanent professors' in each of their
departments, West Point and the Air Force Academy have now also been
authorized to appoint up to 10% of their faculty members as 'tenure
associate professors'. The former have tenure until they complete thirty
years of commissioned service or until the age of sixty-four, whichever
comes later; the latter hold two-year appointments which may be renewed
as long as they are on active duty.

Unlike the other two academies, Annapolis has long employed both
military and civilian personnel in roughly equal proportions. Here, the
thrust toward professionalization has taken two forms: one group of
advocates has pressed to replace officers by civilians except in courses on
naval science; another group has sought to follow West Point and the
Air Force Academy by shifting to an all-military faculty but requiring
its members to take intensive graduate work before they begin to teach.
Neither group has prevailed but faculty standards appear to be rising.

Since interest in research is often taken as an indicator of professionalization, it is significant that the current emphasis on research is one of
the more striking changes at each academy in the past fifteen years. West
Point has created an Academic Board Research Advisory Committee and
is authorized to appoint twelve officers to basic research positions each

28

year. In addition it has established a Science Research Laboratory. The Naval Academy has a Research Council and a program of sabbatical leaves. Its Engineering Department includes a group of young motivated instructors who busily sponsor symposia, encourage midshipmen to undertake professional activities, and clearly benefit from access to research funds and Federal laboratories. The Air Force Academy has an assistant dean for research and its own research fund. In coming years it plans to have one out of every twenty instructors on full-time research status. At present it has about eighty officers and over one hundred cadets in funded research or consulting projects. Military instructors at all academies also go afield in summers, usually to work on service-connected high pay-off projects relating to supply, organization, personnel, weapons or tactics.

As faculty members develop their academic expertise, they simultaneously develop keener interest in professional prerogatives, liberties and amenities. Here they confront the fact that the service academies are not only educational institutions but Federal installations, and military ones at that. Civilians at the Naval Academy are especially likely to be aware of this fact. As civil servants they accrue annual and sick leave at specified rates, and they are subject to performance ratings by their superiors.

As members of a military community they are expected to wear coats and ties in class and to participate in traditional social activities. Requests for sabbatical leave must be approved by the Chief of Naval Operations. When they engage in research and are in doubt concerning the appropriateness of scholarly conclusions which are critical of current American policy, they are expected to submit them to higher authority before publishing.[24]

Inevitably, there is tension between the professional drive for autonomy and the military tradition of centralized command. In 1966, for example, some recently hired civilian Ph. D's at Annapolis concluded that their superior officers were trying to tell them how to grade examinations. In the wake of this incident a new chapter of the American Association of University Professors was born in Maryland.[25] There have also been complaints of undue centralization of power at the Air Force Academy in past years. Some appear to have been directed at the Dean in his relationships with departments, e.g. in the matter of faculty appointments. Others were directed at department heads who allegedly allowed instructors too little discretion in the design of course syllabi or the actual conduct of class.[26]

29

The demand for autonomy implicit in the idea of having 'one's own department' or 'one's own class', will no doubt grow at the academies. So will interest in better office space, more secretarial staff, sabbatical leaves, opportunity to establish closer relationships with students, a larger voice in the determination of educational policy, and that hardiest of all perennials, lighter teaching loads. One or another academy already has a committee on faculty affairs, a faculty forum, a faculty council, even a faculty junior council. It is safe to predict that professional aspirations will be aired in such places with increasing vigor.

THE IMPORTANCE OF SATISFIED CUSTOMERS

A nice parallel to change in the status of faculty is change in the rigorous regimen formerly imposed on students. Substantial changes have been made in the system which horrified a visiting German parliamentarian in the early 1950's – because it struck him as too Prussian! These changes have been prompted by a realization that it is going to be harder to attract and hold the customer unless his rights and privileges are liberalized.

Over the 'battle Ramp' leading from the cadet area to the parade field at the Air Force Academy is the inscription, 'Give Me Men'. During the latter half of the 1960's the academies had cause for concern whether this plea would be sufficiently heeded. While there has been something of an upswing more recently, in February 1969 an evaluation team at West Point reported a decided decline in admissions applications.[27] From 1965 to 1968, discussions between the Superintendent of the Naval Academy and his Board of Visitors were regularly marked by expressions of anxiety over the volume of qualified candidates; this was during a period when other major colleges and universities were deluged. The Air Force Academy continued to have somewhat more pulling power than its two sister institutions. One statistic cited to me by authorities there was that it stood sixth on a list of the most desirable institutions in America in a ranking made by 140 000 male high school students of high intellectual ability.[28] But while formerly very few applicants declined offers of admission, and then largely to enter such universities as Stanford, Yale, or MIT, by 1969 the declination rate had risen significantly, and many withdrew in order to attend substantial but not especially renowned institutions.

This is not surprising. Given the nature of American society, the absence of a post-feudal nobility, and the lure of material values, military life has

30

long been relatively unattractive. Indeed, there is little doubt in my mind that the greatest achievement of the academies, now as in past years, has been their ability to develop a reasonably firm career commitment in a reasonably large number of young men who do not originally have such a commitment. One motive for entering an academy, important in the past, has been weakened by the greater affluence of families and the readier availability of scholarships, including ROTC scholarships, at civilian institutions. Moreover, today's high school students are more demanding, more sensitive to the special characteristics of institutions, more likely to 'shop around'. Some dislike engineering. Others prefer what one officer called 'the California syndrome' – surfing, foreign cars, girls. Many, reared in permissive homes, recoil what they term 'Mickey Mouse' regulations and procedures. Then there is the Vietnam war and the rising anti-militarism of youth.[29] And for wholly unrelated reasons, this time of troubles has coincided with a doubling of the number of spaces the academies must fill to complete expansions planned long ago.

Needless to say, energetic efforts are made to reach prospective candidates. In 1968–69, 615 West Point cadets visited 2, 142 high schools to talk with guidance officers and students. During Christmas vacation hundreds of midshipmen go on similar missions. If the Air Force Academy has a football game in Texas, cadets born in the Dallas area are almost certain to speak at Dallas high schools before the game. Recruiting films are carefully designed to portray athletics, dating, the free exchange of views on a controversial issue in class, a car at graduation, folksinging. One academy has some two dozen members on its public relations staff. But in a larger sense everything that is done is now done with an eye to the potential applicant. In the words of one Superintendent, 'We have to make this place attractive. We have to be able to tell a young man that he can major in a particular branch of engineering if that is what he wants'. Recruitment difficulties are compounded by attrition during the four-year course. This is a long standing problem; one-third of an entering class may fail to graduate. To be sure, average attrition rates are lower than this, and they have been fairly stable of late, but the stability has concealed disturbing changes in the cause of separations and withdrawals. Formerly the major reasons were academic, now they are motivational.[30] Understandably, attrition is greatest in the first year.[31] It is during the initial period of adjustment that the student is most distressed by the tempo at which a dizzying number of requirements must be met; by the rituals exacted by upperclassmen; by the compulsion to support the team loudly; by inability to cut classes; by daily room inspection; by tabus against

31

unkempt hair or clothing when personal sloppiness is in high fashion; and by compulsory chapel when contemporaries proclaim 'God is dead'. All these shocks are experienced by young men whose initial decision to apply to an academy, if admission officials are correct, is more tentative than their predecessors ('I'll try it and see if I like it'), and whose parents are no longer so insistent that their sons stick it out.

External critics have encouraged the academies to review their first year systems. In 1963, the Air Force Academy's Board of Visitors criticized the 'unproductive harassment' of new students and suggested they be granted Christmas leave. A few years later the Under Secretary of the Navy requested a general review of the first year at Annapolis. All academies now discourage sanctions in the form of corporal punishment, denial of food, or humiliation. Students still face special requirements, but the word has gone out that these are to be somewhat more meaningful, businesslike, and 'career relevant'. Privileges are related more closely to performance, rewards are substituted for threats. The trials of 'Beast Barracks' are now history.

The sensibilities of upperclassmen are also considered more carefully. Reveille comes a bit later at West Point these days; Air Force cadets get a slice of unscheduled time in the evening. One academy or another now permits students to wear civilian clothes, drink alcoholic beverages[32], or drive their own car under carefully defined circumstances. All academies, moreover, have begun to be more attentive to student opinion in the formation of educational policy. All are more generous with leave, including long weekends. Each supports a flourishing program of extracurricular activities, the most popular of which seem to be those which enable students to leave the reservation.

The limits of the new permissiveness have been tested by a number of bearers of the contemporary youth culture who have secured appointments. At one academy an observer devised a tripartite typology of students which, though incomplete and simplistic, is nevertheless suggestive. The first category consists of 'engineers'. Less people-minded than thing-minded, they accept the system phlegmatically. The second consists of 'Eagle Scouts' who accept the system enthusiastically. With positive attitudes toward a military career, they identify strongly with the academy, viewing it is 'an island of purity in a sea of corruption'. The third consists of 'mods' and rebels. Though a distinct minority and required to behave circumspectly, this latter element undoubtedly exists.

32

Each of the academies has had an occasional incident involving marijuana. Among students implicated in a cheating scandal at the Air Force Academy in 1967 were some who referred to themselves as 'the cool group' and who, like counterparts elsewhere, sought to distinguish themselves by their taste in music and their preference for ragged clothes and long hair.[33] Aware of how potentially explosive even small incidents can become, authorities at each academy watch these phenomena with some foreboding. One summarized his own sense of current institutional priorities by pointing toward the dormitories rather than the classrooms and stating tersely, 'Our biggest problem is over there'.

THE PROCESS AND LIMITS OF CONVERGENCE

My argument has been that the service academies have become more, not less, like civilian institutions. Convergence, not divergence, is its main theme, although caution prompts the qualification that this is a generalization about the past two decades rather than an assumption about the future.[34] Among the unobtrusive forces for convergence have been junior faculty members. Fresh from major universities where, as one puts it, 'You spend two years in a dorm with eighty "gung ho" graduate students', they have been extremely sensitive to intellectual trends. A few years ago they focused on emerging nations; today they are interested in urban violence, poverty, student unrest and race relations. They, and more senior faculty members as well, have interacted with the faculty of civilian institutions at a growing number of professional meetings. These have included not only large, splashy conferences held at the academies themselves[35], but a great variety of lectures, seminars, and smaller conferences sponsored by their increasingly professional departments.

To be sure, there have been service nuances. But at all three academies curricular changes have enhanced the influence of the specialist, sometimes in ways not wholly anticipated. The advent of electives and majors, for example, has increased the odds that a given student will take two or more courses with the same instructor, or that he will come to meet a faculty member as a research supervisor or departmental advisor. Thus are generated master-apprentice relationships based on shared intellectual interests.

The growth of extreme ideological positions may also have been inhibited by sensitivity to standards and practices accepted by fellow specialists in

33

the larger world. Certainly one cannot detect any systematic effort to indoctrinate students in controversial political, economic or social issues. Indeed, the academies have occasionally invited speakers with whose views they may strongly disagree. The keynote address at a recent West Point conference was given by a man who condemned the Secretary of State's conduct of foreign affairs, castigated the regime in Saigon, doubted that the Soviet invasion of Czechoslovakia posed a threat to NATO, and described the government of Haiti as 'much worse than any Communist government could possibly be'.[36] But at the official level the academies have projected what can only be described as an official view – a conventional, if not actually bland, Establishment perspective. In domestic policy this has been reflected in the reassurance quickly given to a Congressman who inquired whether an academy taught any 'radical new social concepts'.[37] In foreign policy it has been reflected in the galaxy of figures who have attended West Point's SCUSA conferences since 1949. The names of Acheson, Dulles, Harriman, Nitze, Rockefeller and Rusk are supplemented by those of highly senior officers, academicians and foundation officials.

The possibility that students have been affected by such an avalanche of moderation is at least consistent with Lovell's findings on differences between men in their first and last years at West Point. Fewer graduating students believed in the inevitability of all-out war; fewer believed that Korea illustrated a communist intent to dominate the world; and fewer thought that neutralism was a result of lack of moral fibre. More broadly, a shift occurred during the four years from 'absolutist' to 'pragmatic' strategic perspectives.[38]

Lovell has also reported a shift from 'heroic' to 'managerial' orientations. If the Air Force Academy's position is representative, all institutions now officially encourage such a shift. A draft of its 15-Year Plan, January 7, 1970, states:

'The combat-model leadership in which a quality example is offered and unhesitating, unquestioning obedience is demanded, will become more and more rare. Effective leadership will be increasingly predicated upon respect for job knowledge and competence accompanied by the ability to offer sound, rational reasons for the course of action required. The enlistment of voluntary, eager cooperation will be the mark of the leader of the future, rather than the use of fear as a goad to performance. The soldiers and airmen of the future will be more highly educated, more questioning, and more suspicious of authority than in the past'.

Finally, recent research at the Air Force Academy reports a complementary shift from 'concrete' to 'abstract' intellectual and emotional orien-

34

tations. The former are identified with extreme and polarized value judgments, greater dependence on status and formal authority, greater intolerance of ambiguity, and more reliance on stereotypes. The latter are identified with less pessimism, dogmatism, and moral absolutism.[39]

It would be imprudent to speak too confidently about what all this portends for the impact of future military leaders on national policy. I have argued that many forces within the academies have operated to soften the differences between them and civilian educational institutions. Yet, as noted at the outset, the academies draw a special cross-section of American youth and the distinctiveness of this cross-section may well increase in the near future. In 1970, some academies reported an increase in applications. It is reasonable to assume that a number of students applied to them because they were troubled by the unsettled conditions at so many civilian universities; 41% of West Point's Class of 1973 testified that campus unrest had been a factor influencing their desire to pursue a military career.[40] Parents, too, are likely to be influenced by this factor, especially by the uncertain future of ROTC at other institutions; and studies reveal that West Point entrants discuss career plans with parents more than do civilian students.

Since it is most unlikely that the average high school senior is more interested in military service today than he was a year or two ago, the conclusion seems unavoidable that the young men who choose to enter a service academy at this time have a special capacity to be undaunted by the prevailing surge of anti-militarism among their contemporaries. To the extent that this is so, the unique recruitment base of the academies is likely to perpetuate their distinctiveness in the face of the powerful institutional forces which are operating to render them more like civilian universities.

1. *Report of the President's Commission on an All-Volunteer Armed Force* (Washington: Government Printing Office, 1970), p. 72. The Navy drew 6% of its officers from service academies, the Air Force 3,5%, the Army 1,9%.
2. 'Between 80 and 90% of service academy graduates can be expected to remain in the service upon completion of their obligated tour of active duty (now 5 years), as opposed to less than 50% for ROTC scholarship graduates and under 25% for OCS graduates'. *Ibid.*, p. 77.
3. Cf. John P. LOVELL, *The Cadet Phase of the Professional Socialization of the West Pointer*, University of Wisconsin doctoral dissertation, 1962. See also Morris JANOWITZ, *The New Military* (New York: Russell Sage Foundation, 1964), p. 21. It is true, of course, that what goes on there has a great bearing on self-selection.
4. LOVELL, *op. cit.*, p. 96.
5. Walter E. HECOX, *A Comparison of New Cadets at West Point with Entering Freshmen at Other Colleges, Class of 1973* (West Point, New York), p. 31.
6. Gary SPENCER, *A Social-Psychological Profile of the Class of 1973, USMA* (West Point, New York: United States Military Academy, 1969), pp. 5–6.
7. Data in the preceding two paragraphs are taken from HECOX, pp. 20–33.
8. LOVELL, pp. 155–160.
9. Dean E. MANN, *The Assistant Secretaries* (Washington, D.C.: The Brookings Institution, 1965), p. 291.
10. David STANLEY, Dean E. MANN, and Jameson DOIG, *Men Who Govern* (Washington, D.C.: The Brookings Institution, 1967), p. 20. The closest comparison, and it is not wholly satisfactory, is that 2,2% of the West Point Class of 1973 came from private secondary schools which were neither military nor denominational. John W. HOUSTON et al, *Characteristics of the Class of 1973* (West Point, N.Y.: United States Military Academy, 1969), p. 5.
11. STANLEY, MANN, and DOIG, p. 14.
12. HECOX, p. 5. Data on the geographical origins of FSO's are from John E. HARR, *The Professional Diplomat* (Princeton, N.J.: Princeton University Press, 1969), pp. 174–193.
13. HARR, 174–193.
14. *Ibid.*, p. 183. The proportion of *mature* officers describing themselves as 'moderately liberal' or 'liberal ranged' from 1/4 in the Navy to 1/3 in the Air Force.
15. But the question is being studied seriously. See, e.g. Gilbert R. KAATS, 'Development Changes in Belief Systems During a Service Academy Education', *Proceedings of the 77th Annual Convention of the American Psychological Association*, 1969, p. 651.
16. Morris JANOWITZ, *The Professional Soldier* (Glencoe, Illinois: The Free Press, 1960).
17. Because rank is regarded as important in this regard, some observers thought the fundamental character of the Naval Academy might be changed when, in 1960, its mission was restated to omit specific reference to the preparation of *junior* officers.
18. The phrase is Corelli BARNETT's, and the material that follows immediately is taken from his stimulating essay, 'The Education of Military Elites', in Rupert WILKINSON, ed., *Governing Elites* (New York: Oxford University Press, 1969), pp. 195–196.
19. *Five-Year Plan for the United States Air Force Academy*, Headquarters, United

States Air Force Academy, May 1968, pp. 7–8. The 1969 draft plan restated this dilemma: 'Cadets learn that their effectiveness as leaders is enhanced to the degree that a rational justification for their decisions is communicated to their subordinates. But they also learn that loyalty and respect for authority are crucial in military organizations, and that ungrudging compliance with disagreeable directives marks the truly professional officer'.

20. But allowing students graduate credit for advanced courses in its own curriculum, The Air Force Academy enabled them to earn an M.A. at selected universities in less than one year. This plan was a compromise after earlier plans to authorize the academy to give its own M.A. were opposed by its Board of Visitors, the Defence Department, and the American Council on Education.

21. Turn-of-the-century struggles to establish the authority of a chief of staff still linger in the collective unconscious of the Army officer corps.

22. The Air Force Academy has a separate Department of Philosophy and Fine Arts.

23. West Point separated history from English in 1926, while history, political science, economics and English have always been separate departments at the Air Force Academy.

24. *Faculty Handbook* (Annapolis, Maryland: United States Naval Academy, undated) 2nd ed., pp. 24–33.

25. J. Arthur HEISE, *The Brass Factories* (Washington, D.C.: Public Affairs Press, 1969), pp. 114–120.

26. See Special Advisory Committee on the United States Air Force Academy, *Report to the Secretary and the Chief of Staff of the Air Force*, Washington, D.C., May 5, 1965, pp. 31–32.
See also HEISE, chapter 3; and *Administration of the Service Academies*, Report and Hearings of the Special Subcommittee on Service Academies of the House Armed Services Committee, 90th Congress, First and Second Sessions, 1967–1968 (hereinafter cited as *Hebert Hearings*), passim.

27. Middle States Commission on Institutions of Higher Education, *Report to the Superintendent, the Academic Board, the Faculty and the Board of Visitors by an Evaluation Team*, West Point, New York, p. 6.

28. The first five, in order, were said to be California Institute of Technology, Massachusetts Institute of Technology, Rice, Stanford, Harvard.

29. For a frank recognition of such rising anti-militarism, see *Report of the Board of Visitors*, United States Military Academy, May 5, 1969, p. 5.

30. On the drop in the academic flunk-out rate between 1958 and 1968, see *Hebert Hearings*, p. 10311. No doubt students and instructors grew better during the decade, but officials may also have decided they could not let academic attrition continue at the old rate in view of rising motivational attrition.

31. Recent West Point figures were 11% in plebe summer; 7–9% more in the remainder of the first year and an additional 10% in the last three years. The Air Force Academy has reported a total of 25% for the four years.

32. Maryland statutes make it unlawful to give or sell alcoholic beverages to midshipmen within five miles of Annapolis.

33. *Hebert Hearings*, pp. 10909–13.

34. Cf. Charles C. MOSKOS, Jr., *The American Enlisted Man* (New York: Russell Sage Foundation, 1970). Moskos concludes that while the culture of the officer corps, especially in the Air Force, may be converging with civilian culture, that of the enlisted man is diverging. Moreover, he implies that for the military establishment as a whole, the process of convergence has passed its peak. *Op. cit.*, pp. 38, 170.

35. E.g. West Point's Student Conference on United States Affairs, the Air Force Academy's Assembly, and the Naval Academy's Foreign Affairs Conference.
36. *Proceedings of the Twentieth Annual Student Conference on United States Affairs*, United States Military Academy, December 4–7, 1968. The speaker was Bill D. Moyers. Delegates included 216 students from 89 universities.
37. *Hebert Hearings*, p. 10582.
38. *Op. cit.*, pp. 149–162. See also the summary in John P. LOVELL, 'The Professional Socialization of West Point Cadets' in JANOWITZ, *The New Military*, pp. 119–157. 'Absolutists' believe communists are intent on world conquest, nuclear war is likely, massive retaliation is the best policy, neutrals are unreliable, if not potentially hostile. 'Pragmatists' believe the communists are expansionist, some kinds of conflicts are likely, America must be prepared for all contingencies, graduated deterrence is the best policy, and allies may be essential.
39. Gilbert R. KAATS, 'Development Changes in Belief Systems During a Service Academy Education', *Proceedings of the 77th Annual Convention of the American Psychological Association*, 1969, p. 651.
40. SPENCER, p. 11.

The Service Academies as a Social System

C. M. A. HARTMAN*

* Royal Netherlands Naval College, Den Helder, The Netherlands.

This is bound to be a strange paper. Let me explain. Imagine a sculptor who, at mature age, goes to an academy of arts and learns about the aesthetics. And than he is asked to criticize his own work in relation to the 'objective' – whatever that be – norms of this discipline. Or take a psychiatrist and ask him to make an expert analysis of his own psyche. Or think of a naval officer who joined the Royal Netherlands Navy as a 'regular' in 1939; held an executive career till 1960 and at that time was given the opportunity to study sociology at a university. Ask this man, who through his military education and profession must have a 'military mind', to analyse the educational process at the military academy. To complicate his problem, this man as a teacher in the social sciences, is very much involved in this same happening.

This unfortunate man is your speaker who, as a sociologist, is expected to take distance from this object to which he is emotionally bound. The best illustration of his problem is the following case. My colleague at Den Helder asked one of his students: 'Give me an example of role-conflict.' Promptly this midshipman answered: 'Commander Hartman, being a naval officer and a sociologist'. This straightforward, well meant answer gives in fact the quintessence of your speaker's problem.

Now to characterize the topic for this paper, the following might help. Since world war II many military academies – among them the Netherlands – have upgraded their curriculum. In a discussion with colleagues of the Royal Netherlands Military Academy, I formulated the problem of the military education 'new style' in the following thesis: 'Indoctrination teaches the students to think in exclamation marks. Scientific schooling teaches the students to think in question marks. Military education is supposed to succeed in both'.

The original idea for this paper was that I should compile the available empirical data on the process of recent changes to a more abstract level. Alas, the 'poor' availability and the non-comparability of the required data became an obstacle. In this manner I was forced to lean heavily on some contemplative articles and my own 'objective' perceptions. I am well aware of the fact that this lack of empirical input makes the original set-up very scanty.

All the same, I hope to reach a certain level of abstraction so that the specific problems of the various military academies may be recognized in this scheme and to leave enough topics for the discussion and the exchange of information.

To business:

Service academies as a social system; crises in a process.

In my analysis I will survey three periods:

a. The pre-world war II period.
b. The post-world war II period.
c. The coming decades.

In each period I will try to characterize the structural and cultural systems as they appear in the process of change from academies old style to modern institutes. It is my point that round about the transition from one period to the other, a crisis arises in the educational system, resulting in a new social system.

a. THE PRE-WORLD WAR II PERIOD

Let us assume that professionalization of the military career starts somewhere in the 19th century. At this time military education is centralized in the academies. It is at these institutes that the three pillars of professionalization – expertise, ethics and cohesion – can develop and, as an element of military culture, can be made available to the new officer-generations. This form of military education, compared with the pre-existing method of officers enrolment – where one became an officer in the field, with the troop, on the ship – had the great advantage that the ideal of a 'uniform officer' could be approached. Especially the 'ethics' and 'cohesion', but also the 'expertise' – as far as the various weapons did not necessitate specializations – could lead to interchangeable leaders, whose behavior could reach a high degree of predictability. Well defined values and strict norms gave the officercadet a model to which he could identify himself. There is some evidence that this model was idealised, almost to extremity.

Not the reality, but an idealized practice is the guidance for the academies policy. As a seventeen year old cadet I had the aberration to shave my fluffy beard while showering before swimming instructions. 'That is not done' and two days à two hours defaulters drill were the result for my first – not the last – offence. I must admit that nowadays – as a result perhaps – I omit shaving while showering, but it may be because I have an electric razor. The point I want to stress with this anecdote is that a strong social control, in which the negative sanction plays a dominant part, enables the volunteer officers-candidate to conform himself to the 'ideal model'. A special Code of Discipline, adapted to the boardingschool situation, regulates the legal side, supplemented by a system of not-legalized informal house-rules. A comparative research – quantitative and qualitative – between the captain-defaulters record of a

42

military academy and an average military unit would reveal the importance the academies attach to this side of social control. But the positive sanctions are also well developed. Reward for the best cadets of each year, sword of honour for the young keen officer who approximates the 'ideal model'.

On the structural side of the system one finds a homogeneous officer-instructors corps, carefully selected for these positions. In this period there are relatively few civilian teachers. In sofar they occupy important positions, they are either retired officers or civilians who identify themselves strongly with the 'ideal model'. Among the students one finds a very homogeneous cadet-corps. Well guarded mores, strong group solidarity and group cohesion are promoted and sanctioned by the academy staff. Severe aberrant behavior is 'adequately' dealt with. To a certain degree the cadet-corps has an amount of autonomy. Lack of privacy, common dormitories and a social – and often spatial – isolation advance this homogeneity.

An other structural element of the academy is its position in the military organization. Placed direct under the top-command, it gives the institute a high degree of autonomy. Without much trouble it can expel officer-candidates thought unfit with regards to the norms of the self-fixed 'ideal model'. The informal house-rules are easily sanctioned.

In the process of (military) teaching and (military) learning three elements can be distinguished: (intellectual) knowledge, (practical) skill and (behavioral) style. In this period a strong emphasis is laid on Style and Skill, whereas the Knowledge is used as means to facilitate the Skill.

b. THE POST-WORLD WAR II PERIOD

The enormous push in technical know-how, activated in world war II, did not pass unnoticed by the military organizations. Far from it; it compelled the military to keep up to date, to stimulate research and to incorporate the latest findings in their equipment. The times in which technical 'novelties' were viewed with disdainful attitudes, are long passed.

This development forced the military to upgrade the education of their officers and – as seems logical at that time – their academies were entrusted with this task. And here the first crisis was born. It brought to the institutes a staff of scientific teachers, university graduates, either civilian or military. If civilian, they certainly did not bring with them a military mind; nor did they have a notion about an 'ideal model' of a keen young officer. If military, I will not say they lost their military outlook, but they brought with them an other 'ideal model' of a keen young student. And, unintended, their approach in the process of military education is 'specialized', in conformity with their discipline of knowledge and not 'generalized' as might be wished with regards to the 'uniform officer'. The homogeneous instructor-corps got a severe dent. The ideology of the 'uniform officer' got hazy.

This scientific input in the academies had other effects. Or, to put it in a sociological framework: the changing of the cultural system (a change in values, norms and organizational ends) brought changes in the structural system. Contacts with the civilian universities broke open the isolation of the academy. The interference of other authorities than the top-command, lessened the autonomy of the academy. In some cases a board of trustees was installed to supervise the level of education. Relative heavy emphasis on Knowledge, not as a means for Skill, but as an end in itself, made more privacy for the students necessary. The dormitories changed for studies and bedrooms.

Apart from this scientific upgrading of military education, there is another cause which changed the structural system of the academies. A new generation of youth asks for admission. Grossly generalized, the previous generations were motivated to become an officer; among the new cadets a certain category is also attracted to the high technical standard he perceives in the military forces.

Recruitment campaigns and advertising are not foreign for this motivation. These cadets see the officers career as good as any other career. Knowledge is their preference; Skill and in particular Style are an irksome circumstance.

To summarize the situation at the end of this period of the process of change:

The teacher corps is heterogeneous of structure. The 'ideal model' they have for reference is divided. On one side is the idealized practice of the pre-world war II period. But now it can be in disharmony to the reality in the larger military organization. On the other side is an other idealization, also in disharmony to this reality. It is derived from university life with its emphasis on scientific orientation, originality, creativity.

The cadet-corps on the other hand is still homogeneous. The cultural change in the top of the academy has not yet reached the bottom. But this discord is not unnoticed and as a reaction the mores are strengthened and solidarity increases.

The social isolation of the academy is lessened. More liberty is granted. Civilian clothes off duty are allowed. The autonomy of the academy has decreased. It is more difficult to expel an aberrant cadet.

44

And to the close of this period the second crisis appears. The homogeneity of the cadet-corps gets a dent. As a result of all these structural changes, a split occurs. There are students who refer to Knowledge and there are students who refer to Skill and Style (Kjellberg).

And the last hope for an officers generation, characterized by a behavioral uniformity, has disappeared.

c. THE COMING DECADES

I am sorry to say that the title for this sub-part was an eye-catcher. I hope you will accept the fact that I am not a clairvoyant. Neither am I a futurologist. But still, I think we can, through reasoning, get some insight of what the future might bring the academies. Let us first characterize the different types of service institutes. I think we can distinguish four main categories.

I. Military academies which have not upgraded the level of education. Any required extra knowledge in the officers corps is obtained by 'post-graduate' education of selected officers.

II. Military academies which have upgraded their curriculum but which have boarded out the extra scientific part to a civilian university.

III. Military academies which have upgraded their curriculum and meet the requirements for this extra task with their own military, 'regular' teachers.

IV. As III, but which attracted civilian academici for these disciplines. And of course, there are mixtures. So the Royal Netherlands Naval College is a mixture of types II, III and IV.

If I recapitulate the changes, I think that you will agree with the following generalizations.

On the cultural side:

1. The military academies have upgraded their level of education.
2. In the trio Knowledge – Skill – Style, there is a shift from Skill to Knowledge.
3. The model for Style, once inviolable, is changing.
4. The cultural homogeneity of the teachers corps has diminished.
5. The cultural homogeneity of the cadet corps has diminished.

On the structural side:

6. The ratio military teachers: civilian teachers has decreased.

45

7. The ratio teachers: students has increased.
8. The academies are less isolated.
9. The academies are less autonomous.
10. There is a larger variety of motivational categories among the officer-candidates.

These changes have brought the academies in a state of tension. It is my opinion that the degree of tension correlates with the sequence I through IV of the above mentioned categories.

And as a consequence, there will be forces from within the military organization to minimize this tension. Now, and here we come to the future, there are two lines of thought to obtain this minimization.

A. Return – as close as possible – to the pre-world war II period situation. It is my opinion that this course – although it may be very attractive to many an officer 'old style' – is not to be recommended. It replaces the academies in social isolation.

B. Learn to live with the situation that a new officers generation has entered the forces. But this means a more businesslike approach of the military organization, with less pomp and circumstance and perhaps an 'Umwertung aller Werte'.

These two possibilities can be considered as two extremities. Each has its pros and cons. Which course the various academies, with their own particularities, will have to steer to reach calm waters, is difficult to recommend. But I have some – strictly personal – ideas which might be appropriate to those academies which are still in turbulent waters.

1. divide – at least in time, if possible in place – the military indoctrination and the scientific schooling.

2. try to get a consensus of what is expected of the modern young officer. Or in other words, get a clear picture of the objectives of modern military education. The last war was fought with an officers generation of the academies 'old style'. And I think they acquitted themselves very well of their tasks. But it is well to realize that there was a manifold of reserve officers who received but a scant training; and in the underground armies in occupied Europe there were (semi-) military leaders who never had a military training. And both these categories also acquitted themselves remarkably well of their tasks.

These remarks might help to formulate a more realistic model of a modern young officer.

LITERATURE

Morris JANOWITZ, *The Professional Soldier. A social and political portrait.* The Free Press of Glencoe (1960).

Morris JANOWITZ and Roger LITTLE, *Sociology and the Military Establishment.* Russell Sage Foundation. New York (1965).

C. J. LAMMERS, *Het Koninklijk instituut voor de marine.* Van Gorcum, Assen (1963).

J. A. A. VAN DOORN ed., *Beroepsvorming in Internaatsverband. Sociologische beschouwingen en specifieke ervaringen.* Universitaire Pers Rotterdam (1965).

M. R. VAN GILS, *Het Officierskorps. De krisis in een professie.* Boom, Meppel (1969).

F. KJELLBERG, Some Cultural Aspects of the Military Profession. *Archiv. europ. sociol.* VI (1965), pp. 283–293.

'Ich will', *Der Spiegel* – 2 February 1970 nr. 6, pp. 34–41.

Sanford M. DORNBUSCH, 'The military academy as an assimilating Institution'. *Social Forces*, Vol. 33, May 1955, pp. 316-322.

A Military Academy in Transition: A Survey Investigation

J. H. MANS*
M. A. VAN DE SANDT*

* Royal Military Academy, Breda, The Netherlands.

In The Netherlands military education in the seventeenth and eighteenth centuries was given by special professors of military science at various Dutch universities, especially in the field of military engineering. Only at the end of the eighteenth century special Artillery Schools were established which also provided the training of engineering officers. The first Dutch academy for the cavalry and the infantry was established in 1806. In 1828 all these schools were concentrated in the Royal Military Academy at Breda, the first military school in Europe in which military affairs were studied on a scientific basis by cadets of all arms. This academy still exists and today provides military education for all Dutch officers of the army and the air force.

In the course of the nineteenth century, military education experienced a number of changes: the academy developed from a secondary school for military professionals into one offering higher vocational training.

In 1960 the Academy underwent a well-prepared and complete reorganization. The main objective of this reorganization was to give the teaching a firm scientific basis, in particular for those arms which were traditionally the 'non-scientific' ones. Like the technical services, which at an early date received a technological basis, now military leadership and management are provided with a foundation in the social sciences. Henceforth military education is regarded as a branch of higher education. The consequences have been fully accepted. Besides military experts in the field of the social and technical sciences a great number of civilians have been appointed as ordinary or extraordinary professors. The different scientific departments – with the exception of the department of military science – has been placed under civilian direction. At the same time it has been decided to allow the cadets more individual liberty and initiative. The reform of the academy has elicited various criticisms, especially directed against the scientific character of the new training pattern.

It is clear, after ten years of experiment and experience, that the optimal link between vocation and training is not easy (1).

I. THE STRUCTURE OF THE EDUCATION

To get some insight into the problematics under consideration some attention will be paid to the total structure of the education. The academy provides military education for all Dutch officers of the army and the air force.

The education aims at development of insight, knowledge and technical skills which an officer needs.

Therefore the aims of the education are:
a. the development of personality;
b. to give a basic scientific knowledge;
c. to give professional knowledge;
d. to give physical training.

Five different elements of training and education support the objectives mentioned above:
1. Military training;
2. Scientific education;
3. Cadets' Corps;
4. Physical training;
5. Battalion.

Some attention will now be paid to each of these five elements (cf. Fig. 1).

1. Military training

Briefly the military training at the academy is made up as follows.

During the first four months after his admission the cadet gets a military training which is the same for all cadets. At the end of each of the first three years of study this general training is resumed for a period of two months. It comprises among other things combat-training with the commando's, practical leadership training, and – at the end of the second year – a posting with a unit of the chosen arm or service.

The entire last year of the education is devoted to the training in the special techniques of the chosen arm or service. This training takes place entirely outside the academy.

2. Scientific education

The academy has five scientific departments:
a. *The department of military sciences*
   Every cadet attends lectures in this department. Subjects are strategy, logistics, military law etc.
b. *The department of general education*
   Every cadet attends lectures in this department. Subjects are political science, international affairs, history etc. Each cadet chooses one of the modern languages (English, French or German).
c. *The department of technical sciences*
   Every cadet of a technical service attends lectures in this department.

52

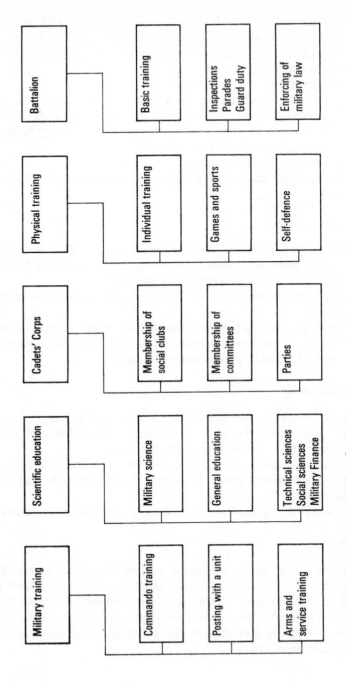

Figure I. The five elements of the education

The course lasts five years. Next to it the department has a four year-training-course for infantry-, cavalry- and artillery-cadets as well as air force cadets of the general services (dependent on primary training at secondary school).

d. *The department of the social sciences*

Every cadet of a supporting service attends lectures in this department. Infantry-, cavalry- and artillery-cadets as well as air force cadets attend lectures in this department too (dependent on primary training at secondary school). It is a four year course.

e. *The department of military finance*

This course is for cadets of the military finance corps only. It takes five years.

3. Cadets' Corps

The cadets' corps is considered an essential part of the education. The ultimate goal is fostering a feeling of solidarity and preparation for the social life of an officer. Membership is compulsary.

Every year a senate of five cadets is chosen. The senate presides the cadets' corps.

Committees and unions (culture, religion and sports) are part of the corps. Sociability is one of the aims too. The outstanding event in corps-life is the annual 'Assaut', pre-eminently the cadets' feast.

4. Physical training

Ultimate goal of the physical training during academy-life is a good condition and insight into the great importance of the military physical training. The training can be divided into two parts:

a. the military physical training as a part of the officers' education. Subjects are athletics, games, swimming, boxing, obstacle race and cross-country.

b. a number of other sports from which the individual cadet may choose.

5. Battalion

The battalion is considered an essential part of the education too. All cadets together form the battalion. The battalion commander (officer) is in charge of the battalion, assisted by a battalion-staff (officers). The battalion is composed of an A- and a B-company as well as a squadron. Important to know is that there is also a battalion-staff (commander included) made up of cadets.

54

In point of fact the battalion is led by cadets themselves. This cadets-staff is responsible to the officers-staff and relatively autonomous.

Summarizing what has been remarked so far, we can say that during his academy life, the cadet is confronted with five important training and education levels. These elements are rather time-consuming and make strong and sometimes conflicting demands on the individual cadet. Naturally this has a strong effect on his behaviour and attitudes. The consequences are hard to define.

To get some insight into these consequences a survey-investigation has been carried out by a research group of the Royal Military Academy. For this purpose, in the spring of 1970 a questionnaire was submitted to

all cadets (N = 438)

all officers (N = 71)

all civilian teachers (N = 55).

A limited interim report will be presented here.

II. RESULTS

1. Opinions about the structure of the education

In order to get some insight into the cadets' opinions about the desired structure of the education they were first of all asked to rank the five elements in order of importance. They were asked which element – in view of their future career as a professional officer – they think the most important, which element comes next, and so on.

Generally speaking we can say that most cadets agree that military training is the most important: 54% rank military training first.

On the whole scientific education averages next but here is less unanimity: 34% rank scientific education first, 37% rank scientific education second. Third, fourth and fifth are, on an average the cadets' corps, physical training and the battalion respectively. A few cadets only think these elements the most important.

There is great unanimity about the battalion: 51% rank the battalion fifth (table 1).

The officers and the civilian teachers were also asked what relative importance they attach to the five elements in view of the future career of a cadet as a professional officer.

55

Table 1. *Ranking of the 5 elements of the education by cadets (N = 436)*

Elements	Percentage per rank					Mean rank
	1	2	3	4	5	
Military training	54	29	10	4	3	1,71
Scientific education	34	37	15	7	6	2,10
Cadets' corps	7	16	28	31	17	3,34
Physical training	2	12	34	29	22	3,54
Battalion	2	6	13	28	51	4,18

All interrelations P < 0,001

Compared with the ranking of the cadets the differences are interesting. The officers and the civilian teachers also rank military training first but they think, on an average, military training a little more important than the cadets do. Scientific education is ranked second by the officers and the civilian teachers as well. The civilian teachers again think scientific education more important than the officers and the cadets do.

There is no unanimity about the cadets' corps. The cadets rank it third, the officers fourth, and the civilian teachers fifth. Half of the civilian teachers think the cadets' corps the least important element (graph 1). Finally the officers and civilian teachers were asked to rank the five elements as they expect the cadets' ranking to be.

Practically the officers' expectations do not differ from the actual cadets' ranking.

The teachers' expectations on the contrary differ on some points. Not only do they expect the cadets' ranking of the military training higher than it actually is, but particularly they expect the cadets' ranking of the scientific education to be much lower than it actually is (graph 2).

To investigate the desired structure of the education a second instrument has been developed. This instrument consists of a series of questions which asks the respondents to say about each element whether it needs more or less attention in comparison with the present situation.

61% of the cadets think military training needs more attention. In other words: in relation with the primary importance, they think the military training does not get the right amount of attention.

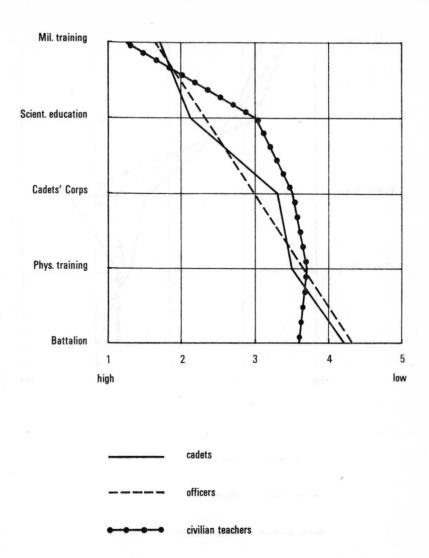

Graph 1. Mean rank of the 5 elements of the education assigned by cadets (N=436), officers (N=71) and civilian teachers (N=51)

57

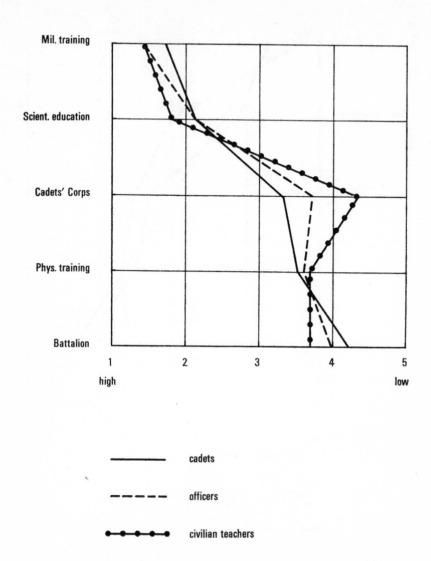

Graph 2. Mean actual rank of the 5 elements of the education assigned by cadets (N = 436), and the mean rank of the elements as officers (N = 71) and civilian teachers (N = 55) expect the cadets' ranking to be

A smaller part of the cadets think scientific education, cadets' corps and physical training need more attention. The battalion, however, forms an exception. Here the amount of attention to be given tends to be less (table 2).

The officers' and teachers' opinions differ to some extent. Most interesting is the fact that the officers – in contrast with the cadets – incline towards giving less attention to the military training.

Table 2. The amount of attention to be given to the 5 elements of the education – as compared with the actual situation – in the opinion of the cadets (N = 438)

| Elements | Percentage of cadets desiring | | | |
	more (score 1)	*equal (score 2)*	*less (score 3)*	*Mean score*
Military training	61	25	14	1,53
Scientific education	47	28	24	1,83
Cadets' corps	40	33	27	1,87
Physical training	47	29	23	1,76
Battalion	26	41	33	2,07

Mil.tr. - sc.ed.	P<0,001	Sc.ed. - ph.tr.	n.s.
Mil.tr. - cad.c.	P<0,001	Sc.ed. - batt.	P<0,001
Mil.tr. - ph.tr.	P<0,001	Cad.c. - ph.tr.	n.s.
Mil.tr. - batt.	P<0,001	Cad.c. - batt.	P<0,001
Sc.ed. - cad.c.	n.s.	Ph.tr. - batt.	P<0,001

Together with the cadets the civilian teachers are inclined towards giving a little more attention to scientific education, an opinion which is not shared by the officers (graph 3).

2. Two types of cadets compared

As has been mentioned before, 54% of the cadets think the military training the most important element of their education. On the other hand 34% of the cadets believe that the scientific education is the most important.

59

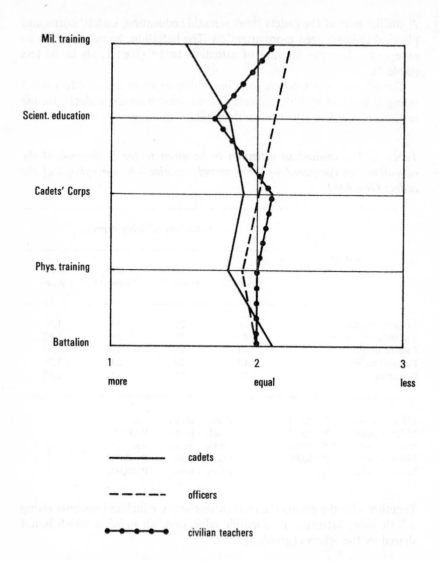

Graph 3. Mean score of the amount of attention to be given to the 5 elements of the education – as compared with the actual situation – in the opinion of cadets (N=438), officers (N=71) and civilian teachers (N=55)

Now we intend to analyse further both types of cadets, constituting together 88% of the population, in order to see, if perhaps they differ from each other in more respects as well. For the sake of brevity we shall henceforth use the terms 'military' type and 'scientific' type respectively.

First of all we checked if both types answered differently to the questions about the attention to be given to the elements of the education. In fact this proved to be the case. The cadets of the military type wish to lay much more emphasis on the military training and on the whole they find the attention actually given to the scientific education satisfactory. Among the cadets of the scientific type the reverse is to be seen: they want more attention to be given to the scientific education and find the military training sufficiently accentuated (table 3).

Table 3. Relation between the assignment of the first rank to either military training or scientific education, and the attention to be given to the 5 elements of the education in the opinion of the cadets

| First rank | Mean score of desired attention to | | | | |
	military training	*scientific education*	*cadets' corps*	*physical training*	*battalion*
Military training (N = 238)	1,22	2,03	1,93	1,77	2,01
Scientific education (N = 151)	1,95	1,38	1,93	1,78	2,17
P	<0,001	<0,001	n.s.	n.s.	0,10>P>0,05

Score 1 = more attention
Score 2 = equal attention
Score 3 = less attention

As in our investigation the scientific education at the military academy occupied a central position, we constructed a scale to measure the cadets' satisfaction with the conditions under which they are studying. The scale consists of a number of sub-scales, each covering a particular aspect of the scientific education, viz.:

61

a. the organization, i.e. the planning and programming of the study;
b. the composition of the study, the relations between the subjects, etc.;
c. the relevance of the study to the future professional duties;
d. the didactics of the teachers;
e. the contacts with the teachers;
f. the study coaching.

Apparently most cadets were satisfied with didactics, coaching and contacts with the teachers, and to a less extent also with the composition of the study. As to the relevance a slight dissatisfaction is shown: in the opinion of a number of cadets the study is insufficiently connected with the actual situation with the troops; not all subjects are of importance for their professional practice; this importance has at least in-sufficiently been stressed; the matters they expect really to need in the future are getting too little attention.

Table 4. Degree of satisfaction with 6 aspects of the scientific education among cadets (N = 438)

Aspects of scientific education	Percentage of cadets scoring on satisfaction scales			Mean score
	Low (scores 1-3)	*Medium (score 4)*	*High (scores 5-7)*	
Didactics	13	31	55	4,60
Coaching	11	34	55	4,57
Contacts	19	33	48	4,43
Composition	27	37	37	4,13
Relevance	37	33	30	3,89
Organization	65	28	6	3,14

Scale 1-7
High score = great satisfaction

Did - coach	n.s.	Coach - organ	P<0,001
Did - cont	n.s.	Cont - comp	P<0,001
Did - comp	P<0,001	Cont - relev	P<0,001
Did - relev	P<0,001	Cont - organ	P<0,001
Did - organ	P<0,001	Comp - relev	P<0,01
Coach - cont	P<0,01	Comp - organ	P<0,001
Coach - comp	P<0,001	Relev - organ	P<0,001
Coach - relev	P<0,001		

Clearly dissatisfied are the cadets with the organization of the study. In general they experience the study as being too strictly organized; the program leaves too little room for personal preferences and interests; the pace of study is dictated too much by the program; not enough time remains for the preparation of the examinations (table 4).

Let's return now to the two types of cadets we wanted to compare. It turned out that their satisfaction with some aspects of the study showed a certain amount of difference too: here the cadets of the scientific type are more satisfied than those of the military type.

Especially with regard to the relevance of the study this leads to an interesting conclusion. On the whole the cadets of the military type are dissatisfied with the relevance of the study for their future professional duties. Among the cadets of the scientific type, on the other hand, the relevance of the study is expressed with a significantly greater frequency (table 5).

Table 5. Relation between the assignment of the first rank to either military training or scientific education, and satisfaction with 5 aspects of the scientific education among cadets

First rank	Mean score of satisfaction with aspects of scientific education				
	Didactics	*Coaching*	*Contacts*	*Composition*	*Relevance*
Military training (N = 238)	4,48	4,56	4,27	3,97	3,71
Scientific education (N = 151)	4,72	4,58	4,62	4,27	4,15
P	$0,10 > P > 0,05$	n.s.	$< 0,01$	$< 0,05$	$< 0,001$

Scale 1 - 7
High score = great satisfaction

Note: Owing to a mistake made in programming the computer, the aspect of 'organization' could not be included in this comparison.

Another factor which gives us an opportunity to compare the two types, is the study attitude and the study motivation of the cadets. Here we cannot give an exhaustive treatment of the meaning of these concepts and their mutual relation (2). Suffice it to say that by study attitude we understand the degree of positive or negative valuation as regards serious study. Study motivation can be defined as the amount of energy expressed in study behaviour. We measured both variables using a series of statements, which in the attitude scale were formulated as opinions about studying, in the motivation scale as descriptions of study behaviour.

On the attitude scale, where we classified the raw scores into five classes, all cadets together got a mean class score of 3,26. Nearly a quarter of the cadets range in the classes 1 and 2, and so show a relatively negative study attitude. The classes 4 and 5, corresponding with a relatively positive attitude, comprise 42% of the cadets. On the motivation scale, classified in six classes, all cadets together got a mean class score of 3,64. Here the classes 1 and 2, corresponding with a relatively low study motivation, comprise 22% of the cadets. A relatively high study motivation (classes 5 and 6) was found with 27% of the cadets (table 6).

Table 6. Study attitude and study motivation among cadets (N = 435)

	Percentage of cadets scoring on attitude scale					Mean score
	1	2	3	4	5	
Study attitude	6	18	33	29	13	3,26

	Percentage of cadets scoring on motivation scale						Mean score
	1	2	3	4	5	6	
Study motivation	9	13	21	31	17	10	3,64

Study attitude
High score = positive attitude
Study motivation
High score = high motivation

To what extent do the two types of cadets distinguished above differ with regard to study attitude and study motivation? In fact the so-called scientific type seems to have a slightly more positive study attitude than the so-called military type, but the difference is not significant. With regard to study motivation, however, a significant difference appears: the cadets of the scientific type show a higher motivation with respect to the study than the cadets of the military type (table 7).

Table 7. Relation between the assignment of the first rank to either military training or scientific education, and study attitude and study motivation among cadets

First rank	Mean score on scale of	
	Study attitude	Study motivation
Military training (N = 238)	3,25	3,56
Scientific education (N = 151)	3,36	3,91
P	n.s.	0,10>P>0,05

Study attitude:
scale 1-5
high score = positive attitude
Study motivation:
scale 1-6
high score = high motivation

Remains the question if it is possible to identify the two types of cadets in clearly indicatable categories. Therefore we checked if perhaps one type is more strongly represented than the other in the different years of study, in the departments of study, in Army or Air Force or in the different arms and services (table 8).

As far as the years of study are concerned, there is a striking difference between the cadets of the first year and those of the following years. In the first year the cadets of the military type form a clear majority: 72% think the military training the most important, only 21% the scientific education.

Table 8. Relation between the assignment of the first rank to either military training or scientific education, and year of study, department of study, forces, arms and services

Categories		Percentage of cadets assigning the first rank to		Level of significance
		Military training	Scientific education	
Year of study	1st (N = 129)	72	21	
	2nd (N = 93)	49	44	
	3rd (N = 86)	53	33	P<0,001
	4th (N = 103)	42	45	
	5th (N = 25)	40	36	
Department of study	Soc. (N = 243)	60	28	Soc.-Techn. P<0,02
	Techn. (N = 161)	50	41	Soc.-Fin. P<0,02
	Fin. (N = 32)	34	50	Techn.-Fin. n.s.
Forces	Army (N = 328)	59	31	
	Air (N = 106) Force	42	45	P<0,01
Arms and services*	Gr. 1 (N = 164)	75	16	Gr. 1-gr. 2 P<0,001
	Gr. 2 (N = 118)	40	47	Gr. 1-gr. 3 P<0,001
	Gr. 3 (N = 91)	41	49	Gr. 1-gr. 4 P<0,001
	Gr. 4 (N = 62)	50	37	Gr. 2-gr. 3 n.s.
				Gr. 2-gr. 4 n.s.
				Gr. 3-gr. 4 n.s.

* Group 1 = infantry, cavalry,
    artillery
  Group 2 = engineers, signal corps,
    techn. service,
    electron. service

Group 3 = army service corps,
    transport, finance corps,
    logistic services AF
Group 4 = general service AF,
    flying service AF

In the following years of study the two types are on the whole nearly equally represented. The small frequency of the scientific type in the first year of study has probably to be ascribed to the fact that the first year cadets have hardly been brought in touch with the scientific education.

Cadets of the military type are more frequent in the department of social sciences than in the departments of technical and financial studies. In the latter departments, on the contrary, the scientific type is more strongly represented.

The cadets of the Army are preponderantly of the military type. In the Air Force both types occur nearly equally.

Finally the military type is much more strongly represented among the cadets of the infantry, cavalry and artillery than of the other arms and services. With the infantry, cavalry and artillery the scientific type, however, is only sparingly represented.

Summarizing: our investigation yielded two types of cadets, cadets who find the military training the most important element of their education, and those who put the scientific education first.

From these two types the first, the so-called military type, shows several distinctive traits. It wants to lay more emphasis on military training, is less satisfied with a number of aspects of the scientific education (particularly with the relevance of it) and shows a less high study motivation.

This type is most frequent among the cadets of the first year of study, in the department of social sciences, among the cadets of the Army and particularly among those of the infantry, cavalry and artillery.

The second type, the so-called scientific type, however, wants to lay more emphasis on the scientific education, is more satisfied with a number of aspects of the scientific education (as well as with the relevance of it) and has a relatively high study motivation.

This type is represented more strongly among the cadets of the senior years, and occurs relatively frequently in the departments of technical and financial studies, among the cadets of the Air Force and among all arms and services except infantry, cavalry and artillery.

III. DISCUSSION

If we regard the military academy as a social system, this system is bound to produce effects, corresponding to the needs existing in the armed forces as well as within the academy. Briefly we can say that the academy has a more or less 'prescribed task' to meet those needs or to realize those effects that are actually desired or necessary.

The ascertainment of expectations inside and outside the academy can make clear what tasks are imposed by the environment and what the 'insiders' see as their own task. It is up to the sociologist to establish if, how and to what degree people know their tasks, and next to establish if and to what degree these tasks have been realized. The facts enable us to do so. Therefore we have to look at (3):

1. The activities and intentions of the military academy;
2. The expectations, opinions and needs of the groups concerned with the academy;
3. The effects the academy actually has upon the others concerned.

The research group has paid some attention to points 1 and 2. In the introduction a summing up is given of the activities and intentions of the military academy. An indication for the expectations, opinions and needs we can find in the results as presented above. It is clear that the groups concerned do not have identical opinions. There are differences between the opinions of the officers, the civilian teachers and the cadets, but also between the opinions (and expectations) of the cadets themselves. This is not remarkable.

We all know that in the armed forces, there is a change in skill structure as well as in professional orientation. Highly sophisticated weapon systems as well as a clear call for managerial expertise have stimulated an increasing input of scientific knowledge and specialized skills.

This seems to be incompatible with the still existing traditional conception of the officer's role as a 'heroic leader'.

The officer still is and will always be a manager of violence. Changes in the pattern of violence have been clearly and well described by military sociologists. It is essential to state that the officer was a so-called 'generalist', skilled as a commander of combat units. This professional type is gradually loosing ground.

A new elite is rising in the military establishment: the technocrats. Yet, the ideal of the 'heroic leader' still persists as an attractive military self-image, as Van Doorn states. 'To mention some research conclusions: the professional orientation of cadets both in the United States and France reflects the coexistence of the technician and the warrior-role. This means that the traditional uniformity of the population of the great military academies has disappeared' (4).

Within the limitations of the design of the present study we may conclude that this is true for the Royal Netherlands Military Academy too.

The tensions, growing out of these different orientations are reflected in the results mentioned above.

The cadets themselves reflect the tension between the demands of a purely military training and the demands of a scientific education adapted to the demands of the increased complexity of the task structure.

Institutionalization of both military training and scientific education seems a hard process.

Since it is clear that the standard model of the profession is outmoded and indistinct, the key problem seems to be how, for the officer of the future, we can find a proper orientation which is reflected in the cadets' education program.

Which of the significant traditional features essential for the military profession are needed?

What kind of education programs at the military academies must be developed: Is it still possible to educate *the* professional officer? Or must there be a shift in the education programs that takes into account the differences within the professional roles to be performed?

In order to answer these questions one thing is needed in any case. To build up a professionally oriented and integrated education program, research has to be undertaken that gives insight into the character, composition and differentiation of the officer's profession.

REFERENCES

1. DOORN, J. A. A. VAN, 'The Officer Corps: A Fusion of Profession and Organization (*Archiv. Europ. Sociol.*, VI (1965), pp. 262–282).
2. CROMBAG, H. F. M., *Studiemotivatie en studieattitude (Study Motivation and Study Attitude)*, Groningen, 1968.
3. MARSMAN, G. W., *De Katholieke dagbladpers in sociologisch perspectief (The Catholic Press in Sociological Perspective)*, Assen, 1967.
4. DOORN, J. A. A. VAN, 'The Military Profession in Transition' (in: WILSON, N. A. B. (ed.), *Manpower Research*, London, 1969).

The Adaptation of Professional Soldiers to New Training Methods

B. FAUCHOIS*

* Bureau for social problems (French Army).

I. INTRODUCTION

This report assembles observations from more than ten years' varied experience on the development of teaching methods.

There have been many reactions to the introduction of active methods for training commissioned and non-commissioned ranks. The original intention was not a deliberate upheaval in traditional military teaching. Some officers had simply come across staff-training methods used in industry and applied them prudently in the army in fully-specified fields.

You will know how these methods evolved: to begin with, the role of the group and the development of self-tuition were emphasised; then a person who 'prompted' or 'facilitated' the development of the group, rather than a 'possessor of knowledge' was insisted upon, as was the lack of a ready-made prescribed solution for the group.

Analogously there has been a constant development in post-war years of audio-visual methods, which have been greatly used for military schooling. Nevertheless these methods were for some time used as an aid to traditional instruction methods, in 'homeopathic' proportions.

Only with the advent of closed-circuit television for education was the need asserted to combat passivity in pupils faced with an influx of images and to combine audio-visual and active methods.

So these two, initially seemingly independent processes meet up and augment one another.

Visual methods help to start the group work up and this is improved with solid groundwork.

The reactions to this challenge have, as we have already stated, been surprisingly animated, from enthusiastic concurrence to set, sometimes rather mystic resistance.

Such emotion can only be explained if, beyond the technical problem of training, there are more fundamental questions: in fact one cannot refer to the education scene without assuming some concept of authority and power. It involves a man's image as a leader, as an officer and the general attitude of the individual towards the problems of human relationships.

Before we compare the traditional concepts of the chief training officer with the new, it is worth recalling the relative isolation of the Army for several decades; it has been a closed world where ideas, at large in other circles, were barred and censored.

This situation may explain why some concepts, which are fully admitted if not well-applied in university and industrial circles, seem almost subversive in a traditional military environment. This reaction is bound up with a whole set of attitudes, and its nature might be an additional item on the Wisconsin scale for radical conservative opinions.

II. THE ARMY, A CLOSED SOCIETY

Sociologically speaking, the Army is a permanent contradiction.

Considering its very purpose, and the fact that its efficiency requirements must be met, it should be a community with an evolutionary calling suited on the one hand to follow, sometimes instigate technical progress, and on the other to adapt to the most varying situations and constantly changing staff, both of which reflect contemporary civilian society.

Yet it constitutes a closed, over-protected society. This is primarily due to a combination of circumstances.

The sociological make-up of the officers corps is not representative of the French population: between 1962 and 1968 the percentage of soldier's sons entering the special Military Academy varied between 38 and 50%. If the sons of civil servants are added, the percentage varies from 45 to 65%.

Moreover, the social mobility of these officers is very weak. Until recently, a young officer entered the Army for his entire career; extremely few reserve officers are taken up into active service if they have a late vocation. The influence of the family circle, the habit of living in a closed environment, the renunciation of a lucrative career all contribute to the soldier's acceptance more or less sincerely of a system of values pertaining specifically to the military profession: order, discipline, service to the nation, disinterestedness.

A certain view of the world emerges for many, a set of ethics often supported by religious values which are opposed to contemporary ideologies.

We could digress at length to discover how the lure of a military vocation marks out particular temperaments and thus defines the characteristics of the military group, or if, on the contrary, the basic principles condition the mentality of the members of the group and separate off the deviants.

An experiment by Professor Mucchielli at the Saumur Cavalry School in 1962 would seem to prove that if there is an ideal officer 'image' expressed in a particular character pattern, the traits of the young officers who themselves defined this stereotype will not correspond to the model and might even be quite varied. Whatever the case may be, we could refer to the professional soldier's 'basic personality' which is modelled by regulations and expressed in daily behaviour and outward appearances, such as ideological choices.

The Armed Forces of different nations might even be found to have numerous common traits and affinities.

These very highly significant circumstances also result from the structural limitations of the Army: strict hierarchism, freely-accepted privation of normal civil liberties, life in isolated camps or garrisons, frequent changes, which impede neighbourly or friendly relations with other categories of the population and widen the gulf separating soldiers from civilians.

This state of affairs explains the attachment to traditional views which have slowly formed at the very heart of the military institution, and the distrust of methods from outside which upset established ideas.

III. THE TRADITIONAL CONCEPT OF THE CHIEF TRAINING OFFICER IN THE ARMY

Since a soldier's object is preparation for combat, this dominates the idea officers have of their rôle: an image of virility, self-assurance, but of drama and exacting demand too. They see themselves as the men who one day may have to lead others into battle (envisaged furthermore in the most violent terms; as hand-to-hand fighting, as skirmishes) and they will have to give orders on which the life or death of their subordinates depends.

The major difficult and distressing problem would therefore seem to be to get such orders accepted and carried out, under conditions where speed of performance is of foremost importance and spontaneous, direct, almost reflex obedience is required.

This acute situation is therefore at the root of the image, even in peace-time, even if one's war-time duties have little chance of leading to direct confrontation with the enemy.

It helps to define a style of command based on the leader's absolute, unquestionable power. He is charismatic; his authority is glorified and he obtains it from his virtues, his personality; the gift of command is demanded of him.

In our military academies the chief training officer is at the same time the hierarchical head, and, where these two roles meet, one overrules to such an extent that the consideration of power, self-assertion, protection of the leader-image often blur the educational concerns.

The chief training officer, in describing to his pupils the ideal portrait of a leader, develops in them an expectation, often present beforehand, as a result of the cadets' family background.

He is obliged to cultivate a stereotyped, exemplary leader and avoid any situation which might disclose the man behind the model.

In practice, whether or not this is in keeping with this temperament, he is induced to adopt an autocratic style of command and in the teaching field to use only communication methods which are essentially unilateral, i.e. didactic.

If the pupils are permitted to be verbally or physically active, by means of questions, the chief officer in the last resort names or confirms the right solution, whether it is the Academy's or from his own experience.

Moreover, quite logically, training officers at Military Academies have long been chosen from among those who have the most exemplary service records, so as to back up their advancement and their authority as instructors with impeccable experience.

Exemplary teaching and the importance of the problem of power are not peculiar to the Army, but here they find the best justification and rationalisation.

IV. THE TRAINING OFFICER'S ROLE IN THE NEW METHODS

Active methods and educative technology based on audio-visual means challenge the traditional links between the teacher and the taught.

The tutor loses his once-acknowledged monopoly to transfer knowledge. He is only one source of information among others: documents, visual aids, groups of pupils.

Teaching in the past centred around the mentor's person; now the interest has moved to the pupil or the group. The concrete results are the disappearance of the teaching dais, the new arrangement of desks so that everyone can see and hear everyone else.

Audio-visual methods put even the teacher in the spectator's seat among the other spectators, i.e. his pupils. All have moved to the 'same side of the fence' and receive, simultaneously, pictures and information made by others.

But although the mentor loses his role of an 'oracle', of the privileged holder of knowledge, he acquires other functions: that of an organiser of information received, a go-between in the exchange of opinions and in group work.

The pupil is no longer considered as an 'empty vessel' which he must fill, but a 'reservoir' of potentialities which can be developed.

76

The teacher has come down from his pedestal, back to his primeval function: to be at his pupils' service assisting them in changing, acquiring ability or knowledge corresponding to the teaching objectives.

V. THE PROBLEMS OF THE NEW METHODS
FOR THE CHIEF TRAINING OFFICER

In the military leader's eyes, the men are a means of fulfilling a mission; he has their interests at heart, but he knows that sometimes he will have to sacrifice them for his mission.

And yet, it is inconceivable that a teacher could even sacrifice his pupils for anything. This is the paradox of the military instructor.

The introduction of new teaching methods in a Military Academy, with both prominence of the group as a 'training agent' and the apparent eclipse of the instructor, would seem, compared with traditional education, to call for the elimination of the leader.

The training officer used to behave like a 'wartime leader' with his pupils, demanding strict discipline, whereby the knowledge he was instructed to convey had to be accepted as combat orders would have been.

Henceforth he will have to differentiate between his two rôles and play them alternatively.

The new pattern of education far from represents a convenience for him: the pupils' expectations are determined by the institutionalisation of longstanding models.

Their passivity used to be very well, too well, accepted by most; the expression and initiative required in 'active' education meet with resistance.

Therefore, the training officer does not only have to fight himself to shake off his old habits, but sometimes his pupils too, who are flustered by the new demands, disappointed in their expectations and will beg for the 'good old authoritative lecture'.

We must bear in mind that teaching cannot be reduced to a private talk between the master and his pupils.

The institution and its set-up are making the full weight of their inertia felt and oppose new methods with all the traditional reflexes of resistance to change.

Can in fact renewal of teaching methods change the processes restricted in time and space to the training sessions?

Theoretically the chief training officer might find some flexibility in his rôles so that he can keep his autocratic style in command, but restore to the group all its scope of expression in the training periods.

In fact, the leader who has used active methods undergoes an irrevocable change, whereby he can no longer command AFTERWARDS AS BEFORE. He becomes aware of the individuals' merits and of the group's creativity as such and thus acquires a permanent need for 'feed-back' and does this whenever he can.

Command is no longer his prerogative, nor the gratification of prestige he must claim, but a vital function in the group which someone must carry out in the interests of all.

A radical change ensues in the atmosphere surrounding leader and subordinates; there is still not sufficient generalisation of active teaching methods to test its repercussions on the military institution on a large scale.

Yet it is not premature to imagine they will be considerable. Nor is it blindly optimistic to expect positive effects on the cohesion and efficiency of units, in peace and in war.

Social and technological
influences
on military organization

Military Training and Civilian Employment

J. A. JACKSON*

* Professor of social theory and institutions. The Queen's University of Belfast, Northern Ireland.

This paper is mainly concerned to explore the overall occupational pattern in which the military career is placed in most contemporary societies. For all but a very few who take up the profession of arms today there is no prospect of a lifetime career but instead only a partial commitment for relatively few years in any occupational life history. Although this situation is not altogether new it has a particular relevance in the circumstance of an increasingly technologically oriented profession devoted to the preparation and training for wars which must not happen.

Extensive consideration has been given both within and outside military organizations to the effective use of skilled manpower within the services and to the training and recruitment of appropriately qualified personnel. Competition with industry makes this recruitment difficult while the cost of specialised training within the services demands that some return is shown for the investment. It is here that the short-term commitment to the military career provides special problems. As Kurt Lang pointed out in this context nearly ten years ago: 'The short military service expectancy of the new enlistee is, on the average, only about one-tenth the working expectancy of an eighteen year old civilian male worker entering the labor force. The shorter the utilization period, the smaller the return to the services for their investment. A short-term military establishment with a rapidly rotating base of poorly trained manpower will contain hidden costs.'[1] It is indeed the problems of recruitment and training in these specific skills that have led to the investment of growing military resources to the problems of the redeployment of service personnel in the civilian sector; preparation for a second career and compensation for redundancy and premature retirement.

In conscript armed forces all males, and in some cases such as Israel females also, have an obligation to spend a period in military training before pursuing their civilian career. In such a situation the military commitment can be interpreted as an extension of the educational process, equally compulsory and implying the view that each citizen must be equipped with the basic military skills and techniques to allow him, should the need arise, to defend the state. This concept of 'every citizen a soldier' is one important strand in the development of a discussion of the proper functions of military training. With such a system there is a need for a small corps of career personnel but for the large majority military service represents a period of further socialization before their *real* occupational life commences rather than a specific preparation for it. The period of compulsory military service is then a 'training for life' rather than the first stage in the commitment to a chosen military career.

In countries which maintain their military forces by voluntary recruitment the practice has increasingly developed of limiting the commitment to a terminal commission of five, twelve or fifteen years with various possibilities of re-enlistment. Here again, few can confidently expect to make a lifetime commitment to a military career. After fifteen or even twenty years' service the question of the second career assumes an increasing importance in relation to streamlining of the military organization itself.

Since service and training in army, navy or airforce cannot offer the 'cradle-to-grave' assurance that is characteristic of many civil service appointments it becomes relevant to question the relationship of the military section of an individual occupational history to what follows it. There is, unfortunately, a sad lack of research on the actual occupations followed by those who are retired from or voluntarily leave military employment. Such figures as exist for Britain only cover a period of some three years following the termination of a service commission though they do indicate the general features of the resettlement process.

The Officers Resettlement Survey conducted in 1968 by the British Ministry of Defence covers 4,076 officers who had retired from the three services during 1965, 1966 and 1967.[2] In spite of the short period that had elapsed since they left the service one quarter had already changed their employment at least once and a further 10% were unemployed at the time of the survey. Although the period is too short to indicate the development of a consistent second career pattern the occupations followed by those who had found employment suggest that the transition to civilian life may not be without very real difficulties of adjustment for the individual and in terms of broader issues of the use of manpower may not always represent a maximum utilization of resources.

So far as the areas in which officers find post-service employment the survey indicated that one third took a clerical job, a quarter found professional employment and one fifth became either salesmen or managers.[3] These broad employment categories conceal a wide range of particular employments and levels of responsibility and remuneration. Half the sample expressed themselves 'very satisfied' with their present job[4] but it is clear that aspirations were directed often as much, if not more, towards the choice of a salubrious area in which to live (54.7% wished to live in the South and West of England) rather than a specific second career.[5] The average salary enjoyed by these officers on leaving the service was £1,500 per annum which suggests that for many a service pension is assumed to make up for a drop in real rewards once service benefits are given up.[6]

The details of this survey cannot be fully reported here but sufficient

84

has perhaps been mentioned to suggest a range of questions about the broad problem of resettlement of ex-service personnel.

Being a member of a military organization confers a status and qualification which is to a large degree lost when one leaves it. Purely 'military' skills are not directly transferable although certain incidental skills may be such as the capacity to fly aeroplanes or 'manage men'. For the officer corps especially as Feld has pointed out 'the authoritative position of the officer is based on the political utility of the organization he directs'... 'The range of rewards and inducements of a military career are limited by the fact that military service is a public monopoly. Within his social system, the organization he belongs to is the only one to which the soldier can legitimately sell his skills.'[7] One has seen particularly over the past twenty-five years as modern military establishments have developed more towards the *constabulary*[8] or *fire brigade*[9] concept of a deterrent and preventive function they have been deprived more and more of their professional glory and objective aims. The process noted by Feld leads to a situation where 'the secularization of society has intensified both the professionalism and the alienation of the military'. In this situation 'expertise replaces tradition, the ascriptive processes discard absolutistic standards in favour of secular ones.'[10]

The effects of this process on the subsequent career of service personnel lies chiefly in the disappearance of those ascriptive qualities conferred by a service career which were, it was assumed, transferable to the civilian sector. 'Once a soldier, always a soldier', 'You can tell it by his bearing' and other catch phrases designed to identify the ex-military or service personnel when off duty are marks of the recognition of a distinctive ascriptive status. Most significantly the fact that military rank was also considered transferable outside the organization and carried status attribution was a further mark of the validation by civilian society of the criteria of the military profession and life style. Today the organizational isolation and alienation of the military has served to diminish and limit any particular reference to military status outside the organization. Rank becomes a functional and specific rather than universalistic quality. Exceptions of course exist for some of the higher ranks and in some areas such as Northern Ireland where even a relatively low rank such as Captain or Major appears to have continuing political significance and worth in the civil sphere. The British Ministry of Defence survey indicates that rank may still be a factor taken into account by possible employers particularly if it is at a high level.[11] However the survey finds that purely military qualifications did not affect a man's search for employment or the point at which he obtained it but together with civilian qualifications they are directly related to employment prospects, initial salary and responsibility levels.[12]

The tension between ascriptive and achievement professionals in the military organization has been stressed in a recent paper by Harries-Jenkins with particular reference to engineers in the Royal Air Force. He demonstrates that the incorporation of achievement professionals trained outside the organization which uses their training leads to a conflict situation between their commitments to the civilian professional organization and the military organization. They approach the position of the doctors, dentists, chaplains and similar branches who are 'essentially civilians who happen to perform their professional function within a military environment.'[13] For these 'free professionals' the autonomy and professional commitment they enjoy in relation to their specific professional function greatly eases their eventual transfer to a civilian occupational environment. For the ascriptive military professional, on the other hand, not only is no such easy transfer of functions possible but also their dependence on the organization and its comprehensive structure of hierarchical control and specific ascriptive training limits any transfer to occupations outside it.

The proportion of service personnel having qualifications of a professional kind which would facilitate transfer to an alternative civilian career is still in any case relatively small and particularly so outside the technical branches. The Officers Resettlement Survey did not include in its terms of reference doctors, veterinary surgeons, dentists, chaplains and lawyers but the findings for the remaining sections indicate that there is a considerable variation between the technical branches and the general service branch. In their sample 55.3% of officers in Engineering and Education sections had a University degree, 18.2% in Supply and Secretariat sections and only 14.4% in all other branches.[14] Even within technical branches such as the Full Career Engineering Officers in the Royal Air Force in 1969, considered by Harries-Jenkins, 50.8% lacked a university degree or any further formal qualification and consequently were only recognised for their technical abilities within the sphere of the military organization itself.[15] On the basis of these indications it is clear that one cannot assume that many service officers are by definition readily equipped to make a transfer to a civilian career demanding the same or equivalent technical skills and experience to those for which they are utilised in the military sphere.

Even those who are so qualified may hold in reality only the prerequisite educational qualifications, such as a degree but lack the specific applications and experience that would be relevant to a post in civilian life.

In spite of these difficulties there has been a tendency for the military, especially in its recruiting campaigns to emphasise its attractions as a training ground for particular skills and professions. This is a legitimate claim so far as many skilled and semi-skilled crafts are concerned (truck drivers, mechanics, clerks, cooks, etc.) but particularly for the general service soldier at officer level the training is necessarily specifically geared to the needs of the organization itself. Consequently apart from the claim to 'train managers' offered by the British Army there is little evident civilian equivalent toward which a Service career can be oriented. These officers are most vulnerable to redundancy precisely because their career expectancy is tied solely to the organization in which they serve and on its arbitrary decisions they stand or fall. For them any future, non-military career, means a total reorientation of their occupational skills, goals and ambitions and life style.

Change of career and the choice of a second career are problems which occur widely outside the military sphere but it is precisely because of the nature of the total commitment to a military career, even a relatively brief career, that it is distinguished from any other job. It is characteristic of military organizations that they are total institutions providing comprehensively for the welfare of their personnel and requiring equally total commitment on the part of these personnel to the ideology, normative discipline and aims of the organization. The notion of the military as a total institution has been discussed fully elsewhere but in terms of the basic elements of the model the contractual obligation of labour is absolute and the successful functioning of the organization depends on the maintenance of high levels of discipline in response to the demands of senior personnel. Apart from boarding schools and possibly prisons and hospitals, no other organization in which an individual is likely to find himself provides quite so total an environment.[16]

Certain quasi-military bodies such as the police or the fire services approximate in certain respects to the military model but it is notable that even in the more relaxed climate of contemporary Western armies the essential characteristics of this model are maintained. Although there has been a clear movement towards the idea of the military career as simply 'another job' it remains a functional distinction that military personnel are 'always on duty'. The ascriptive, life-style vocational elements of the 'whole man' or training for life conception remains dominant over the achievement, task-specific division of labour within the organization.

The transfer from a military career to a second or subsequent career outside the military organization while having intrinsic problems of its own also raises questions about the general framework of occupational sociology and manpower studies. Even in discussions of social mobility there has been a tendency for a rather static, snap-shot comparison to be made between fathers' and sons' final achieved occupations rather than in terms of a total occupational profile. The status, income level and rewards of a second career may reflect a marked downward shift from that of the first career especially for those who make the move at ages of forty plus. Even allowing for pension and other compensatory awards such as the lump sum payments on redundancy – the Golden Bowler of the British Army, for instance – there would appear to be a relative decline in income for a significant number of ex-service personnel.

It is, however, extremely difficult to assess the value of many of the fringe benefits enjoyed as part of the Service career which are given up at retirement. Biderman citing a study in 1963 shows that in the United States although the mean figure of active duty pay and allowances is compared with the mean total of retirement pay and the earnings from civilian employment, the median figure shows the average officer to be slightly disadvantaged.[17] The British Ministry of Defence sample, while it does not attempt any direct comparison, indicates an average initial salary of £1,500 for Army and Air Force personnel and £1,600 for Navy personnel. The difference is explained by the larger number of Navy men who have University degrees which carry higher initial salaries. The highest average initial salaries are earned by those in the thirty to thirty-nine age group (£1,700); the forty to forty-nine age group average £1,600 while those under thirty (£1,300) and over fifty (£1,400) average lower initial salaries.[18] It must of course be borne in mind that these are initial salaries and in many cases quite considerable increments can be expected once an officer has demonstrated his capacity in the civilian employment.

The assumption that an occupational profile would ideally consist of a steady progression in rewards and responsibility from school leaving until final retirement at an age of about sixty-five is not closely supported by examination of the problems of the second career in the military sphere. In civilian employment a shift toward earlier attainment of earning peaks with, for the large majority, a subsequent decline in second and subsequent careers is also evident. Large corporations share some of the problems of the military in terms of their need to recruit able young men from whom after ten or fifteen years' service only a few will survive to reach senior executive positions. For the remainder who become redundant at ages of thirty-five or forty a similar problem exists to that of ex-military personnel although in some cases their skills may be more easily transferable.

That the second career has some risks attached to it is recognised by the buffer effect of military pensions on the one hand and the high rewards paid to high redundancy risk occupations in the civilian sector such as that of air line pilot on the other. Whether in terms of the most effective redeployment of manpower the situation is entirely satisfactory is another question. Biderman comments on the attractions of teaching as a second career for many American officers, particularly since some aspects of the job would be consistent with work already undertaken in the Service career.[19] The large number in clerical occupations in the British sample (33.2%) similarly suggests fields in which some transfer of tasks may be possible. But viewed from an overall perspective one must ask whether ten, fifteen or twenty years of military service and training is the most satisfactory way to train a teacher or a clerk.

Equally one may perhaps ask whether the relief of post-career anxieties is an important military function. The extension of this concern, closely related to recruitment considerations suggests a conflict between the view of the military organization as a 'total welfare body' and as 'a competitive industrial organization'. Abrams has described fully the development of the Resettlement Service in Britain as a product of the reorganization and streamlining of the structure of the services.[20] To the extent that this streamlining has suggested increased organizational efficiency and has offered to those who aspire to be employed within it 'a job like any other, only more interesting', this paternalistic concern may be misplaced. However, most military organizations, especially those operating without conscription, need to impose arbitrary limits on the freedom of their employees to move freely between the services and alternative employment particularly if they are to gain maximum utility from their investment.

Quite apart from these considerations most will recognise necessary limitations on the degree to which it is desirable to maintain that there is an identity between military training and capacity for civilian employment. As Biderman has pointed out 'Too much stress on the adaptability of military personnel to civilian pursuits... may tend to undermine the peculiar features of profession, identity, and mystique on which the distinctive claims of the military rest. This is particularly true at a time when its special claims to expertise are being challenged by the increasingly significant roles of civilians for various defence activities.'[21]

The military profession must be pursued within an organizational framework which constrains and prevents its exercise in any alternative situation. To the extent that the streamlined military organization cannot offer a full career commitment to those it employs while still demanding in the period the individual is employed a total commitment to the organization, it inhibits a ready flow of personnel between military and alternative employment.

Further, by virtue of the emphasis on the recruitment of youth and the 'whole man' concept of professional socialization, there is an assumption in the modern military organization that the military is necessarily the 'first career'. This assumption is certainly one that may need to be questioned in terms of the most effective transferability of skilled personnel into and out of the military organization. Where a general 'national service' military commitment operates for the whole population it may be possible to bridge the gap between the military and the civilian occupational ethos more freely. In that case a much greater emphasis could be placed on a military force capable of recruiting those in older age groups with requisite skills which could be employed within the military framework rather than the converse.

It is inconsistent with the increasing technological requirements of a contemporary military force to consider the possibility of even wider use of non-military trained personnel for specific task fulfilment in the military sphere. Also it is somewhat heretical in terms of security factors to open more widely the flow of personnel from outside the military sphere if the 'whole man' concept of career commitment is sacrificed. In spite of this one is tempted to consider whether a far more flexible structure involving secondment of personnel at various levels throughout the occupational career pattern might not provide an answer to some of the problems of the modern military organization. Particularly with the minimal military training provided by an initial 'pre-career' period of conscription it does not seem impossible to envisage a military force increasingly staffed by personnel seconded from regular civilian commitments for short service appointments. Without the present commitment to youth as the prime requirement of the recruit the expertise of industrial and civil service middle management might readily be applied to military purposes.

Clearly such a development would mean the disappearance of the 'military career' as such – even in its present truncated form. It would lead to the ultimate fear of the autonomous military profession that it would become 'civilianised' and 'secularised'. However it is increasingly doubtful how much of the mystique of the military profession is any longer sufficient to justify its claim to offer a distinctive professional career in arms to those that it employs.

In any case many of the 'purely military' roles in which contemporary service personnel find themselves employed call for skills of a 'constabulary' or 'fire brigade' kind closely involved in community relationships in the civilian sector which further serve to weaken the distinctive military role in relation to civilian alternatives.

The possibly bizarre notions depend on the implication that the present situation is unsatisfactory so far as the second and subsequent careers of military personnel are concerned. Such evidence as we have does not yet provide a full picture extending over the whole occupational life history until retirement. This longitudinal research is now badly needed in order to assess the full implications of the present transfer from military to civilian employment.

NOTES

1. LANG, Kurt, 'Technology and Career management in the military establishment' in JANOWITZ, M., *The New Military*, Rusell Sage Foundation, New York 1964, p. 49.
2. *Report of the Officers Resettlement Survey*, Ministry of Defence, London, 1969, p. 7. A report of a study of other ranks will be available shortly and a further survey of officers is planned.
3. *Ibid.*, Table 25, p. 68.
4. *Ibid.*, Table 43, p. 91. A further 39.2% expressed themselves as 'fairly satisfied'. However, since the question was asked in relation to 'present job' it does not take account of initial dissatisfaction felt by those who had already changed jobs at the time of the survey.
5. *Ibid.*, Table 46, p. 99. A comparable clustering was found to occur in the U.S. situation examined by BIDERMAN, A. D., 'Sequels to a military career: the retired military professional' in JANOWITZ, M., *The New Military*, Russell Sage Foundation, New York, 1964.
6. *Ibid.*, Section 3.8.1., p. 73. Section 6 of the Second Series of Supplementary Tables of the Officers Resettlement Survey should also be consulted since these figures on salary are analysed more fully there.
7. FELD, M., 'Professionalism, nationalism, and the alienation of the military', in VAN DOORN, J. (Ed.), *Armed Forces and Society*, Mouton, The Hague, 1968, p. 55.
8. JANOWITZ, M., 'Armed Forces in Western Europe: Uniformity and Diversity', *European Journal of Sociology*, VI (1965), p. 231.
9. JACKSON, J. A., 'The Irish Army and the Development of the Constabulary Concept', in VAN DOORN, J. (Ed.), *Armed Forces and Society*, Mouton, The Hague, 1968, p. 126.
10. *Op. cit.* FELD, M. D., p. 65.
11. *Op. cit. Report of the Officers Resettlement Survey*, Table 34, pp. 77, 134, 135, 150. 33.3% of officers have military qualifications and 55.7% have civilian qualifications (A-level or above).
12. *Ibid.* pp. 129, 130 and 149. One officer in three had some kind of military qualification. Those holding a University degree (27.8%) varied between the services and by age and length of service.
13. HARRIES-JENKINS, G., *Dysfunctional Consequences of Military Professionalization*, unpublished paper presented to the Working Group on Armed Forces and Society, Seventh World Congress of Sociology, Varna, September 1970, p. 1.
14. *Op. cit. Officers Resettlement Survey*, Table 61, p. 124.
15. *Op. cit.* HARRIES-JENKINS, G., p. 6.
16. *Op. cit.* BIDERMAN, A. D., p. 319.
17. It must be said that the apparent 'Japanization' of some sectors of British industry suggests that there may be a move toward a more total organizational model. See for example SOFER, C., *Men in Mid-career*, Cambridge University Press, Cambridge, 1970.
18. *Op. cit. Officers Resettlement Survey*, Tables 31 and 32, pp. 73 and 75.
19. *Op. cit.* BIDERMAN, A. D., p. 314.
20. ABRAMS, P., 'Democracy, Technology and the Retired British Officer' in HUNTINGTON, S. P. (Ed.), *Changing Patterns of Military Politics*, Free Press, New York, 1962.
21. *Op. cit.* BIDERMAN, A. D., p. 302.

92

Some Sociological Aspects of Recruitment, Vocational Training, and 'Second Career' of Long-Term Soldiers

H. BENNINGHAUS*
H. RENN*
A. ROSNER*

* Research associates, University of Cologne, W. Germany.

1. PERSONNEL STRUCTURE AND PERSONNEL PROBLEMS OF THE BUNDESWEHR

Since 1956, the year of the set up of the Armed Forces of the German Federal Republic, all males of German nationality are liable to military service on reaching their eighteenth birthday[1]. At present the duration of the basic military service is 18 months[2]. According to official announcements the government intends to retain compulsory military service[3].

In spite of the compulsory military service the Bundeswehr does not rely exclusively on conscription. The active military personnel of the Bundeswehr consists of: (*a*) officers and non-commissioned officers who are regulars or volunteers, (*b*) long-term privates, and (*c*) conscripts[4].

1.1. *The Deficit of Long-Term Volunteers*

With the existing recruitment system the Bundeswehr has not been – by far – able to win sufficient number of long-term volunteers. The 'unhealthy proportion of regulars to long-term officers and non-commissioned officers'[5] has been viewed as one of the most urgent problems of the Bundeswehr for many years. The armed forces need – as the recent survey of the minister of defence showed – far more enlistees, i.e. soldiers who enlist for 2 to 15 years, and soldiers who remain in the services until they reach their special age limit of about 40 years (e.g. jet pilots)[6].

At present, the deficit of long-term officers amounts to 2 600 or 9 percent, whereas the deficit of non-commissioned officers runs up to 26 000 or 18 percent[7]. Especially the deficit of non-commissioned officers is viewed as 'alarming'[8].

For the following reasons the Bundeswehr is forced to direct its attention to the recruitment of volunteers with a length of service of three or more years[9]:
— Since the set up of the Bundeswehr the extraordinarily large need of long-term volunteers could not be met, with the exception of the first two years.
— The trend for volunteers to enlist only on a two years term of service is increasing[10].
— In the next three years a large proportion of departures are expected since non-commissioned officers with a 12 or 15 years length of service will be retiring.
— The intended increase in the proportion of long-term soldiers according to the structural model of the Bundeswehr heightens the need for long-term privates and non-commissioned officers.

Figure I reveals the intake of long-term volunteers since 1956.

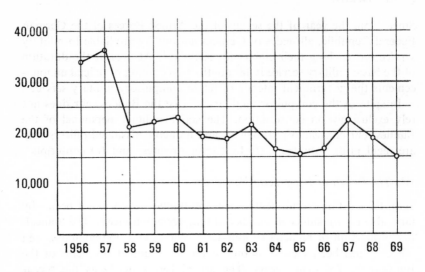

Figure I

When the Bundeswehr was set up in 1956/57 and candidates from many age classes enlisted, the intake of long-term volunteers was exceptionally high (average 35 000). Already in 1958 the intake decreased to 21 000, held out until 1963, and then fell off sharply in 1965. In 1967 financial restrictions largely reduced the possibilities of enlistment and reenlistment of soldiers on a two years term but, in the same year, resulted in an increase of applications on a three or more years term. In 1968 however, a new downward trend begun[11]. The number of volunteers with a three or four years term decreased from about 19 000 in 1968 to about 15 000 in 1969[12].

After reducing the length of service for volunteers to a minimum of two years in 1962, many young men enlisted for that length of time[13]. The certainty of being called up for basic military service and the attractive financial rewards made them well-disposed towards a length of service which exceeded the legally prescribed service by only six months. These volunteers can be called 'quasi-conscripts'[14]. The advantage is that a certain proportion of these short-term volunteers will later reenlist for a three or more years tour[15]. However, that advantage is somewhat offset by the fact that the applications for a short-term tour automatically reduce the applications for a longer term. Besides this, as the Defence

Commissioner of the Bundestag puts it, in a two-years tour 'proper training and its useful application is not possible'[16].

1.2. *Planning of the Ministry of Defence*[17]

In the face of this situation concerning the proportions of long-term volunteers, the planning of the ministry of defence seems scarcely realizable. Such planning is based on the assumption that the Bundeswehr cannot manage without a sufficient contingent of long-term volunteers because the military training and the maintenance and operation of highly developed weapon systems require special knowledge and skills which can only be acquired during a long period of service.

Given these military requirements and the available financial resources, the ministry of defence has outlined a model of personnel structure (see appendix, fig. C). This structural model calls for a ratio between long-term soldiers and conscripts of 60 percent to 40 percent and is rated as 'economically reasonable and militarily suitable'[18]. Figure C shows how far off the Bundeswehr is from its planned target. There are at present 49.5 percent long-term soldiers as against 50.5 percent conscripts. As the most recent official report of the ministry of defence states: 'These figures illustrate one of the main problems of the Bundeswehr'[19].

1.3. *The Special Status of the Long-Term Volunteers*

Other western armed forces have similar concerns and are striving to do away with the deficit of long-term volunteers[20]. But if their efforts are restricted to measures which raise the attractiveness of the careers or increase the financial incentives, in the long run the prognosis must turn out to be unfavorable. Those measures provide necessary but not at all sufficient conditions for removing the deficit of long-term volunteers.

Most of the long-term volunteers spend only a limited phase of their gainful activity in the armed forces. As the military can merely take over a limited proportion of them as regulars, the great majority has to retire after about 3 to 15 or 20 years of service. Consequently, the long-term volunteers must realize that they will spend only a relatively short but decisive phase in the services. They are forced to orientate themselves to their second career at the right time. This must be taken into account not only by the long-term volunteers but also by the armed forces. For: 'Over the long run, the ability of the military to recruit and retain superior

97

talent depends in part on the success of the military retired personnel in civilian economic and social life'[21].

Accordingly, armed forces which are unable to recruit enough long-term volunteers must pay attention to the factors which determine the success of the second career of retired volunteers. These factors will be analyzed in the following section.

2. DETERMINANTS OF A SUCCESSFUL RESETTLEMENT INTO CIVILIAN WORKING LIFE

There are two main determinants facilitating the reintegration of long-term volunteers into civilian life. The first is a socio-structural one which depends on the structure of the military organization and the general occupational structure of society; the second is an individual one which depends on the structure of the personality.

Obviously, the distinction between these determinants is only an analytical one, that is to say, there are only different grades of valence but no pure types in reality. Accordingly, an extensive analysis would isolate the interaction effects of the two factors, but limitations in the data hinder this in our case.

The first of the alleged determinants refers to the 'structural similarities' of the occupational activities in the military and the civilian sector of the society and to the 'interpenetrability' of these structures[22]. In the case of soldiers on limited engagements the salient point is the question of whether knowledge and skills acquired in the military setting are transferable into civilian life. The answer to this question depends mainly on the occupational experiences of the volunteer during his time of service. These experiences are of two different kinds: (a) knowledge and skills acquired through daily work, and (b) knowledge and skills gained through participation in special vocational training programs carried out by the military organization.

A 'lack of transferable skills'[23] is not the only reason for a failure in resettlement. Various findings indicate '... that it was not necessarily the retiree whose background was "more military", rather than "more civilianized", who had the greatest problems of transition'[24]. Moreover, it is not so much the 'absence of marketable skills' which is problematic in this connection 'but rather the difficulty of translating individual skills and experience gained in the military setting into civilian terms so that they can be "matched up" with employer needs'[25]. Therefore, the individual's readiness and ability to utilize his occupational knowledge and skills appears as an additional determinant of a successful transition[26]. Consequently, the successful resettlement of soldiers depends on two requirements: 'transferable skills' *and* 'translating skills'. Obviously, resettlement fails if both are absent; the lack of readiness and ability to apply knowledge and skills operates as a psychic obstruction preventing transfer. On the other hand, only for a limited time good 'translating skills' can make up for the absence of marketable knowledge and skills. Figure II shows these relationships.

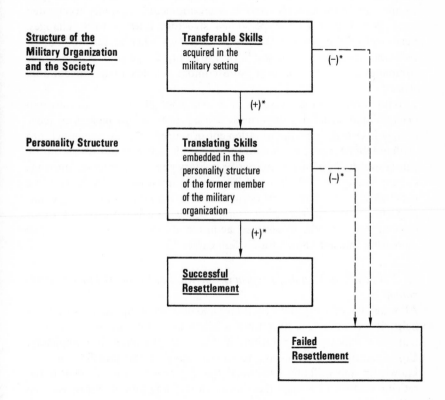

* Signs symbolize presence (+) or nonpresence (−) of skills

Figure II

2.1. Socio-structural Factors

To begin with the first determinant we have to ask what socio-structural realities are relevant in the society and the military establishment of the Federal Republic of Germany.

2.1.1. Convergence of Military and Civilian Occupational Structures

Like other industrial societies the society and military establishment of the Federal Republic has witnessed a process of increasing complexity of technology. In the military sector this development has rapidly accelerated since World War I. The personnel structure mirrors these changes: personnel of the pure military type decreases whereas the number of technical specialists increases[27]. In 1964 only 29 percent of the whole personnel of the Bundeswehr were combat soldiers in a conventional sense[28].

With regard to the question of convergence of military and civilian occupational structures the crucial consequence of this increasing technology is that it helps the resettlement of retired military personnel into civilian labor force. Such a convergence is also evident in the case of the Bundeswehr: 71 percent of the active military personnel practice functions corresponding to 250 different civilian occupations[29]. As Kurt Lang concludes: '... the decline of occupations with no civilian-military counterparts ... suggests increasing overlap between skills required in the two sectors. As a result, experience acquired during military service has increasing transfer value in a civilian career'[30].

2.1.2. Vocational Training Programs Carried Out by the Military Organization

Although the convergence of military and civilian occupational structures helps the resettlement of retired soldiers even without any assistance from the military organization, it does not guarantee it completely. Consequently, it is necessary to further enhance the transfer value of knowledge and skills by vocational training programs which enable the retiring soldiers to change their roles without any loss of status. But the still existing structural dissimilarities are not the only reason for conducting vocational training programs. Independently of the degree of convergence these programs are very important in another respect. At present – and probably in the future – the recruitment of long-term volunteers by the Bundeswehr will depend largely on those who either need vocational training or wish to take the opportunity for upward mobility made possible through enlistment[31].

Legally the Bundeswehr must facilitate the movement of the retiring soldiers from the military setting into civilian life. In this connection it is given the task of initiating measures which will make possible a taking up of an occupation after the end of the service or after the end of a subsequent vocational training[32]. The institutional instrument for the realization of this legal mandate is the 'Berufsförderungsdienst' (Office for Vocational Furtherance) of the Bundeswehr. It has the following main goals:

— personal guidance,
— vocational furtherance to maintain former occupational knowledge and skills (study groups engaged in vocational training, vocational courses, financing of correspondence courses),
— financing of vocational training after the end of the service where the length of the training depends on the term of service[33],
— financial support whilst making the transition from military to civilian life, and
— rehabilitation of injured soldiers.

Moreover, long-term volunteers can attend certain schools of the Bundeswehr before or after the end of their service[34]. Summarizing we can state that there are strong socio-structural factors in society and in the military establishment of the Federal Republic of Germany which facilitate the resettlement of long-term volunteers. The increasing technology not only of the military organization but also of the civilian occupational life leads to a convergence of both sectors. Beyond that the Bundeswehr has at its disposal occupational programs with civilian orientation. Whether these programs guarantee the successful reintegration of retired soldiers and whether such programs help attract new recruits will be dealt with in a subsequent part of this paper.

2.2. *Personality Factors*

As mentioned above, the successful resettlement depends not only on whether long-term volunteers possess transferable knowledge and skills; but also depends on their individual abilities to utilize such knowledge and skills in civilian life.

In our analysis[35] direct measurement of translating skills was not possible. Instead we chose two personality factors which are components of the theoretical construct 'translating skill'; i.e. the achievement orientation which may facilitate successful resettlement, and the commitment to the military setting which may inhibit the successful reintegration of the retired soldier.

101

In the following we intend to inquire whether these factors are characteristically found in the personality structure of long-term volunteers and not in that of other types of military personnel.

2.2.1. *Achievement Orientation*

In spite of the lasting discussion about the relationship between achievement orientation and occupational success[36], we follow the hypothesis '... that strength of achievement motive is an important personality factor contributing to occupational mobility'[37]. Starting from this standpoint, we measured the achievement orientation of the sampled soldiers making use of eight statements[38]. The answers to these statements were combined in an index of 'achievement orientation' and dichotomized at the median. The measured achievement orientation of the soldiers was related to their military status. Figure III shows a

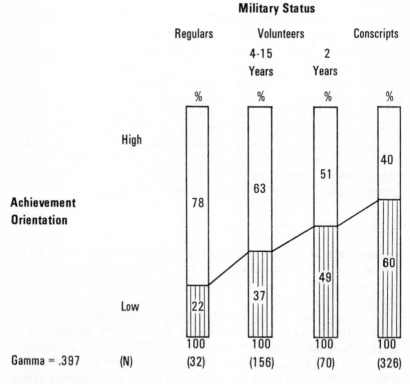

Figure III

rather strong positive association (Gamma = .397)[39]. The ascertained relationship is nearly linear.

The proportions of the achievement orientated soldiers (proportions above the median of the distribution) vary from 40 percent of the conscripts, 51 percent of the 'quasi-conscripts', 63 percent of the long-term volunteers to 78 percent of the regulars. On the one hand, the long-term volunteers have to except more difficulties in transition from military to civilian life, on the other hand, they indicate an orientation which will facilitate a successful beginning of a second career.

2.2.2. Commitment to the Military Organization
As compared with achievement orientation, commitment to the military organization is a personality factor which inhibits successful resettlement of long-term volunteers.

In our analysis the strength of commitment was measured in two steps. First of all the soldiers were asked to evaluate 14 aspects of an occupational activity[40]. These aspects were to be rated as 'very important', 'rather important', 'less important', or 'unimportant'. Afterwards the soldiers were asked to indicate whether these aspects were to be found more in the Bundeswehr than among civilian employers. If positive evaluated aspects were rated as typical for the military organization rather than for civilian employers, this was interpreted as indicating a strong commitment to the military organization[41].

In the first instance our results reveal that all aspects in question received a positive evaluation[42], although there were some differences in the degree of importance[43]. The proportions of 'very important', as shown in figure IV, I, do not vary much between the different types of enlistment. The corresponding curves wind round an imaginary mean line lapsing from the right upper to the left hand corner of the diagram. Correspondingly, there is hardly any relationship between the evaluations of certain aspects of an occupational activity and the military status of the soldiers. This relatively high agreement in the evaluations between different types of enlistment is also indicated by the coefficients of association for ungrouped categories: only 5 of these 14 coefficients exceed the value .100, and only two the value .200.

However, in judging the chances of finding these aspects as being greater in the military than in the civilian sector, there is a far lesser degree of

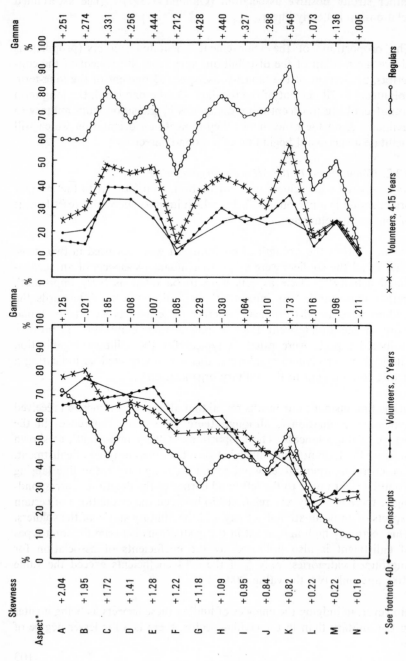

Figure IV

agreement between the different types of personnel (see fig. IV, II). Here the coefficients of the relationships between types of enlistment and judgments in question were all positive. This means that soldiers enlisted for longer terms attributed positive aspects more often to the Bundeswehr than conscripts or 'quasi-conscripts'. With the exception of three, all coefficients exceed the value .200, and out of one coefficient all were greater than the Gamma-values of the relationships between types of enlistment and the evaluations of these aspects of an occupational activity.

These results can be seen as an expression of differing commitments to the military organization of the various groups studied: the longer the type of service, the stronger was the commitment to the military setting. Nevertheless, figure IV, II shows that it was the strong commitment of the regulars in particular which caused the relatively high Gamma-values. In this connection the regulars differ sharply from the other types. In comparison the difference between the long-service volunteers on the one hand and the conscripts and the 'quasi-conscripts' on the other hand were much smaller, as expected, although the diagram shows certain dissimilarities.

Summarizing we can state that, compared with conscripts and 'quasi-conscripts', long-term volunteers show a higher achievement orientation, but are more strongly committed to the military organization. However, their commitment is very much lower than that of the regulars. With regard to both personality factors studied, the majority of the long-term volunteers show a psychic disposition which furthers rather than hinders a successful transition from military to civilian life.

3. 'SECOND-CAREER' – PREPARATIONS AND REALITY

Three major results have been outlined hitherto:
— There is a general convergence of occupational structures in civilian and military sectors.
— In addition, a training program – called 'Berufsförderungsdienst' – directed to civilian occupations is available to the Bundeswehr.
— The long-term volunteers especially are characterized by a relatively favorable readiness and ability to individual adjustment.
Considering that on the one hand there are still some structural differences between military and civilian sectors, and that on the other hand a pro-

portion of volunteers intends to get training for a new profession within the Bundeswehr, one must discover the efforts volunteers make to use the available chances for vocational and advanced training. Simultaneously, one must ask whether these chances are suitable for the special situation of volunteers.

3.1. *Participation in the 'Berufsförderungsdienst'*

Among the most important means available to the 'Berufsförderungsdienst' one can find, in addition to personal counselling, training which takes place during free time of the soldier while still on active duty as well as financing of professional training once the soldier has left the armed forces. There is a lack of empirical material concerning the participation rate of volunteers in study groups for vocational training within the scope of the 'Berufsförderungsdienst'. But from the available data it can be inferred that activities performed during service time are of little importance. An investigation undertaken in 1966 reports that of about 1 000 ex-volunteers, only 25 percent had participated in these study groups during their service time[44].

Results of our analysis are even more negative. In June, 1970, 95 percent of N = 627 active soldiers indicated no participation in study groups at that time; further 87 percent of all interviewed soldiers had not participated at any previous time. Although such activities are largely disregarded, they will – if at all – be used by soldiers having to expect more difficulties in making the transition to civilian life. Of the long-term volunteers, 14 percent participated in study groups at the time of investigation as compared with 2 percent of conscripts; while the 'quasi-conscripts' and the regulars did not participate at all. Nevertheless the 'Berufsförderungsdienst' points out that the success of vocational furtherance measures performed during service time may be seen in the fact that about 39 000 special examinations were passed during the last 10 years[45]. Unfortunately there is no standard of comparison available. Therefore, these figures do not say so much.

Between 1960 and 1969 about 85 000 volunteers had made use of vocational training immediately before or after the end of their term of service[46]. In this case the question of proportion of participants to all volunteers who could legitimately participate remains open. Yet the already cited study undertaken in 1966 shows that only 35 percent of ex-volunteers had made use of vocational training at the expense of the

106

Bundeswehr after the end of their term of service[47]. However, of these ex-volunteers 82 percent had only 6 months available for vocational training – too little time for thorough training.

3.2. Adequacy of the Offered Furtherance Measures

Even a superficial examination of the 'Berufsförderungsdienst' will show some deficiencies. In this connection the personnel of the 'Berufs-förderungsdienst' must be called insufficient. In 1969 there were only 150 officials in the 'Berufsförderungsdienst' confronted with 165 000 volunteers. It is hard to imagine how qualified guidance and care of volunteers together with their preparation for the 'second career' can be performed under such conditions.

It is especially disturbing that measures for the upholding of vocational skills and knowledge are almost exclusively carried out within the leisure-time of the soldiers and that the crucial part of vocational training is postponed until the end of service time. This displacement of the focal point to the end of service time handicaps especially those soldiers who have enlisted for 10 to 15 years and leave the forces at 30 to 35 years of age. They are supposed to begin training for a new occupation while others have already reached their occupational goals or they are supposed to attend schools while their children are in school already[48].

Even if we disregard these problems – which could be ignored because they are the results of personal decision – the following considerations speak in favour of a revision of the present conception of vocational furtherance in the Bundeswehr. Accomplishing training within relatively short time and under the strain of uncertainty (horror vacui) on the boundary between military and civilian occupation can hardly guarantee the best results for successful completion of training. Whereas training relying on more steps and spread out over the whole term of service would not only give more possibilities (including the possibility of repeating unsuccessfully accomplished parts of the training program), but also this kind of training would considerably reduce the danger of deciding for a wrong occupation.

3.3. Recruitment and Social Mobility

These problems cannot be ignored by the military organization – because as Janowitz and Little rightly state – the number of applications, over the long run, depend in part on the successful reintegration of ex-volunteers in the economic and social life. In this regard the situation will probably become more problematic for the Bundeswehr within the next years. Not so much because the 'Berufsförderungsdienst' had failed as an instrument for preparation of volunteers' reintegration – we neither can definitively confirm nor disprove this – but because the military will lose its attractiveness for some groups as means of social mobility[49].

Two considerations are central in this connection. First, the results of different investigations identically show that the possibility of undergoing vocational training is an important reason for joining the armed forces. This reason had been indicated by a substantial proportion of the interviewees (between 33 and 55 percent)[50]. Even if one takes into account that these arguments are, in part, rationalizations of past decisions with motivations surely more complex as can be seen from these answers, it is evident that armed forces are perceived as an institution which makes upward mobility possible through vocational training.

On the other hand, there is a more easily practicable channel for upward mobility in the German Federal Republic since 1969. While, up to now, the Bundeswehr held at least four years of commitment as a prerequisite for eligibility to a six-months vocational training, now every employee is entitled to individual grants[51]. Not only does the civil administration bear the costs of vocational training wholly or in part, but also the participants get a considerable grant for up to 2 years so that today the participation in civilian vocational training programs is not associated with a substantial reduction of income.

This development should not be an isolated trend in the German Federal Republic. The similarity of problems faced by industrialized nations will result in similar educational measures. Therefore, one may expect that an important argument in favour of the recruitment of long-term volunteers will lose a good deal of its strength.

NOTES AND REFERENCES

1. See *Wehrpflichtgesetz* (Conscription Law) of July 21, 1956.
2. Before 1962 the length of basic military service was 12 months.
3. See Bundesminister der Verteidigung (ed.), *Weißbuch 1970. Zur Sicherheit der Bundesrepublik Deutschland und zur Lage der Bundeswehr*, Bonn 1970, p. 61. The military system recently indicated by the minister of defence as an option for the late seventies – consisting of a professional army component and a citizen army component – is also based on the conscript system, although with a shorter duration of basic military service.
4. See appendix, figures A and B.
5. *Weißbuch 1970, op. cit.*, p. 49.
6. *Ibid.*
7. *Ibid.*, p. 85 and p. 90.
8. See FÜRSTCHEN, Rolf, Nachwuchslage und Bedarfsdeckung – Unteroffiziere und Mannschaften, in *Truppenpraxis* 4 (1969), p. 289.
9. An examination of military sociological literature indicates that studies on problems of recruitment of long-term privates and NCOs are not so frequent as studies on problems of recruitment of officers. See among others ABRAMS, Philip, Technology and the Retired British Officer, in HUNTINGTON, Samuel P. (ed.), *Changing Patterns of Military Politics*, Glencoe, Ill. 1962, pp. 150–189; DOORN, Jacques van, The Officer Corps: A Fusion of Profession and Organization, in *Archives Européennes de Sociologie* 6 (1965), pp. 262–282; KJELLBERG, Francesco, Some Cultural Aspects of Military Profession, in *Archives Européennes de Sociologie* 6 (1965), pp. 283–293; ZALD, Mayer N., and William SIMON, Career opportunities and Commitments Among Officers, in JANOWITZ, Morris (ed.), *The New Military. Changing Patterns of Organizations*, New York 1964, pp. 257–285. In a bibliography of military sociological literature among 29 studies under the heading 'Social origin' 22 deal with social origin of officers. See ZIEGLER, Rolf, Ausgewählte Literatur zur Militärsoziologie, in KÖNIG, René (ed.), Beiträge zur Militärsoziologie, *Kölner Zeitschrift für Soziologie und Sozialpsychologie*, Special Issue 12 (1968), p. 359.
10. See *Weißbuch 1970, op. cit.*, p. 91.
11. See FÜRSTCHEN, *op. cit.*, p. 291.
12. See *Weißbuch 1970, op. cit.*, p. 91.
13. See appendix, figure A.
14. In 1964 67 percent of interviewed volunteers of the Army gave as reason for their enlistment: '... I would have been called up anyhow, and by voluntarily joining I could improve my financial standing'. (Cited in ROGHMANN, Klaus, Soziologische Analyse von Militär und Gesellschaft in der Bundesrepublik Deutschland, *Schriftenreihe Innere Führung*, Wehrsoziologische Studien, Vol. 1, Bonn 1967, p. 51). Moreover, regarding soldiers with two years of service as 'quasi-conscripts' is justified by a lot of other similarities (e.g. attitudes, behaviors) with conscripts.
15. Only 15 percent of the soldiers with two years of service reenlist and become NCOs. See *Weißbuch 1970, op. cit.*, p. 87.
16. See Deutscher Bundestag, 6. Wahlperiode, Drucksache VI/453, *Jahresbericht 1969 des Wehrbeauftragten des Deutschen Bundestages* (Annual Report 1969 of the Defence Commissioner of the Bundestag), Bonn/Bad Godesberg 1970, p. 33.
17. See *Weißbuch 1970, op. cit.*, pp. 69–81; Appendix, figure C.
18. See *Weißbuch 1970, op. cit.*, p. 90.

19. *Ibid.*
20. *Ibid.*
21. JANOWITZ, Morris, and Roger LITTLE, *Sociology and the Military Establishment,* rev. ed., New York 1965, p. 72.
22. See BIDERMAN, Albert D., and Laure M. SHARP, The Convergence of Military and Civilian Occupational Structures. Evidence from Studies of Military Retired Employment, in *American Journal of Sociology* 73 (1968), p. 383.
23. See BIDERMAN and SHARP, *op. cit.*, p. 384.
24. *Ibid.*
25. See U.S. Senate, Committee on Armed Forces, *A Study of the Military Retired Pay System and Certain Related Subjects* (prepared by the Study Committee of the University of Michigan, July 6, 1961) quoted according to BIDERMAN and SHARP, *op. cit.*, p. 384.
26. Analogously, reference can be made to the distinction between 'functional' and 'extra-functional skills'. 'Extra-functional skills' are defined as skills which enable the individual to manage as the circumstances may require while exercising his 'functional skills'.
27. See HEISELER, Johannes Heinrich von, Militär und Technik, in Georg PICHT (ed.), *Studien zur politischen und gesellschaftlichen Situation der Bundeswehr*, Vol. II, Witten und Berlin 1966, p. 75.
28. See MOSEN, Wido, *Eine Militärsoziologie*, Neuwied und Berlin 1967, p. 24. Shifting in the ratio of NCOs to rank and file indicate similar changes. In 1913/14 this ratio had been in the German Armed Forces 15:85; in the Bundeswehr (March, 1970) this ratio is 23:77 for the Army, for the technically more advanced Air Force and Navy 40:60 and 43:57 respectively. Sources: OBERMANN, Emil, *Soldaten, Bürger, Militaristen*, Stuttgart 1958, p. 122; *Weißbuch 1970, op. cit.*, p. 89.
29. See MOSEN, *op. cit.*, p. 24. These figures do not say that the proportions of occupations are identical in both military and society. Here considerable differences may be suspected.
30. LANG, Kurt, Technology and Career Management in the Military Establishment, in JANOWITZ, *op. cit.*, p. 47.
31. This can be seen from the answers to the question: 'What are you going to do after leaving the Bundeswehr?'

Intentions	Type of Enlistment			
	Conscripts	Volunteers		
		2 Years	4 Years	6–15 Years
	%	%	%	%
Return to the former job	69	50	27	5
Get a new job	7	11	25	31
Attend a school	9	15	24	31
Study	10	18	6	9
Do not yet know	4	6	17	23
Other	1	–	1	1
(N)	100	100	100	100
	(347)	(72)	(81)	(75)

A specification revealed that 168, i.e. 74 percent, of these 228 volunteers had already completed professional training as skilled workers or as clerks before joining the armed forces. Only 53, i.e. 32 percent, of these 168 volunteers definitively intended to return to their former jobs. For details on sampling see footnote 35.

32. See *Soldatenversorgungsgesetz* (Law Governing Pensions and Grants for All Ranks of the Armed Forces) of August 8, 1964.

33. Volunteers engaged for less than four years of service are not entitled to financing vocational training after the end of service time. All other volunteers have the following legal claims for vocational training:

— after 4 to 5 years of service   up to 6 months
— after 6 to 7 years of service   up to 12 months
— after 8 to 11 years of service   up to 18 months
— after 12 and more years of service   up to 36 months.

During this time ex-volunteers get at least 90 percent of their last monthly salary. See *Weißbuch 1970, op. cit.*, p. 134.

34. Normally volunteers with less than 8 years of service are not entitled to attend special schools of the Bundeswehr. After 8 to 11 years up to 12 months, and after 12 and more years up to 18 months of attendance are financed immediately before leaving the armed forces. If vocational training (see footnote 33) and attendance of special schools of the Bundeswehr are used together the first will be reduced by the amount of time spent for attending schools.

35. These data, gathered in June, 1970, are part of the larger study 'The Soldier and his Leisure'. A stratified sample consisting of 20 companies of the Army, Air Force, and Navy of the Bundeswehr was used in this research. All participating soldiers (N = 1,878) filled in a largely standardized questionnaire in a classroom situation. Lack of time leads to random choice of only one third (N = 627) of this material analyzed in this paper.

36. See, e.g., McCLELLAND, David C., *The Achieving Society*, New York 1961, as opposed to KAHL, Joseph A., Some Measurement of Achievement Orientation, in *American Journal of Sociology* 70 (1965), pp. 669-681. Both positions are confronted by SCANZONI, John, Socialization, Achievement, and Achievement Values, in *American Sociological Review* 32 (1967), pp. 449-456.

37. See CROCKETT, Harry J., Jr., The Achievement Motive and Differential Occupational Mobility in the United States, in *American Sociological Review* 27 (1962), pp. 191-204.

38. The soldiers had been asked to indicate to what extent they agreed or disagreed with each of the following statements ('strongly agree' = 1, 'partially agree' = 2, 'partially reject' = 3, or 'strongly reject' = 4).

A. When a man is born the success he's going to have is already in the cards, so he might as well accept it and not fight against it.

B. The secret of happiness is not expecting too much out of life, and being content with what comes your way.

C. All a man should strive for in life is a secure, not too difficult job, with pay to afford a nice car and eventually a home of one's own.

D. Nothing in life is worth the sacrifice of moving away from one's home.

E. When looking for a job one should make sure that you will live near your parents, even if it means giving up a good job opportunity elsewhere.

F. The best kind of job to have is one where you are part of an organization all working together even if you don't get individual credit.

G. Planning only makes a person unhappy since plans are very seldom realized.

H. Nowadays, with world conditions the way they are, the wise person lives for today and lets tomorrow take care of itself.

The scale ranges from 8 to 32 points; the higher the score, the higher the achievement orientation. The parameters of the distribution (N = 587) are: median = 22; mean = 21.97; mode = 23.

39. See GOODMAN, Leo A., and William H. KRUSKAL, Measures of Association for Cross-Classifications, in *Journal of the American Statistical Association* 49 (1954), pp. 732–764.

40. Vocation, one is ready to perform for a longer time, should in any case make sure that one can obtain...

A. ... recognition of personal performance
B. ... personal recognition
C. ... good provision for one's old age
D. ... a secure position
E. ... a good chance of promotion
F. ... satisfaction from one's job
G. ... varying tasks
H. ... and make use of good special knowledge and skills
I. ... and make use of good general knowledge
J. ... recognition by one's superiors and colleagues
K. ... personal responsibility
L. ... prestige
M. ... challenge in one's work
N. ... good financial reward at an early stage

41. This interpretation relies on the theory of affective-cognitive consistency by Heider. See HEIDER, Fritz, Attitudes and Cognitive Organization, in *Journal of Psychology*, 21 (1946), pp. 107–112; reprinted in FISHBEIN, Martin (ed.), *Readings in Attitude Theory and Measurement*, New York-London-Sidney 1967, pp. 39–41.

42. The skewness as a statistical measure of deviation from symmetry was positive in each of the cases. This means that each aspect has been regarded as important (see fig. IV, I).

43. This can be read off from the numerical value of skewness. In figure IV, I all aspects have been ranked according to ascribed importance.

44. See WARNKE, Rudolf, Der ehemalige Zeitsoldat, *Schriftenreihe Innere Führung*, Wehrsoziologische Studien, Vol. 4, Bonn 1968, pp. 84-85.

45. See *Weißbuch 1970, op. cit.*, p. 133.

46. *Ibid.*, p. 134.

47. See WARNKE, *op. cit.*, p. 94.

48. These deficiencies were also recently criticized by the voluntary professional organization of Western German soldiers, Deutscher Bundeswehr-Verband e.V., to which more than 80 percent of long-term soldiers (volunteers and regulars) belong. See Deutscher Bundeswehr-Verband e.V. (ed.), *Der berufliche Förderungsplan für Soldaten auf Zeit*, Bonn 1969, esp. pp. 6-12.

49. It cannot be said with certainty to what extent the Bundeswehr serves as a mobility channel today. Warnke, however, reports that 65 percent of interviewed ex-volunteers had changed their former occupational positions after service. Generally, these ex-volunteers now executed more non-manual jobs than before service time. See WARNKE, *op. cit.*, pp. 105–117.

50. See ROGHMANN, *op. cit.*, p. 51; Wehrsoziologische Forschungsgruppe, Die Anpassung des Rekruten an das militärische Leben während der Allgemeinen Grund-

ausbildung, Teil III: *Die Bereitschaft zur Weiterverpflichtung*, Köln 1968, p. 20 (unpublished manuscript); WARNKE, *op. cit.*, p. 30; Der Bundesminister der Verteidigung, *10 Jahre Berufsförderungsdienst der Bundeswehr*, December 31, 1969, mimeo.
51. See *Arbeitsförderungsgesetz* (Vocational Furtherance Law) of June 25, 1969.

Appendix

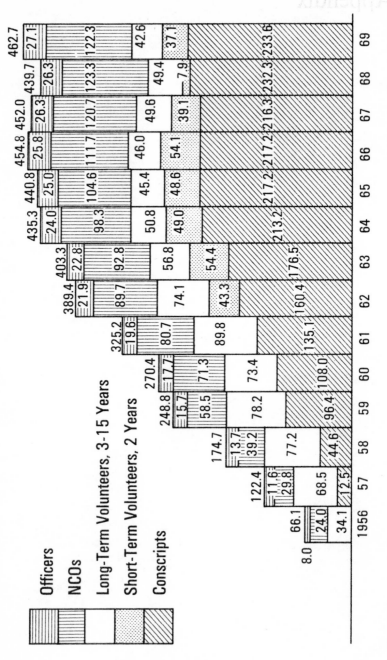

Figure A

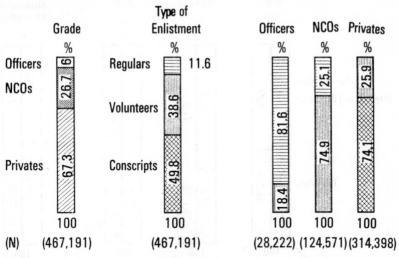

	Grade	Type of Enlistment	Officers	NCOs	Privates
%	%	%	%	%	%

Grade: Officers 6; NCOs 26.7; Privates 67.3

Type of Enlistment: Regulars 11.6; Volunteers 38.6; Conscripts 49.8

Officers: 81.6 / 18.4
NCOs: 25.1 / 74.9
Privates: 25.9 / 74.1

(N)   (467,191)   (467,191)   (28,222) (124,571) (314,398)

▤ Regulars (Berufssoldaten) = Soldiers who serve until they reach their age limit of 52, 54, 56, 58, or 60 years (jet pilots until the special age limit of about 40 years) and then are due for retirement

▥ Volunteers (Zeitsoldaten) = Soldiers who serve about 2 or 15 years

▩ Conscripts (Wehrpflichtige) = Soldiers on an eighteen-months term of basic military service.

Figure B

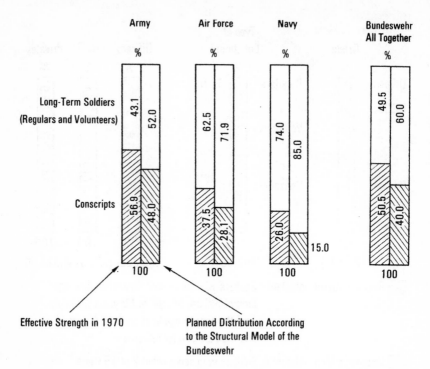

	Army	Air Force	Navy	Bundeswehr All Together
	%	%	%	%
Long-Term Soldiers (Regulars and Volunteers)	43.1 / 52.0	62.5 / 71.9	74.0 / 85.0	49.5 / 60.0
Conscripts	56.9 / 48.0	37.5 / 28.1	26.0 / 15.0	50.5 / 40.0
	100	100	100	100

Effective Strength in 1970

Planned Distribution According to the Structural Model of the Bundeswehr

Figure C

118

Military Technology and Expertise: Some Chinks in the Armor

K. LANG*

* Professor of sociology, State University of New York at Stony Brook, Stony Brook, New York.

The military, like many other traditional professions, is caught up in the throes of a far-reaching technological and organizational revolution. This revolution, long in the making, is closely linked to progressive improvements in the power, range, and accuracy of weapons and to equally dramatic increases in troop mobility. These developments came to a head with the rise of strategic air power and the advent of nuclear arms in World War II, a war that also opened a new chapter in combined operations. But there has been no slowdown in technological progress since. Whole generations of weapons valued primarily for their deterrent effect have passed through the entire cycle from the drawing board to the 'junk yard' without their effectiveness for combat ever having been tested except under simulated conditions. The present technological arms race is clearly of the qualitative type and, as such, increases the rate at which past experience becomes obsolescent.

It is in the character of the strategic forces, particularly in the preeminent role assigned to air power and to submarine-based missiles, that the changes are most visible. Yet the present-day U.S. force structure also testifies to the complex arrangements necessary to assure the material and logistic support of conventional forces adequate to the world-wide commitments of the United States. In these and other respects, the technological and organizational facets of the revolution are closely interlaced.

The effects on the organization can be summarized in a simple phrase: the military establishment is shifting in its orientation toward greater concern with resource management. The shift is partial and one of degree. Combat and operational support activity are still important and they continue to provide the rationale for the other activities. One nevertheless observes in the military, no less than in other sectors of society, the growth of a 'tertiary' sector. I am referring to the many scientific, administrative, information-gathering, educational, and quasi-political activities only indirectly related to the actual direction of fire power. These activities, although vital to the maintenance and effectiveness of the organization, have become partly autonomous of the primary mission. They also call for expertise different from, or in addition to, the traditional expertise of the military.

The current officer occupational structure, shown in table 1, gives a crude approximation of the diversity of occupational roles professional military must nowadays fill. Attention is drawn in particular to the close correspondence in the rank order of frequency, if not in the actual proportions, of the major groupings within each of the services. Positions involving responsibility for combat or otherwise closely related to tactical

121

Table 1. U.S. officer distribution by occupational groups: 1970 (in per cent)

	Total	Army	Navy	Marine Corps	Air Force
1. General Officers and Executives	1	*	3	3	*
2. Tactical Operations	41	49	23	57	38
3. Intelligence	4	5	3	1	4
4. Engineering and Maintenance	15	12	19	9	17
5. Scientific and Professional	4	3	6	1	6
6. Medical	9	9	11	–	8
7. Administrative	12	11	15	7	12
8. Supply, Procurement, and Allied	6	6	7	8	6
9. Other Basic	4	–	–	13	8
10. Unidentified	4	3	12	*	–
Total**	100	100	100	100	100

* <.5%
** Some percentages do not add up exactly to 100 because of rounding.

Source: Department of Defence.

operations are still the largest category but, except in the Marine Corps, a minority everywhere. This category, which accounts for slightly over forty per cent of all positions, includes the basic ground combat arms (like infantry and artillery) and all close ground combat support, pilots and their crews, the commanders of ships, missile and similar units, and officers on operations staffs. The 'engineering and maintenance' category is everywhere the second largest.

Officers in jobs of this category perform duties closely related to the new technology. Together with those classified as 'scientific and professional', they account for about a fifth of all officer positions – somewhat more in the Air Force and Navy and somewhat less in the Army and Marine Corps. Administration and various logistic support activities (categories 7 and 8 in the table) also demand a considerable share of officer personnel. The proportion of officers in the latter type of jobs provides a rough index of organizational complexity, especially since only about one per cent overall are identified by the Department of Defence as military managers, i.e. as general officers or executives not elsewhere classified.

Because the classification was based on similarities of the duties in positions, as these were described in service manuals, some differences between the services may only reflect what each chooses to emphasize in writing the specifications for any particular job.[1]

Others arise from special arrangements. The Marine Corps, for example, has no medical corps of its own but has such services provided by Naval medical personnel. Beyond that, the occupational complexion of each service is affected both by how missions are allocated among them and by current commitments; the fluctuating demand for certain types of ground combat troops in Viet Nam illustrates the latter.

Insofar as ground combat, despite some very considerable gains in fire power and troop mobility, remains unchanged in its fundamentals, it stands to reason that the requirements of the new technology should manifest themselves more clearly in the occupational structure of the Air Force and Navy than in that of the Army and Marine Corps. The first two have significantly larger proportions of officer personnel not only in the engineering and maintenance fields but also in jobs in the scientific and professional as well as in the administrative and logistic support categories.

The trend has gone farthest in the Air Force, which has the highest percentage of officers to total strength. Equipment, like airplanes, requires small crews. These consist almost exclusively of officers who are classified as employed in tactical operations, whereas the enlisted airmen, unlike their counterparts in the other services, perform mostly the various maintenance, support, and other subsidiary functions. With the aircraft inventory – not counting helicopters, which operate principally as ground combat support – greatly reduced from the level of ten years ago, the tasks of technological and resource management predominate even more strongly than appears from the occupational breakdowns of only officer positions.[2]

CAREER OPPORTUNITIES

The officer occupational structure has an evident bearing on the opportunities open to young men at the beginning of their military career. An occupational career typically consists of a sequential pattern of movements through positions in the work world, positions that in the normal order of things offer the incumbent a progressively wider range for his skills, more responsibility, more authority, and commensurate increments of prestige, remuneration, autonomy to regulate his activities, and so

123

forth. The concept is close to everyday usage and requires no more formal definition than this.

Past studies of officer careers have usually focused on the relatively few who achieved high rank or gained entry into the inner nucleus of decision makers.[3]

But the elements around which unusually successful careers are built have only limited validity for the careers of the overwhelming majority of officers. Opportunity *within* the military is largely defined by the rank structure, and the chances for even regular and career officers to attain general or flag rank, unless in a cohort that benefits from wartime mobilization, are really quite small. Statistics for 1970 indicate that more than a third of all officers in the u.s. Army and Air Force with twenty years of prior service, and hence eligible for retirement benefits, still had not at this point advanced beyond the rank of major; the proportion in the Navy still lieutenant commanders after twenty years was over one half. The period of what the service career development plans define as the 'maximum contribution', toward which the pattern of rotating assignments is geared, still lies ahead of these officers, should they choose to remain, as many do, but the modal rank even at the twenty-five year point is still only lieutenant colonel (or commander in the Navy).

Some accommodation of the rank structure, which determines the opportunities for young officers in the military, to the new skill structure has nevertheless taken place. Promotion does come more rapidly today than it did in the 'pre-technological' era. Advancement to the rank of captain (or lieutenant in the Navy) has become just about routine for all who remain on active duty beyond their initial obligatory or contractual tour. This is in recognition, on the one hand, of the higher level of general education attained by the current officer input and, on the other, of the broader range of knowledge demanded in many assignments.

The upgrading has extended to positions in tactical operations – for example, that of commander and of other flying personnel in Air Force pursuit squadrons. The equipment for which these officers shoulder responsibility has become more costly and complex since World War II, and they must retain parity of status with the large number of diverse staff specialists whom they may be called upon to direct.

As a general rule, the number of positions in the middle ranks of an organization measures the complexity of its internal division of labor. Although the officer rank structure exhibits some tendency toward a bulge at the rank of captain, that of the Army has, since 1950, reverted back to the traditional pyramid (table 2). This is because present distributions are somewhat 'distorted' by the continuing disproportionately

124

Table 2. U.S. Army and Air Force officer grade distribution (in per cent)

| | 1920 | 1950 | | 1970 | |
	Army	Army	Air Force	Army	Air Force
General	.4	.8	.5	.3	.3
Colonel	4.1	9.4	4.3	4.4	5.0
Lt. Colonel	4.7	11.5	10.0	11.3	12.2
Major	14.9	20.7	17.8	16.9	21.8
Captain	35.9	34.9	34.6	26.1	33.8
Lieutenant	40.0	22.7	32.9	41.0	26.9
	100.0	100.0	100.0*	100.0	100.0

* In these and other tables, percentages do not always add up to 100.0 due to rounding.

Sources: 1920 and 1950 – M. Janowitz, *The Professional Soldier. Op. cit.* 1970 – U.S. Department of Defence.

large exodus of junior officers, the results of which are most visible in the Army. There the shortages at the company-grade level have been so severe that many lieutenants now hold commands that actually call for the rank of captain, and vacancies have had to be filled with officers without the seniority to qualify for the rank this position formally carries. This situation, with its depressive effect on grade distributions, is rather different from that prevailing in 1950, when both the Army and the Air Force, each in its own way, were still reeling under the impact of rapid mobilization followed by nearly as sharp a retrenchment after the war. For this reason, the growth in the number of lieutenant colonels and colonels over the past fifty years has been neither as dramatic nor as uninterrupted as might seem when the grade requirements of particular specialities are examined.

The structures within which individual officers develop their careers are the product of centrally managed personnel systems. The assumptions behind these personnel systems differ somewhat from service to service, but all incorporate in one way or another the principle of frequent rotation between command and various staffs or between tours at sea and shore assignments, with courses at service schools or advanced academic education coming at crucial points in an officer's career. The system predicated on the assumption that experience in a broad variety of assignments in the best way of grooming officers for higher levels of responsibility, is clearly geared to the development of military managers. The basic problem that all services, even though not all are affected by it to the same degree must meet in one way or other, is how to provide an opportunity structure that offers suitable rewards to an increasing number of diverse specialists. A rank system meant to articulate levels of hierarchical authority must converge toward the top. Yet the pyramidical distribution no longer accords with either the actual skill distribution or with the aspirations of officers whom it is in the interest of the services to retain. The present system makes only grudging concessions to the specialist. The services are exceedingly reluctant to relinquish an idea they have long cherished; namely, the idea that professional military judgment is founded, above all, on operational experience.

The problem is compounded by two other trends: generally rising aspirations among the young men embarking upon a career and, the opportunities for a lateral movement increasingly available to those among them who have attained the level of schooling the technical and professional typical of most officers today.[4]

That the excess of voluntary attrition over forced separations (because of non-selection for promotion) has affected most strongly some of the very specialties in which the most rapid growth is anticipated is something of which those in personnel management are acutely aware. Many positions have had in fact to be filled with men only marginally qualified, thereby greatly improving the advancement opportunities for officers with skills in the area of shortages. Selection to the rank of colonel has actually come somewhat more rapidly for officers in some scientific and engineering fields in the Air Force and for some in the Army specialist programs than for officers whose primary specialty was in operations.[5]

I shall now proceed to examine, briefly, how occupational requirements are reflected in the types of job to which officers are assigned and in the professional specialties they acquire at different phases of their career. My attention shall be confined to the Air Force and Navy – the two services on which the impact of the new technology has been greatest – using such data as are used by the services themselves in order to monitor their personnel systems.

Existing distributions, it must be kept in mind, are always the result of three separate processes: differential attrition, selective advancement, and career development. The separate effect each has in the aggregate is something difficult to estimate.

The personnel system of the Air Force incorporates a clear-cut division between the 'operational rated-pilot career' and a career in the technical and support area with practically no crossover after the grade of major and nearly all of it away from operations. The Air Force officer requirements for the mid-1960's (as defined through a computerized model) in three broad occupational groupings are shown by rank in table 3. The basic division is between the operations area, the technical management fields (which include assignments in security, intelligence, information, and various aspects of material, financial, and personnel management), and the various scientific and engineering specialties.

Table 3. U.S. Air Force officer requirements by grade and major occupational category, 1966 (in per cent)

	Colonel	Lt. Colonel	Major	Capt./Lt.
Operations	37	43	43	55
Technical	37	32	30	24
Scientific/Engineering	26	25	27	21
Total	100	100	100	100

Source: U.S. Air Force, AFPDP.

Some categories, like medicine, law, the chaplaincy, and band leaders, were not included in these tabulations. There is a distinct shift at the higher ranks, where apparently more officers are required, proportionately, for the technical management positions and fewer for tactical operations. Those in the scientific and engineering categories exhibit little variation with rank.

Productivity in an organization with a highly complex technological base depends less on those who man and operate the machinery – though minimal standards have obviously to be met – than on continuous improvement and development. A large staff of administrators becomes ever more essential to provide the engineer and the scientist as well as the organizational planner with the resources and information that will make the effort pay off. A somewhat top-heavy administrative structure is,

127

according to Vollmer and Pederson, an essential attribute of what they call a 'technology management organization'.[6]

The actual pattern of distribution in 1970 among the three major groupings had only a loose resemblance to the requirements as defined. (See table 4). Instead of a progressive decline toward the higher ranks, the

Table 4. U.S. Air Force officer occupational assignments by grade and years of prior service, 1970 (in per cent)

Grade	General	Colonel	Lt. Colonel	Major	Captain	Lieutenant
General Mgt.	100	16	4	*	*	0
Operations		29	47	62	50	39
Admin., Logistic, & Intell.		34	27	18	25	31
Science & Engrg.		21	22	19	24	30
	100	100	100	100	100	100

Years of prior service	23 + above	18–22	12–17	4–11	0–3
General Mgt.	18	3	1	*	0
Operations	31	46	63	50	39
Admin., Logistic, & Intell.	33	25	18	26	31
Science & Engrg.	18	24	19	24	30
Total**	100	100	100	100	100

* $< .5\%$.
** Some percentages do not add up exactly to 100 because of rounding.
Source: Based on data provided by the U.S. Air Force.

operations category exhibits a sizeable bulge at the rank of major and accounts for a disproportionately large share of the officers even above that rank. The situation is reversed for the two lowest ranks of lieutenant and captain, where the number in the scientific and engineering as well as in the technical management categories is considerable in excess of authorizations to compensate for the deficits in the higher ranks. The overall strength in such specialized fields as research and development, communication and electronics, civil engineering, and cartography where grade allocations are generally advantageous, has been kept close to that

authorized by the overassignment junior officers, usually without aeronautical ratings, many of whom have little commitment to remain. In
other words the discrepancy is caused either by a lack of qualified personnel at the higher officer levels or by the deliberate avoidance of these
assignments by officers who remain long enough to rise. Reading the
data on length of service against those on rank certainly accords with
either explanation; they are not, in any event, mutually exclusive.

The particular professional qualifications of Air Force officers are
revealed to some extent by the fields in which they hold their academic
degree (see table 5). All Air Force officers nowadays must have the B.A.
at the time they are commissioned and those previously commissioned

Table 5. Academic majors of U.S. Air Force officers by grade, 1970
(in per cent)*

Undergraduate	General	Colonel	Lt. Col.	Major	Captain	Lieutenant
Admin., Mgt., & Mil. Sci.	47	43	33	30	28	25
Engineering	18	14	17	18	14	18
Biol., Phys., & Math.	10	8	13	17	19	19
Soc. Sci.	15	19	18	16	22	23
Other, no inf.	10	16	19	20	17	14
Total**	100	100	100	100	100	100
Graduate						
Admin., Mgt., & Mi. Sci.	35	33	40	36	28	27
Engineering	19	18	20	32	31	35
Biol., Phys., & Math.	8	7	9	10	13	17
Soc. Sci.	37	33	14	9	11	17
Other, no inf.	2	10	16	14	16	5
Total**	100	100	100	100	100	100
Proportion with Grad. Degrees	.31	.29	.30	.19	.12	.06

* Excludes officers with degrees in medicine and law.
** Some percentages do not add up exactly to 100 because of rounding.

Source: Based on data provided by the U.S. Air Force.

without it are under pressure to make it up. On the other hand, an officer with a graduate degree is almost certain to have obtained it while in the service. Generally rising levels of education notwithstanding, the proportion with advanced degrees is greater among those senior both in rank and in age and length of service than among junior officers.

What holds for officers in general, however, does not hold with equal force for officers whose degrees have been taken in certain fields. The effects of attrition on officers whose degrees, graduate as well as undergraduate, were in the natural sciences or mathematics or who have specialized in engineering to the point of obtaining a graduate degree are evident from the progressively smaller proportions with such degrees among the officers at each rank. Only generals represent an exception to this trend. The exception supports our previously made contention that having the right specialty can give an officer a distinct advantage in the competition for promotion. On the whole, some training in a technical or applied field is probably useful as a foundation on which to build a military career, but specialization in a technical field can easily become excessive to the point where it interferes with the internalization of organizational perspectives. The specialist is apt to identify himself with civilians who ply the same trade as he does.

Officers through the rank of lieutenant colonel, if they did obtain a graduate degree, most frequently took it in administration, management, or military science and next most frequently in engineering – all of them fields with high applicability to some specific job. By contrast, there is among those who have made colonel or general clear evidence of a movement toward one of the social sciences, subjects that do not usually involve overspecialization but are nevertheless considered to be highly relevant to military and political planning. These subjects also provide officers with a set of concepts and a vocabulary for dealing with civilians and would be of particular utility in a second civilian career.

Students in the service academies likewise seem to be experiencing the appeal of the social sciences more than they did in former times.

The point is that even if he remains in operations, an officer must change his orientation in order to advance. Only a diminutive percentage of those classed as pilots, navigators, and bombardiers hold a rank higher than major. Those in operations who do are most often assigned to positions on staffs, usually as directors of operations, while the even smaller number in command of Air Force organizations appear in our table as military managers. But of all the major commands the one with the highest concentration of officers above major is u.s. Air Force Headquarters; the assignments there are more often in technical management than in operational planning. The rank distributions in high-prestige organizations like the Air Force Systems Command, the Office of Scientific Research, and the Air University, in which scientific and intellectual activity predominates, is only somewhat less favorable. Although their work is basic to many operational activities, it is unlikely that, given the relatively small size of these organizations, they will in the near future become havens for more than a minority of senior officers.

THE NAVY

The distinction between unrestricted line officers and others individually designated for either restricted or special duties, including those in the several staff corps (like the Civil Engineering Corps, the Supply Corps, the Medical Corps, and so forth) approximates in some ways that between rated and non-rated officers in the Air Force. All unrestricted line officers are considered to have the same primary specialty: naval warfare. No specially designated career paths linking several assignments within some defined occupational area are therefore provided for them. On the contrary, all are equally subject to mandatory rotation between sea duty and a whole variety of shore assignments. Partly exempt from rotation requirements are officers not of the unrestricted line, who serve as engineering, aeronautical engineering, or special duty officers in such fields as cryptology, public affairs, hydrography, and so forth. An officer, once so designated cannot succeed to command except ashore and this only upon special authorization. Separate career lines are also foreseen for officers in the staff corps, who are specialized in some broad functional area.

Navy requirements for manpower more professionally trained in fields outside the operations career area could be met in either of two basic ways:

by designating more officers for the restricted and special duty categories and enlarging the staff corps, or by directing unrestricted line officers into paths of education and assignments that correspond to functional career fields. Each has its advantages. An officer freed of rotation requirements could assume duties in a specialty over a longer period and thereby make it possible to satisfy the same requirements with smaller inventories of professionally trained personnel. However, the removal of a large number of line officers from the unrestricted duty list runs contrary to Navy ideology. Command at sea remains the preeminent goal toward which professional development is directed. As a Navy study[7] of the officer situation in 1969 noted, the majority of the billets in some twenty

131

professional manpower utilization fields examined had been written for the unrestricted line. This was true of such new and developing specialties as Operations Research/Systems Analysis and Information Systems where present shortages will no doubt be aggravated by especially large future growth. Large growths were also expected in the various engineering specialties but these are already dominated pretty much by restricted line billets.

The concept of a 'subspecialty' has served as a tool for combining the elements of a traditional career with the requirements for more and more officers with significant qualifications outside their primary naval warfare specialty. Such a qualification can be acquired through a combination of formal education, functional training, and practical experience. Many positions nowadays are defined by both rank and one of fourteen subspecialties, ranging from the natural sciences and operations analysis, through the various engineering and technical management categories, to public and international affairs.

The overwhelming number of officers in the Navy – well over 75 per cent those in the medical, chaplain, and judge advocate corps are removed from consideration – are unrestricted line officers and as such presumed to be qualified in the whole range of war and cold war operations. Our analysis is thereby forced to rely on the subspecialty specifications attached to unrestricted line billets, which probably represents a lower

Table 6. *U.S. Navy officer requirements by grade and major subspecialty category, 1966 (in per cent)*

	Captain	Commander	Lt. Cmdr.	Lieutenant
General Mgt. (Planning)	3	1	*	*
Operations (none)	79	77	80	90
Technical	5	5	3	3
Scientific/Engineering	13	16	17	7
Total**	100	100	100	100
Proportion with subspecialty	.21	.23	.20	.10

* $<.5\%$.

** Some percentages do not add up exactly to 100 due to rounding.

Source: Based on data in the appendices of the Secretary of the Navy, Study of Career Management, Washington, D.C., August, 1967.

level of specialized competence than a similar classification in the Air Force. Comparing these requirements by rank (table 6), one notes a sharp jump in subspecialty billets between the rank of lieutenant and that of lieutenant commander. Until the latter level is reached, so it appears, few positions entail duties outside the operations area calling for any significant degree of specialized expertise, and this continues to be the case for nearly eighty per cent of the positions of lieutenant commander and above. Positions without subspecialty requirements have been classified as in operations.

As regards the subspecialties themselves[8], those in science and engineering dominate throughout but more strongly in the upper middle ranks than in that of captain. The technical management area gains in importance and what the Navy calls the Political/Strategic/Military Planning Subspecialty gains even more. It must nevertheless be remembered in interpreting these statistics that many positions in the scientific and engineering and in the technical management categories are filled with officers with specially designated career lines. Officer inventories indicate, moreover, that some positions are being filled with 'non-selectees' passed over for promotion but retained by the Navy in jobs they have been specifically trained for though not necessarily one demanding a subspecialty qualification.

Table 7. Subspecialties of U.S. Navy officers by grade, 1966 (in per cent)

	Total	Unrestricted line officers				
	Flag	*Flag*	*Capt.*	*Cmdr.*	*Lt. Cmdr.*	*Lieut.*
Political/Strategic/ Military Planning	39	48	7	4	*	0
Operations (none)	30	9	55	56	70	89
Technical Mgt.	40	38	23	26	22	7
Scientific/Engineering	30	16	15	14	8	4
	100**	100**	100	100	100	100

* <.5%.
** 70 Flag officers and 55 Flag officers of the unrestricted line have more than one subspecialty qualification.

Source: Based on data in the appendices of the Secretary of the Navy, Study of Career Management, Washington, D.C., August, 1967.

Table 7 shows that the proportion of unrestricted line officers qualifying for a subspecialty in one of the technical management fields is far greater, at every rank, than that qualifying in one scientific and engineering subspecialties. More officers are, in other words, conversant with and expert in the techniques relating to some aspect of management than with the technology and scientific principles that underly the particular components they may direct. The balance of the officer inventory thus appears the reverse of requirements set forth in the billet structure. Although some special competence beyond operations is advantageous, if not a near-necessity, for an officer's promotion prospects, there is some change toward the higher ranks. Thus nearly half the unrestricted line officers of flag rank but only one out of every fifteen captains have qualified as planners in the political, strategic, and military area where diverse components have to be adjusted to one another.

This subspecialty, either by itself or in conjunction with some other, is what sets the general manager and flag officer apart from those below. By contrast, an officer with a subspecialty in the technological area is more likely, if he achieves flag rank, to do so as a specialist in the restricted line or special duty category.

CONCLUSIONS

It is always easier to rework traditional notions when they no longer accord with reality than to discard them. Technology has caused some chinks in the military career as traditionally prescribed.

Among the cherished principles, which none of the services is prepared to abandon, is that a career centered around operations is essential to the professionalism of the officer corps. Accordingly, the officer with an aeronautical rating personifies the truly professional Air Force officer; the Navy builds its self-image around the officer of the unrestricted line, while officers in the Army, regardless of their particular specialty, are still commissioned and assigned to commands within one of the traditional branches.

These images correspond less and less accurately to what officers actually do, particularly at the higher ranks.[9] Moreover officers in the Air Force, if they remain pilots have a below-average chance of rising beyond major; duty ashore is becoming more important in the Navy; and the Army is confronted with so severe a shortage of commands in Viet Nam that, in order to make room for others, most officers are rotated to staff positions even within the course of their normal twelve-month tour in the theatre. The belief nevertheless persists that outstanding performance in combat, at sea, as a leader of troops or flying personnel is the real measure of a man and more readily identifiable than performance in other areas.

In the light of this assumption, career development built on rotation had a distinct advantage but only as long as few officers at the higher ranks were specialists. Today, it interferes with the filling of many positions with adequately qualified personnel. The effects of the existing career structure are mutually reinforcing. On the one hand, most officers are forever new to their jobs and constantly learning; on the other, the sequential assignments necessary for a full-fledged specialty are often resisted as limiting an officer's area of future utilization and hence as not enhancing his prospects for a successful career – it therefore takes larger inventories, often of minimally qualified officers, to staff the same number of positions.

There are limits to the ability of the military to adapt itself to the new requirements. For one thing, operations remains the distinctly military specialty. One also needs to be conscious that the more the technology of weapons advances the greater the degree to which it will be the product of civilian, rather than specifically military, thinking. Few military officers, even those with scientific training, have the technical know-how to invent a new weapon. If the weapon has never been actually used, the estimation of its effectiveness is likewise a matter of scientific conjecture. Left for the military to cope with are, above all, the internal structural implications of these devices. Attention thus shifts from the primary and secondary sectors, of military activity concerned as they always have been with the direction of troops and with their logistic and material support, to the management of technological innovation, of resources, and of the personnel systems on which continued organizational effectiveness increasingly depends. The new roles and specialties flow less from the weapons themselves than from organizational requirements. In other words, the 'tertiary' sector begins to become the dominant one.

The tertiary sector is to some extent independent of the specific mission assigned to each service. At the very time combined operations are causing specific service viewpoints to fall into obsolescence, there is a reluctance to fathom careers along functional lines that cut across the traditional divisions among the arms. Instead each service explores a variety of managerial devices designed to develop the number of specialists it needs from among its own officers, who remain responsive to service viewpoints.

Notwithstanding all the changes, the military career remains a parochial one in the strict sociological sense of being incompatible with inter-organizational mobility. Generals must be internally recruited. As long as this remains the practice and the conviction – both not entirely without sound grounds –, the education and development of officers cannot be geared exclusively to the specific requirements of operations, of weapons technology, or of military administration. There is some indication that those who rise do indeed, in one way or another and no doubt at some cost to organizational efficiency, acquire broader perspectives. Elites almost always distinguish themselves in this way. In the military it means, however, that many essential jobs in the scientific and engineering and in the technical management areas are relegated either to the short-term reserve or to the low performers among the regulars. There is obviously some measure of incompatibility between the expert needed to keep the military running and the military statesman qualified to be the advisor on the major strategic issues confronting his country. One may question the extent to which a life-time spent in the military, as compared with other experiences, improves one's capability to fill the latter role, but there can be no doubt that a major share of the talent is being and will have to be directed to fill functions generated within the organization itself.

NOTES

1. The categories are those in the Department of Defence Uniform Conversion Code of occupational specialties.
2. See the US Budget Summary FY 1970.
3. For example: M. JANOWITZ, *The Professional Soldier: a Social and Political Profile.* New York: The Free Press of Glencoe, 1960; P. P. VAN RIPER and D. B. UMWALLA, Military Careers at the Executive Level, *Administrative Science Quarterly*, 9 (1965), pp. 421–36; and D. R. SEGAL, Selective Promotion in Officer Cohorts, *Sociological Quarterly*, 8 (1967), pp. 199–206. Janowitz in particular has popularized the notion of 'adaptive' career characterized by assignments that affords unusual opportunity to innovate within the more or less formally prescribed framework. To rise to the highest level an officer had, in other words, to acquire qualifications and visibility beyond that common to most in his cohort. Outstanding combat performance usually has this effect, but the opportunity for it exists only during war. Consequently, the peace-time equivalents are an officer's close association with a new weapon either during its development or in formulating ideas for its effective use or, alternatively, service in a position of a quasi-political nature requiring the deft handling of sensitive negotiations. Both help an officer widen his contact beyond the circle of his normal associates.
4. The problem is highlighted in M. N. ZALD and W. A. SIMON, Career Opportunities and Commitments among Officers. In M. JANOWITZ (Ed.), *The New Military.* New York: Russell Sage Foundation, 1964, pp. 257–285.
5. See also the evidence in VAN RIPER and UMWALLA, *op. cit.*
6. H. M. VOLLMER and W. C. PEDERSON, The Role and Career Development of the Scientific and Engineering Officer in the Air Force. *R & D Studies Series, Stanford Research Institute*, Menlo Park, California, January 1966.
7. Future Professional Manpower Requirements Study (FPRMS), Report to the Chief of Naval Operations, May 1969.
8. The Navy itself uses a different breakdown both in classifying its billets and its subspecialties from the one used here, which attempts to adhere 'as closely as possible to the uniform conversion code (see footnote 1). To illustrate: the conversion code defines all flag billets as managerial positions; the Navy, on the other hand, considers over 40 per cent of its flag billets to be in operations with the remainder divided among four major subspecialty groupings – engineering, administrative management, natural sciences, and public and international affairs.
9. See also A. D. BIDERMAN's comments on what is military at the conference on selective service held in Chicago, December 1966. In S. TAX (Ed.), *The Draft.* Chicago: University of Chicago Press, 1966.

The Functional Significance of the Military Socialization Process for the Internal Stability of the Military Organization

D. SCHÖSSLER*

* University of Mannheim, W. Germany.

In the military process of socialization all members of the military organization acquire all the behavioral qualifications which are needed for their integration into this social system. We think of organizations as formalized social systems of activity which have to perform specific '*internal*' and '*external*' tasks if they are to survive. This implies the need for *external legitimation* (= '*adaptive*' *problem*) as well as for physical and social support (by which the problems of technological and social change become '*inside*' *problems* of the military social system) and for the internal legitimation of the military authority structure (= '*integrative*' *problem*). Despite a formal 'liberal' ideology, the educational strategy in the Bundeswehr – especially in the Army – is mainly orientated toward the functional and motivational requirements of a traditional hierarchical (= bureaucratical) model. Therefore no educational concept exists which in fact helps reduce those pressures resulting from the accelerated change in technology and in societal environment. This thesis deserves more detailed consideration...

In Western society 'particularistic' interest seems to be more legitimate than interest propagated by a governmental institution. Public administrations are forced to 'sell' *decisions*. Military administrations are in a difficult situation because they have to legitimize a 'deviant' purpose: namely 'the management and application of military resources in deterrent, peacekeeping, and combat roles in the context of rapid technological, social and political change.'[1] Especially in the German post-war situation this perceived 'incompatibility' of civilian and military values forced the Bundeswehr to make a special effort to adapt itself to this 'external' situation. That means the Bundeswehr had to transform its membership conditions into an 'adaptive' concept.[2] Consequently the official socialization concept describes the conditions by which the Bundeswehr fits into the civil culture. For this reason the military innovators – such as Graf von Baudissin – developed a human relations concept which was claimed to be well adjusted to the requirements of a modern military organization. The perceived conflict between 'alienated' individuals and the bureaucratic organization was expected to be solved by the introduction of teamwork and the cultivation of primary group attitudes.[3]

Paradoxically, this concept legitimates its contradiction: as a concept of rigorous adaptation, the Innere Führung tacitly accepts the penetrant bureaucratization of the Bundeswehr because civil control can only be conceived in terms of bureaucratic control. In spite of its liberal attitude, the Innere Führung has an authoritarian bias: the penetrant bureaucratization induces some 'circuli vitiosi' which are more applicable to the

141

members' 'behavior' than the officially expected 'liberal' attitudes. To describe the two most important processes we will go back to some analytical categories of Talcott Parsons. He differentiates between three major levels in formal organizations:

1. the *technical* level, where the actual 'product' of the organization is manufactured or dispensed;
2. the *managerial* level, whose primary concern is to mediate between the various parts of the organization and to coordinate their efforts;
3. the *institutional* level, which connects the organization with the wider social system.[4]

It appears that the third level is chiefly concerned with problems of 'adaptation' and the second with 'integrational' problems. The first level 'realizes' the purpose of the organization. Which kind of role expectations are connected with each level? This question leads us to an approach which we consider useful.

First, we should differentiate between value orientation and instrumental orientation. The 'institutional' level, which operates for the 'external' legitimation, is dominated by a *civil* value orientation and therefore by a civil instrumental orientation as well. Instrumental orientation on this level means *bureaucratic* orientation. The members of the 'technical' system are mainly orientated 'outside' the organization because the skill structure is more similar to that of civil professions. The main direction of value and instrumental orientation corresponds to the main orientation on the 'institutional' level, but presumably with emphasis upon the instrumental perspective. On the other hand, the members of the 'managerial' system do not have such a civil reference system. In one aspect, they orientate themselves 'upward' (= to the 'institutional' level), which implies a mainly *civil* orientation. 'Downward', the 'managerial generalists' have more opportunity to succeed in their military way of behavior. This situation produces conflict:

| Subsystems | Role expectations | | |
	Value orientation	Instrumental orientation	Dominant orientation
institutional	civil	civil	value o.
managerial	civil vs. military	civil vs. military	value
technical	civil	civil	instrumental

142

If we study this diagram, we observe two main situations of conflict:
1. The institutional-managerial conflict, which is a civil-military dissent in *value* orientation (level of 'external' legitimation).
2. The technical-managerial conflict, which is an internal military dissent in *instrumental* orientation (level of 'internal' legitimation).

The recently published papers of General Schnez clearly reflect these conflicts.[5] The papers (the authors of which had important positions in the military socialization process, people such as General Karst and General Schall), were very much in favor of the 'institutional' system and therefore expressed, in the first place, the officially desired value orientation: 'Personnel management and military order in the forces based on the principles of the "Innere Führung".'[6] The 'pluralist democracy' is seen as a 'historically necessary high stage in the political development of our social and economic system.'[7] *Conflict* arises if this societal view is confronted both with the 'problem of balancing diverging interests and also with the needs of the common weal. In cases of doubt, the former must have more significance for armed forces.'[8]

This perspective, which reproduces a latent Hegelianism, is ideological because of its function in the 'internal' legitimation of the traditional hierarchical model: 'Upward' (toward the 'institutional' system), this interest is legitimated by the need for more military efficiency.[9] 'Downward' (toward the 'technical' system), this hierarchical interest is legitimated by the need for a face-to-face relationship between superiors and subordinates.[10] In both ways this articulation opposes the *bureaucratic* process: as regards the first situation of conflict, it clearly touches on the importance of civil values, as the 'top level' of the managerial system is inextricably woven into the 'institutional' system. It would be interesting to find out the motivational basis of this astonishing reproduction of the Trettner case.[11] On the second (technical-managerial) level of conflict, this articulation must be seen as an attempt to replace the bureaucratic reduction of complexity[12] by a *hierarchical* organization.[13]

Summing up the various educational elements of the Schnez papers, the authors attempt to re-establish an 'equilibrium' between military 'mission' and military education. This 'integrative' intention of the Schnez papers still requires a societal context which is in keeping with a traditionally organized military system. Compared with the real situation in post-war Germany, this assumption seems Utopian. Another Utopian dimension of the Schnez paper is its professional perspective: The 'sui generis' premise implies only a small, traditional role set. For comparison, A. A. Jordan's definition seems more complex: 'The military has the same general characteristics as the other professions, namely, a specialized knowledge acquired through advanced training and experience, a mutually defined and sustained set of standards, and a sense of group identity and corporateness' (Janowitz, 1960). In addition, the military profession has several characteristics not shared by other professions such as law, education, or medicine; it is, for example, bureaucratized, with a hierarchy of offices and a legally defined structure (Huntington, 1957) and it is a uniquely public profession marked by its members' commitment to unlimited service, extending to the risk of life itself.[14]

We may therefore state that there exists a latent 'cooperation' between the bureaucratic (=civilian) and hierarchic interests which altogether decelerate a better adaptation of the military to social and technological change. The most dangerous 'circulus vitiosus' must be seen at the technical-managerial level: As R. Warnke points out, the Bundeswehr motivates persons with typically non-technical skills to join the military organization,[15] because of its bureaucratic character (and a therefore alimentary system of gratification). This non-technical type enters the organization with a view to taking up an administrative position. The Bundeswehr, however, needs a highly qualified 'technician' who enters the Bundeswehr for some years and then returns into the industrial society. But the non-technical type orientates himself in a hierarchical-bureaucratic way in the hope of staying as long as possible in the military organization. This 'circulus vitiosus' definitely reduces the technical-managerial conflict (as the recruitment pattern of the technical system is also bureaucratic) but intensifies adaptation problems between organization and 'environment' (society). Consequently, the Bundeswehr is forced to increase its programs for the technical 're-education' of its personnel, procedures which strengthen the administrative 'bias' of the military organization. The table on the next page may illustrate this process.[16]

This means that, while there is a relatively 'stable' quota of 'Zeitsoldaten' (short-term commissions) – about 20 per cent –, the 'mixed' quota has been reduced in favour of the 'non-genuine' type. This might be considered a 'latent trend toward a professional army' (R. Warnke).

But there is another 'circulus vitiosus': because of the bureaucratic 'alimentary' structure of the organization, the Bundeswehr not only 'prefers' the bureaucratic 'generalist' but punishes the technical 'specialist'

Structure of length of service
(non-commissioned officers)

Type	Length of service	1962	1963	1964	1965	1966	1968
'genuine'	2–4 years	22.7	20.4	20.7	24.5	21.8	16.9
'mixed'	5–8 years	66.1	64.6	53.4	38.2	31.0	28.8
'non-genuine'	9–15 years	11.2	15.0	25.9	37.3	47.2	54.3
		100	100	100	100	100	100

in so far as the bureaucratic pattern only rewards 'performance' by 'promotion.' But promotion within a bureaucratic 'pyramid' means: permanent rotation of staff and therefore a permanent shortage of qualified personnel. 'The logic of rotation is a powerful means of developing higher officers. Its impact on the system, however, is pervasive, since it demands the constant utilization of personnel who are *new* to their assignments. As a result, the solutions that must be found tend to be based on a *general formula* rather than on specialized ones' (K. Lang).[17] The military version of the 'pyramid climber' type is therefore recommended to acquire a 'generalistic' orientation in his own interest to advance in this respect. In other words: the longer a period of service commitment lasts the more 'functional' is a 'generalistic' (=bureaucratic) orientation in a military person's career.

'Loyalty' then replaces 'performance' where the latter only functions as official ideology: 'Upward' (toward the institutional system), the stress for conformity results in a 'societal' orientation. The members of the military organization develop a 'liberal' attitude. This orientation pattern can be demonstrated by the table on the next page.

This table shows that there is a correlation between rank and attitude: the higher the rank, the more 'liberal' is the attitude.[18] On the instrumental level, therefore, the attitude must be civilly orientated which means: bureaucratically orientated. We can conclude that, obviously, career success and a liberal-bureaucratic attitude tend to correlate. 'Downward', there is increasing opportunity to succeed if one has a *military* mind and a military instrumental (= hierarchical) orientation. The authors of the Schnez papers clearly expressed these interests. We see

*Results of the dogmatism-scale**

Rank	Durchschnittl. Skalenwert	Varianz	Anzahl der Befragten
Rekrut	4.56	0.53	1089
Gefreiter	4.58	0.57	1310
Unteroffizier	4.43	0.52	573
Feldwebel	4.49	0.60	296
Offizieranw.	4.11	0.45	526
Leutnant-Hauptmann	4.01	0.42	105

* See: E. WALDMANN, *Soldat im Staat*, Boppard, 1963, p. 247.

here some processes which tend to 'reduce' the technological and social complexity (of the technical system) by authoritarian mechanisms.

SUMMARY

The 'latent cooperation' between civil-bureaucratic and military-hierarchic interests generates a characteristic mind and induces some social processes which, on the whole, seem to prevent the Bundeswehr from adapting more readily to accelerating social and technological change. It is especially a problem of attitude, as the bureaucratic structure penetrates the whole socialization process. New members therefore accept and internalize these role expectations. This process of integration is accelerated because the positive attitude toward these roles is reinforced by the 'alimentary' preference of the new members. A *real* change can only be achieved, if (1) the military educational system is not only 'manipulated' but 'revolutionized'[19] and if (2) the bureaucratic-hierarchical structure is replaced by a more flexible management system.

REFERENCES

1. JORDAN, A. A., Officer Education, in: LITTLE, R. W. (ed.), *A Survey of Military Institutions, The Inter-University Seminar on Armed Forces and Society*, Inc. 1969, Vol. I, p. 171.
2. See as a general approach LUHMANN, N., *Funktionen und Folgen formaler Organisation*, Berlin, 1964.
3. BAUDISSIN, W. Graf von, *Soldat für den Frieden*, München, 1969.
4. PARSONS, T., *Structure and Process in Modern Societies*, Glencoe, 1960, pp. 16–96.
5. The first paper was finished in spring 1969 (= 'SCHNEZ paper I'), the second in summer 1969 (= 'SCHNEZ paper II').
6. 'SCHNEZ paper II,' item 1.
7. 'SCHNEZ paper I,' p. 9.
8. *Ibid.*
9. 'SCHNEZ paper II,' esp. part 4.
10. 'SCHNEZ paper II,' item 13.
11. 'SCHNEZ paper II,' item 27.
12. This was characteristical in the 'Starfighter'-incident – 1965/66.
13. 'SCHNEZ paper II,' item 13.
14. JORDAN, A. A., *op. cit.*, p. 170.
15. WARNKE, R., *et al.*, *Die Bundeswehr als Arbeitsplatz auf Zeit*, Bonn, 1968 (Schriftenreihe Innere Führung, Wehrsoziologische Studien, Heft 3).
16. *Ibid.*
17. LANG, K., Technology and Career Management in the Military Establishment, in: JANOWITZ, M. (ed.), *The New Military*, New York, 1964, p. 51.
18. WALDMANN, E., *Soldat im Staat*, Boppard, 1963, p. 249.
19. A new concept of military education (esp. officers' education) is published by SCHUBERT, K. von, Zur Ausbildung des Truppenoffiziers, in: *Wehrkunde*, Heft 7, Vol. 70, p. 368 ff.

The Mobility of Non-Commissioned Officers*

J.P. THOMAS**

* This text has been based on research carried out in compliance with agreement no. 108/67 between the Minister of Defence (directorate of research and test methods) and the National Foundation for Political Sciences.
** Fondation Nationale de Sciences Politiques.

It will be difficult to list in a few pages all our hypotheses for working out the total research into the environment of non-commissioned officers. The comments which follow were suggested by two series of preliminary interviews among non-commissioned officers in the Air Force, and Naval petty officers; they include general statistical studies, individual records, non-focused interviews, opinion polls with random samples. We are, therefore, concerned with presenting the results, reconstructing them tentatively and examining suitable methods by which to verify them.

I. POSSIBILITY OF GIVING UP REPRESENTATIVE SAMPLE POLLS

This study entailed two sets of non-focused talks with Air Force NCO's (Spring 1968) and petty officers (Autumn 1968) and contact with local commanders who accompanied them. From these talks the main lines for research emerged. The statistical study of individual dossiers also contributed to a lesser degree. At this stage we shall only single out five points from the mass of information obtained.

1. The ends of the military institution, as experienced by non-commissioned officers, are as follows:
— *defence:* little identification in this respect; does not appear in the classical form of 'pride in service' or 'search for an ideal'. It may be substituted by 'professional conscience' sometimes displayed with aggressiveness. This leads us to the second end.
— *addition to national education* through professional training and apprenticeship for a trade. This idea of the 'professional' (at the expense of the 'military') as regards the NCO's position was dominant in the Air Force and is also spreading in the Navy.
— *a refuge* (an 'island retreat') for marginal categories of adolescents, maladjusted to civilian life, who find in the forces a life and social structures on which they can depend. This has been overdone by the applied psychology section of the Navy (cf. the percentage of volunteers who originate from broken homes).

2. Non-commissioned officers *do not constitute a 'corps'*. In their own words they are 'passing through' the forces. The setting up of an officers corps of engineers, interpreted as 'topping off' and 'creaming off' has helped to devalue the idea of the 'corps' among the Air Force NCO's. If we weigh up an average NCO life, one point is manifest: in the most favourable case, with voluntary enlistment at the age of 17 (Navy), a

25-year military career and civilian retirement at 65, the active civilian life, allowing for possible apprenticeships before enlistment, lasts as long as a military career. The scales are unquestionably in the civilian's favour, the average military career being 15½ years. These figures suggest that the importance and image of civilian society greatly determine the interviewees' conduct.

3. The third point follows on naturally from the preceding ones. Non-commissioned officers are divided, at the very heart of military society, between *two worlds and two reference systems:* the 'professional' world which is allied to the civilian society: the acquisition and practice of high-level technical specialisation; the 'military' world: their inclusion in the hierarchy and participation in traditional military activities.

This dualism, found in every non-commissioned officer, encourages the development of two types of behaviour. The first is connected with the search for a civilian profession and will eventually end in anticipated departure. The second type of behaviour is linked with the pursuit of a military career. What is the consequence of each type of behaviour for each individual? To what extent, and why, is one preferred to another? The general economic situation and the interest of the man's current post in the forces, personal relationships, sometimes favour his departure to industry, sometimes his attachment to the military institution.

4. The behaviour we have just discussed, the preference for one form rather than another, presupposes a 'plan of campaign'. To what extent is the behaviour conscious and voluntary? Is there a rational forecast of the future? Can one make allowance for social determinism and the autonomy of the individual's will? On what information and experience do non-commissioned officers base their decisions? What are the rules of this 'strategy game'?

5. The simple word, the forces, stands for a complex society divided into many groups. It is as well to distinguish between reglementary or administrative stratifications, determined by prescribed parameters: ranks, specialised branches in the forces, corps, units..., and the divisions resulting from spontaneous, informal sociological groups, whose limits do not coincide with the foregoing divisions. The difficulties that the formal groupings entail are clear from the individual dossiers (the many specialised groupings mean that each is represented too little to warrant statistical study); the analysis of the non-focused talks has revealed the importance of the latter (informal groupings).

152

The 'context' in which the non-commissioned officer lives is made up of 'combinations' of these groups, and these variables determine his answers to the questions relating to the foregoing points.

How can these observations guide research?

Points 1, 2 and 3 led to the plan for a mobility study: social mobility between *generations*, professional mobility within *a generation;* points 4 and 5 led us to resort to the methods of 'contextual' analysis. And this choice will affect considerably the composition of the sample for the final inquiry and will lead us to add outside variables to the facts obtained from questionnaires.

We finally chose behaviour and 'context' (background) rather than motivation and values. This choice is also justified in view of the vagueness surrounding the ability to memorise and the verbal expression of the latter type of information. A mobility study does not have the same epistemology as a motivation study.

II. MOBILITY 'PROJECTION'

A. The 'ideal type' in the mobility 'projection'

This second stage in the hypotheses will mainly be borrowed from Weber's epistemology. The spread of facts in time (differences in years of service) and their breakdown on the date of the inquiry (into stratification according to grade, specialisation, type of assignment) make it impossible to grasp them directly and organise them: they need some guideline. This could be found by forming 'ideal types'.

Max Weber[1] believes that 'the characteristic ideal concept aims at forming a judgement by deduction: it is not itself a hypothesis, but seeks to guide the working out of hypotheses', or again 'there is only one meaning, that of a purely ideal concept, by which reality is assessed in order to clarify the empiric content of certain important elements and with which it is compared'.

Preliminary inquiries among non-commissioned Air Force officers and Naval petty officers resulted in the choice for the mobility 'projection' of a characteristic central ideal concept which empiric data will illustrate.[2]

How shall we define the 'mobility projection'? In the case in question it corresponds with the individual's course via two points: 1. the decision to join up; 2. the decision to quit. We can describe the 'projection' by analysing these two decisions. The former falls within the domain of past

153

behaviour. The latter, on the other hand, is in the domain of hypothetical behaviour. It should appear at a future date as the main outcome of the subject's 'plan of campaign'. We shall have to try to discover the mechanisms of this strategy from the replies to the questionnaire, taking into account the NCO's circumstances.

Four 'ideal types' have been established:
institutional 'projection'
individual, or industrial 'projection'
community 'projection'
instable 'projection' or none at all.

One of the main difficulties in the inquiry was to find a *definition* for these 'projections'.

1. *Institutional 'projection':* the wish to make a career and the search for security. Good merging with the norms of the institution and identification with it. This concerns non-commissioned officers with an 'old retainer' vocation, found primarily in the classical specialist branches which offer moderate possibilities of re-integration in the civilian sector.

2. *Individual (or industrial) 'projection':* the wish to obtain good professional qualifications and the search for satisfaction in employment. Refusal of military norms and good identification with professional norms. Service identified with professional conscience. These will be non-commissioned officers who would like to be 'passing through' the forces, found mainly in 'top' specialist branches which offer good possibilities for employment in the industrial civilian sector.

3. *Community 'projection':* the wish to do something which would be difficult, or impossible in civilian life: piloting fast planes, parachuting, commando training etc., search to enter a more limited, more closed community than the military and associated essentially with the activity in question. These people will challenge the general norms of the institution, but adhere the (non-written) 'code' of the restricted community. They will be non-commissioned officers in very varying groups, ranging from Air Force navigating staff, parachute units or Naval commandos.

4. *Without 'projection'* (or inconstant projection): short-term utilitarianism and search for security. Indifferent identification with the norms of the institution; service governed by fear of sanctions. These will be very different types: the volunteer who is too frustrated to adapt to the developments in the forces, or the adolescent in pre-delinquency; the

154

common denominator will be the mediocrity of potential (intellectual or moral) and lack of adjustment.

B. Mobility 'projections' and the final cause of the military institution

Let us see if the proposed descriptions can be made more systematic. Table I which follows relates the projections to the above-mentioned final courses/ends of the military institution. This is a diagram for information purposes, devoid of any subtle differences. What conclusions can one draw? The connections between the individual projection and the motive of completing one's education, and between no projection and the motive of refuge, are evident and exclusive.

Table I. The mobility 'projections' and the final causes/motives in the military institution

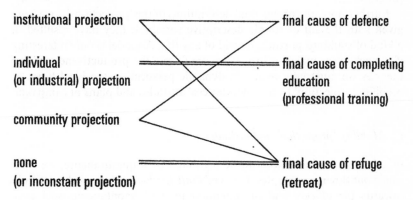

One will note above all that the connections concerning the institutional and the community 'projections' resemble one another: the final cause of defence will be explicit in the first (identification with the norms of the institution and adoption of the pertaining vocabulary) and implicit in the second (specifically military activities of the community). The refuge motive corresponds to the search for security in the institutional 'projection', within the exclusive framework of the military institution. In the community 'projection' it corresponds to a double action: search for an occupation which is not possible elsewhere and search for the 'setting' offered by the 'delinquent community'. The diagram mainly shows therefore the relationship between the institutional and community

155

'projections', the latter appearing to some extent as the pathology of the former.

These observations provoke several comments.

First of all, the validity of the final causes attributed to the military institution may be queried. This is undoubtedly the weakest point of the analysis. The almost entire absence of the defence motive in the talks does not mean it has vanished, but perhaps that it has been concealed by behaviour patterns and a new vocabulary. This phenomenon has some bearing on Robert Pages' observations regarding a study on Merchant Navy officers.[3]

The teleological illusion is dangerous because it makes the investigator use notions which are not as revealing as the 'model' which he is supposed to make (thus the 'mission', a military word, is not a 'social fact' in the Durkheim sense of the word. It should therefore fall to the investigator to construct variables which enable him to take this into account in his programme.)

Furthermore, the provisional descriptions of the 'projections' have been given with the aid of simple descriptive variables: they have resulted in a kind of standard portrait, devoid of any life. A model is only interesting if a mechanism makes it live. If we are to test the productiveness of our theories we must now relate, in dynamic perspective, the ideal types of mobility 'projection' to the interviewees' attitudes and plans of campaign.

C. Mobility 'projection' and attitudes

Of all the attitudes which can be registered by a questionnaire, we shall single out three as examples: the man's *satisfaction in his work*, his attitude towards the *officers* and his intention to *quit*. Spontaneous sociology would easily admit the convergence of these three attitudes: satisfaction would be linked with a favourable attitude towards the officers, and to the intention to make a career. This can be gradated by means of the types of 'mobility'.

1. Satisfaction/Dissatisfaction

Satisfaction is not synonymous with adaptation: on the contrary, as Crozier has shown, aggressive dissatisfaction may be a sign of a certain adaptation. In that adaptation signifies the integration of the norms of the institution and the adoption of the institution as a privileged group of reference, one could in fact admit that the more demanding the persons concerned (i.e. dissatisfied) the more involved they are.

156

We propose, therefore, the following hypotheses:
— institutional 'projection': dissatisfaction with the institution ('deceived lover complex') – participation;
— individual (or industrial) 'projection': satisfaction in work and professional conscience – indifference towards the institution;
— community 'projection': satisfaction with respect to the 'delinquent community' but opposition to the overall military institution – variant adaptation;
— without (or inconstant) projection: indifference or anomic adaptation.

The questionnaire for the preliminary Naval inquiry should verify the two first hypotheses (dissatisfaction in the institutional 'projection'; satisfaction in the individual).

2. Attitude towards officers
In this respect we only expect a negative attitude, with the following interpretations:
— *institutional* 'projection': disappointment with superiors who are not of the classical stereotype (any longer);
— *individual* (or industrial) 'projection': the technical man's scorn for the 'incompetence' of representatives of the military hierarchy;
— *community* 'projection': adoption of the 'patrons' of the 'delinquent community' (charismatic leadership), retreat from outside representatives of the military hierarchy;
— without (or instable) project: primary hostility towards the superior who hands out sanctions.

3. Anticipated departure
Let us now consider the intention to leave the forces and suppose that we are dealing with a group of non-commissioned officers who express in their replies to the questionnaire their intention to depart for good: these would seem to be voluntary, anticipated departures.

What has brought about these decisions?
— institutional 'projection': the anticipated departure is voluntary, with negative motivations. The non-commissioned officer is going to leave the forces feeling 'let down'; which does not mean he has made a 'happy landing' in civilian life. At all events this concerns a member whom the Army would no doubt have wanted to keep.
— individual (or industrial) 'projection': this is a voluntary departure with positive motivations. The NCO is leaving his military station

157

because he has found a more suitable post for which he is trained too. He is an expert with an expensive training; the Army will do its utmost to keep him (speed up promotion, create an engineer officers corps, etc. We shall find out later how to interpret such measures).
— community 'projection': voluntary departure is a rationalisation for enforced departure. The 'community's' activity requires young staff with special aptitude, the effect of age-limits is very strong here. NCOs who no longer meet the conditions required will not necessarily be tempted by 'military bureaucracy' and general service: that would be a come-down. Their qualifications are hard to convert into monetary terms on the civilian employment market, where their personalities are, however, appreciated. Some may be tempted by the mirage of adventure or by marginal jobs (pilots for small African airlines, frogmen for public works companies etc.)
— no projection (or inconstant projection): voluntary departure is a rationalisation for enforced departure. The mediocrity of the qualifications obtained, slowness of promotion, the threat of the contractual ties not being renewed or the fear of not reaching the rank of career petty officer or NCO will often cause the serviceman to take this decision. These are generally instances of 'dead weight'; the Army is not likely to try to hold on to them.

These examples show that seemingly similar attitudes may be the outcome of different processes; a group of people defined by a common opinion may in fact harbour opposed sub-groups.

The Army cannot durably affect the manner of serving and loyalty by working on one of the elements in the satisfaction/attitude towards officers/intention to leave 'trilogy', but by seeking to detect the sociological sides to the NCOs' circumstances in military and in general social terms.

D. Mobility projection and personal plan of campaign

Before we develop the second set of examples borrowed from the 'plan of campaign' theme (cf. I, point 4), we should like to outline the general problems and suggest a few definitions.

We first need to know who is involved in the plan of campaign: an individual, or groups of people (all those in a specialist branch, all the NCOs in a unit, a particular 'graduation' year, or even a small, informal, spontaneous group?). Let us assume that in the vast majority of cases the individual is concerned.

158

Secondly, we must discover the objectives of the plan of campaign. We would be wrong in suggesting that they are strictly utilitarian and economic: the interviews have revealed the need for esteem, the search for security and interest in work.

Thirdly, where is the plan of campaign 'enacted': is it limited to the military institution (internally – e.g. 'making a career') or does it extend to the whole of the society (externally – the search for social resettlement)?

Our fourth question concerns the 'rules' which govern this tactical game. There are 'mechanisms' which maintain the balance in the system and keep it going. The 'actors' do not necessarily notice them. The NCO, in developing his own plan of campaign, allows for elements which are accessible, i.e. familiar to him: personal experience, the examples of friends, advice from superiors, regulations etc. Similarly he runs up against factors whose power and effect he does not know and which are beyond his control: we shall call these *areas of uncertainty*. And all the forces which govern these we shall call *social control*[4].

The 'area of uncertainty' and the 'social control' differ greatly from one 'plan of campaign' to another. If it is within the military institution (i.e. 'internally') the areas of uncertainty are clearly confined within its limits: fluctuations in budget, change in the administrative rules, creation or suppression of special branches or units connected with a new definition of missions etc. Social control is mainly (but not entirely) identified with the voluntary, conscious action of the Command. This we shall term *institutional social control*. (One can, incidentally, reintroduce into the inquiry the idea of 'mission' by the double mediacy of the notions of 'individual strategy' and 'social control': 'budget' and 'mission' are, ultimately, the essential determinant factors for institutional social control.)

On the other hand, if we are dealing with an 'external' plan of campaign, the areas of uncertainty extend beyond the institution to the vast sectors of industry, even to the entire civilian society. Social control will therefore be different, both comprehensive and anonymous, as are the rules of supply and demand: it will be more like a 'regulatory mechanism' than organised control. This we shall term *external social control*. We shall give it two dimensions: *economic* (the general situation on the employment market) and *political* (the attitude of the civilian population towards the military and Defence – 'antimilitarism'). A few illustrations are called for here.

1. Strategy and dissatisfaction

We have already noted that *aggressive dissatisfaction* could be a paradoxical sign of a certain adaptation. This could be reformulated as follows: the 'institutional projection' (vocation of 'old retainer') develops an 'internal' plan of campaign. The person concerned comes up against internal (i.e. institutional) areas of uncertainty and suffers institutional control without understanding or knowing all the rules. Defence mechanisms reply to the pressures caused by a situation like this: the fewer the alternatives, the stronger they are (to some extent a 'back to the wall' situation). Establishment in the military society is the sole objective, the possibility of quitting (withdrawal position) is not considered.

2. Strategy and the search for security

The *security* theme evoked above will serve as a further illustration. The institutional and individual 'projections' occur in the Navy and in the Air Force. In the present stage of preliminary enquiries the former would seem to occur more frequently in the Navy, the latter more in the Air Force. The need for security does not appear to be the same. Petty officers attach extreme importance to admission into the rank of career petty officer and frequently mention in the interviews the possibility of the contractual ties not being renewed. Air Force NCOs, however, are less concerned about entering the rank of career NCO and seek to extend short contracts (6 months), which enable them to leave the forces quickly if the opportunity of civilian employment arises. In the first case it is more likely to be the institution that will make use of the ties, in the second the person concerned will do so. In other words, the petty officer will run into 'internal' (institutional) areas of uncertainty, the Air Force NCO will face 'external' uncertainties. These are only hypotheses which the final inquiry will have to test. We mention them to show how analysis of these 'plans of campaign'/strategies could help to define the mobility 'projections'.

3. Strategy and access to the engineer officers corps

Let us continue by examining a measure of institutional social control: the setting up of an *Engineer Officers corps* in the Air Force. It was mentioned in many of the interviews with Air Force NCOs, amongst whom it appeared to be rather unpopular. We are hardly likely to betray the military authorities' intentions if we view this measure as a tentative effort to keep some categories of NCOs in the forces whose departure would constitute a costly loss.

This institutional social control is conscious and voluntary. Everything should proceed as if access to the officers ranks were a sufficient social

160

promotion for NCOs not to be tempted into the civilian sector. The following suppositions might explain partial failure of this system.

— Institutional 'projection': 'internal' (institutional) strategy, 'internal' areas of uncertainty. The people concerned are solely NCOs under institutional control, that is, those who should be most sensitive to a measure like this. The unfavourable reactions observed can be divided into two groups. The better subjects considered the limitation of an engineer officer's three stripes in the future as the sign of inadmissible discrimination. The Engineer Officers corps would represent a come-down compared to recognised promotion by rank. The less brilliant subjects did not make the comparison with other procedures for entering officers ranks, but with the ideal career of NCO: appointments to the Engineer Officers corps would entail 'topping off' or 'creaming off' of the NCO rank. The stereotype of old regimental sergeant major 'who is a personality at the base' is recalled; they would rather become 'a whale among the minnows, than a minnow among the whales'.

— Individual (or industrial) 'projection': 'external' strategy, 'external' areas of uncertainty. These are NCOs who are less sensitive to institutional control. The social control which is to affect the plan of campaign in the 'individual projection' springs from outside the institution. The internal measures taken by the Forces do not define for these people the real 'rules of the game' (the action of supply and demand on the employment market etc.). The creation of the Engineer Officers corps is a promotion measure within the framework of the institution, the effects and conditions of which stay within its limits; open perspectives are foreign on the subject's horizons and the measure becomes entirely pointless.

— Community 'projection': the mechanisms of the observed reactions would be fairly similar to those in the 'institutional projection'. Nevertheless, when promotion means breaking the ties with the 'delinquent community', a similar situation is produced to the 'individual projection': the measure moves outside the subject's horizons and arouses no interest. (Take the case of a navigating engineer for whom a commission means leaving the navigating staff, for there are no officers ranks in this branch.)

— No 'projection' (or inconstant): for 'sour grapes' reasons.

There would seem here to be some contradiction, inherent in the system itself: the creation of an engineer officers corps stems from the 'classical' values of the military institution which want an officer to be superior to

161

a non-commissioned officer and promotion to be a good thing in itself. Continuing within this traditional hierarchical system, we shall however discover that its final cause reveals a different system. A particular qualification will be ratified, even though the person concerned is not necessarily endowed with the vocation for command (an outline for a functional hierarchy perhaps?). With regard to the 'institutional projection' the principle of 'equality for all without a commission' is not compatible with the system of adopted values, no more than the pyramid of non-commissioned officers. With the 'individual projection', however, the first aspect of the system is incompatible with the norms of the industrial organisation. And on similar lines is the occasional fear that the 'polyvalence' attached to the rank of officer renders useless a hard-won specialised skill.

We have gone into this example in some detail because it shows the interest of an inquiry into the connection between the mobility 'projection' and social control. This will be a foremost objective of the final inquiry.

4. Strategy and search for power
The last illustration in this context deals with *power*. Some company sociologists, Crozier in particular, see the search for power, or a modicum thereof, as an essential objective in the strategy of individuals confined in an organisation. Our problems are different, in that we have concentrated on mobility processes. The quest for power is not entirely unrelated, however, to this subject. It may be a compensation of a failure: how does a petty officer who has become master-at-arms (marine) experience this function? Power is not necessarily exerted within the official hierarchy: what is the dependence of 'operationals' compared with 'engineers'? Crozier has analysed this (the power of 'maintenance workers' in a State industry).[5]

Power corresponds in both cases to an objective within the military institution, proving a 'closed' plan of campaign. Analysis of the interviews shows that the quest for power is one of the main motive forces in the 'institutional projection' strategy. For the master-at-arms we mentioned above, it might represent the force to pass from the 'community projection' to the 'institutional projection'. For the engineer exerting power outside the hierarchy, it will correspond to the desire for a functional hierarchy parallel to the classical military hierarchy: the quest for power might therefore be the force to pass from the 'individual (or industrial) projection' to a *new* 'institutional projection', corresponding with a *new* way of serving and adaptation to *new* missions in the forces.

It is as well to emphasize, at the end of this section, that the ideal

162

mobility 'projection' is hardly ever found complete, nor experienced entirely univocally. Likewise one might suppose that officership favours the passing from 'no projection' (or 'inconstant projection') to the community, or even the institutional 'projection', or that a good training in the Forces alters it into the individual (or industrial) 'projection'. So some individuals, by historical chance or personality, pass from one type to another. These are accidents of the 'institutional journey'.[6]

Table II in the following pages recapitulates the elements which have helped us work out the ideal types of mobility 'projection'. This is the second stage in the hypotheses.

III. THE FINAL INQUIRY

The next step is to verify the projection empirically; to proceed from a provisional description to an operative definition. The final inquiry gathers together two sets of data. The first set (morphology and ecology) refers to the 'life story' preceding voluntary military enlistment; the second (conduct and opinions) relates to hypothetical behaviour, attitudes and norms perceived on the day of the inquiry. The definition of the projection will comprise elements from both sets of data.

The inquiry was thwarted by two restrictions, concerning the make-up of the experimental group and the compilation of the background ('contextual') data. We shall deal with these in turn.

A. The problems of setting up a sample

The rejection of opinion polls as a research method will explain the rejection of representative samples. A second, decisive argument is the dispersal of the group of people studied (as a result of length of service and specialist branch).

The preliminary inquiries have shown that these two variables are of cardinal importance; the hypotheses cannot be understood unless they are taken into consideration. Moreover, we substituted the representative sample of all NCOs by a series of experimental sub-groups of constant numbers, defined by two single parameters: length of service and specialist branch.

163

Table II. Second stage of hypotheses

	Institutional projection	Individual projection (or industrial)	Community projection	No projection (or inconstant)
1. Teleology	– Final cause defence – Final cause refuge	– Final cause completing national education	– Final cause defence – Final cause refuge	– Final cause refuge
2. Attitude towards the institution	– Adaptation – Participation – Identification with military norms	– Indifference – Refusal of military norms – Identification with professional norms	– Deviation – Closed solidarity with the 'delinquent community' – Challenge of norms of institution – Adoption of the community 'code'	– Marginality – Retreat
3. Attitude towards employment (everyday experience)	– Dissatisfaction – Aggressiveness	– Satisfaction – Professional conscience	– Satisfaction – Search for 'prowess'	– Passivity
4. Conception of leadership and attitude towards officers	– Authoritarian leadership – Deception with officers who do not correspond (any longer) to the stereotype	– Democratic leadership – Technical man's scorn of military hierarchy	– Charismatic leadership – Adoption of a 'patron' within the community – Challenge of external military hierarchy	– Authoritarian leadership – Primary hostility towards the superior who hands out sanctions
5. Organisation of future and attitude towards change	– Medium-term utilitarian calculation (career) – Refusal of change	– Long-term utilitarian calculation (profitability of qualification) – Rational anticipation of change	– Short-term utilitarian calculation in the community – Awareness of change	– Short-term utilitarian calculation (immediate elementary needs) – Refusal of change

Table II (continued)

	Institutional projection	Individual projection (or industrial)	Community projection	No projection (or inconstant)
6. Reference group	– Military institution	– Industrial society	– 'Delinquent community'	– Primary group (immediate context)
7. 'Location' of strategy	– 'Internal' strategy (focused on the institution)	– 'External' strategy (open to industrial society)	– 'Internal' strategy (focused on the 'delinquent society')	– Lack of strategy
8. Areas of uncertainty	– Within the institution	– Outside the institution	– Within the 'delinquent community'	– Within the institution
9. Social control	– Effective institutional social control	– *Ineffective* institutional social control – External social control preponderant	– *Little* effective institutional social control – Community social control preponderant	– Effective institutional social control
10. Intention to leave forces	– Voluntary departure for negative reasons	– Voluntary departure for positive reasons	– Rationalisation of enforced departure	– Enforced departure
EXAMPLES	– Classical specialist branches of long standing – Middle-grade technicians (e.g. secretaries, assistants to quarter-master sergeant, motor mechanics etc.)	– 'Top notch' specialist branches – High-grade technicians (e.g. experts in detection devices; all specialist branches connected with electronics, etc.)	– Occupations which do not exist in the civilian sector – Occupations restricted to lower age groups (e.g. pilots of fast planes, commando marines, paratroopers, underwater combatants etc.)	– Simple specialist branches – Low-grade technicians – Rejects from other categories

B. The compilation of 'contextual' data

1. In search of social compatibility

The relevant 'contexts' in this inquiry are civilian society, which 'places' the decision to join up, military society, which 'places' the decision to leave the forces. It is practically impossible to construct a stratified sample, with one strata being collective civilian units. On the other hand, we can resort to 'social compatibility' and add to the data obtained by our questionnaire, figures based on external statistical or empiric data. The 'ecology' of the decision to join up led to the study of the demographic and geographical backgrounds, based on figures from the National Council for Statistics and Economic Studies (INSEE).

It is not much easier to make a sample with a strata made up of military 'groups'. *The unit or corps is the immediate context/background.* An NCO does not spend all his military life in one unit. *The specialist branch is a better guide to context/background;* it is both manageable and generally permanent.

Recourse to mechanised administration indexes giving military social compatibility adds some figures pertaining to the military background, to the running and the sophistication level of the sample group, to the rate of departures for civilian life, etc.

Table III gives a diagram of our sources.

Table III. Final inquiry – Experimental groups (individual data) and social compatibility

$$P_1$$

$$P_3 \qquad P_2$$

$$P_4$$

P_1 = Experimental group to whom the inter-Forces questionnaire was applied for the final study

P_2 = The entire NCO corps, for whom social compatibility is known from the card indexes of the Chiefs of Staff of the Air Force and the Navy

P_3 = The entire French population, for whom social compatibility is known from the National Council for Statistics and Economic Studies

P_4 = Experimental group in the INSEE study into the training and qualifications of the French population. The study, carried out at the end of 1963, registered the essential stages in the careers of 27,000 persons. *Etudes et conjoncture*, No. 2, February 1967 (22 years) page 3–110.

166

2. The background ('contextual') statistics

Two sets of background statistics were established. The first relates to the origins of the subjects. They were taken from the INSEE: the study of the training and qualification of the French population in 1963 (P_4) supplied figures on the father's 'socio-professional class'. The 1962 census (P_3) gave the figures on 'county ('département') of residence at time of enlistment'. If we take into account the NCO's years of service, division of the sample into periods of 5 years' service and the fact that the final study questionnaire was conducted in March 1970, the dates 1962 and 1963 are acceptable.

The second set of figures relates to the military background and administration. It was drawn up from statistics obtained in 1968 by the Air Force and Navy Chiefs of Staff (P_2). As the basic data were not obtained by the same methods, we could not supply a joint list for both forces. Nor are all the figures of equal significance; many are merely experimental. Three points were important, though impossible to assess exactly:

— speed of promotion
— level of qualification in years of service
— proportion of departures according to years of service.

CONCLUSION

These concluding remarks sum up the particulars of the preliminary studies.

1. *Economic problems* (pay, annuities, etc.) apply for all NCOs alike; however, they are only really crucial for young men who are getting married. Nevertheless they are experienced as *symbols*, even as a necessity: the symbol of a lack of consideration of which NCOs are thought to be victims; the symbol of the deterioration of the military 'station'; the symbol of failure in social promotion.

2. *Social mobility* emerges as the pivot for the 'NCO problems'. It does not only reflect economic and financial aspects.

3. Developments in the last few decades would seem, entirely pragmatically, to have cast two different, even opposed types of 'military station' in a common legal mould: the *traditional* military 'station' founded on the concepts of corps and hierarchy, and a *new* 'station', based on the concepts of profession and post. The values of the former are lasting and involve a

withdrawal into the institution; those of the latter are geared to change and involve an opening out towards industrial society.

4. This dualism is in effect a contradiction with the unity of principle. An unstable equilibrium arises, which explains the ceaseless dialectic between resistance from the sociological milieu and social control exerted by the military authorities.

The problem, therefore, is to know whether this new reality should be ratified by new legal principles or if only the principle of the unit is compatible with the military 'mission'.

One final observation is necessary. The methods and 'concept' tests applied in the 'mobility study among non-commissioned officers' might well be used for studies into other environments. We noted in particular when studying recruiting for the Military Academy and professional guidance of cadets (regarding the choice of military destination) phenomena which the mobility projection might take into account. Comparable mobility studies of other ranks could help to work out a theory on military standing.

Thus these few hypotheses are to our mind but the groundwork for a more elaborate project.

1. cf. Max WEBER: 'L'objectivité de la connaissance', in *Essais sur la théorie de la science*. Paris, Plon, 1965, pages 180 and 185.
2. One can consult the following on the concept of mobility: KARPIK, Lucien, Trois concepts sociologiques: le projet de référence, le statut social et le bilan individuel, in *Archives européennes de sociologie*, VI, 2, 1965, p. 191;
   TOURAINE, Alain, *Sociologie de l'action*, Paris, Éditions du Seuil, 1965, 508 p.;
   TOURAINE, Alain et RAGAZZI, Orietta, *Ouvriers d'origine agricole*, Paris, Éditions du Seuil, 1961, 128 p.
3. KANDEL, Liliane, MICHELAT, Guy, PAGES, Robert, BABINET, Marie-Ange, *Des dirigeants marginaux? Étude préliminaire sur la situation socio-professionnelle des officiers dans la marine marchande*. Laboratory of social psychology – Faculty of Human Arts and Sciences of the University of Paris. February 1964, stencil, 156 p., page 145.
4. 'Area of uncertainty' and 'social control' are borrowed from Michel CROZIER's vocabulary in *Le phénomène bureaucratique*, Paris, Éditions du Seuil, 1963, 414 p.
5. Cf. CROZIER, M., *op. cit.*
6. The expression 'institutional journey' has been taken from Crocq: 'les dimensions sociologiques des conduites inadaptées en milieu militaire' (the sociological dimensions of maladjusted behaviour in the military environment). *Le médecin de réserve*, 61st year, No. 5–6 (Nov.-Dec. 1965) p. 142.

Evolution of the Military Community. 'Associate' Groups - Reference Groups

M. GATINEAUD*

* Centre d'Études de Sociologie Militaire, Paris.

The military community and development therein cannot be studied without constant reference to the changes within society as a whole. These changes relate both to the structure of the military institution and the mentality of the men who comprise it, especially their feeling of integration.

One must admit that the military world, characterised by the values it implies, takes on the individual as a person, but also as a member of a hierarchical society into which he must blend. However, this society, which has been formed to realize an indirect, sometimes ill-perceived mission, requires total involvement of the individual for the nation's benefit. The nature of the 'mission' imposes obligations on each person involved.

Thus the military institution means more for the individual than a way of life, since it does not only order his activities and behaviour, but his personal status too, and it determines his duties and his 'rôles'. So we can aver that it forms for him one of his fundamental 'associate' groups (i.e. those to which he belongs), even if this belonging is not fully experienced.

Every individual should place his aspirations at the core of this associate group, where two worlds can be found, one typically military which sets the aims and the style of living, the other professional which determines the actions to reach these aims.

But this is not so. Many soldiers evaluate their position or circumstances in relation to groups outside the military institution. If the comparison is made at the individual's level, this reference may be presented as a model for his 'rôle'.

So one might think that by studying the position of the reference groups inside and outside the 'associate' group, the individual's integration into his social environment might be discovered.

Similarly we shall proceed to show how military society has developed, bearing in mind developments in society at large.

DEVELOPMENT STUDY

The military community has long formed a self-sufficient society, in which each person could realise his material and moral aspirations.

Further, the activities at the heart of the Forces were of a specific nature, having no connection with those in society as a whole. The military and professional worlds were one.

Little by little the whole of society has become organised, often along

173

military lines, the structures have become similar and the technical progress of arms has meant that many professional military jobs have come to resemble civilian activities.

The last twenty-five years have been particularly marked by this technical development, but by new ideas too. Thus the concept of national defence is not as clear as it was, and its necessity has even sometimes been queried.

The Armed Forces have been obliged to adopt a very similar organisation to that of an industrial enterprise for the use of their 'matériel'. They gave society a structural pattern and now they are organising themselves along similar lines to the industrial concerns.

Within the most technical sections of the forces (aviation and naval corps and some sections of the army) there is staff specialisation and allocation of duties. The individual is integrated into a new group with a well-defined mission, often construed, however, in terms of technical output and no longer as a participator in the completion of a wider mission, which is that of the Forces as a whole. The military and professional worlds are separate and, though the groups to which these persons 'belong' are still in the military society, these technicians choose their reference groups outside.

This severing of the groups is complex and occurs in different forms, depending on the individual, his aspirations and the type of mission entrusted to him.

If we make a rough distinction between two types of recruiting – rural and urban – characteristic behaviour patterns emerge. In the first instance, the 'positive' reference groups start off mainly within the associate group; the 'negative' references are outside.

The army in fact constitutes security for these people, who come from a 'sub-divided' community, and within the army they will achieve their aspirations, assessing their personal success against the other members of the group. They will be very sensitive to all aspects of promotion, the more so because the circles they come from and to which they hope to return some day still recognize the prestige of rank.

On the other hand, people of urban origins will acquire more systematically groups outside the military community as their references. They will be hindered by this world to which they do not really belong, reject its obligations and develop a feeling of refusal towards it. They will consider themselves primarily as technicians, and will voice their opinions as such; they will assess themselves, rightly or wrong, in comparison with technicians outside the forces.

So in extremely general terms: we shall find in specialist branches where

174

the professional character closely resembles or is confused with the traditional military character more persons of rural origins. The opposite will be the case in more advanced specialist branches. This threatens to produce a split at the very core of military society, the more so as urbanisation is speeding up, thus leading to a change in the make-up of the military environment.

A further distinction can be made with regard to the academic level of those entering the forces. Research among NCOs has shown that, at least during the first years of service, at the lowest levels one finds those who are at the same time most attached to the institution, and the most critical of it.

The forces for them were a means to personal achievement which should allow them to make up for their basic handicap. Their reference groups will therefore be within this military society, since by climbing its ladder they will ascend in the social scale. Only when they have reached a certain level might they assume outside groups of reference, especially if they have sited their initial references too high and feel let down. This then is a case of a transfer of reference group to outside the associate group.

The advance of schooling in society as a whole reduces this effect and more and more young people are entering the forces with a very high level of aspiration from the start. They may feel that the possibilities offered by the group to which they belong and particularly by accession to a particular rank, do not correspond to what they think they have found in other groups. So they reject a priori the military world, yet are not hostile towards it, since their 'internal' reference groups make them practically disregard an 'associate' group, in which they feel 'in transit'.

However, when this category achieves some seniority in the forces, and if they plan to follow a military career, some will transfer their groups of reference to within the group to which they belong. These persons become increasingly critical of the military institution and either develop a feeling of comparative frustration or, on the contrary, a desire for greater integration which, criticism aside, appears as compliance with the values of the group's most admired and respected core.

So certain phenomena in society as a whole – technical progress, urbanisation, academic progress – bring about new phenomena in the military community, especially the breakdown of 'associate' groups and reference groups.

Let us now consider new states of mind.

We have already mentioned that the military world was isolated for a long time, living solely by its own rules and satisfying all the aspirations of its staff.

These days, divisions are tending to disappear and military staff are inclined to question the rules concerning their professional activities in military surroundings; they consider the restrictions due to their membership of the forces out of date and hard to tolerate.

So if we follow technical progress in the forces, we see groups forming around the professional activity in which either the desire to maintain the traditional way of thinking is strong, or there is evidently an effort to adapt traditional military values to the new trends in society as a whole.

PRESENT SITUATION

Even if we admit that all the military staff are aware of what is going on outside the forces, especially in view of advances in communication media, we must nevertheless consider the special nature of the Army, the Navy and the Air Force, as regards their missions, staff and degree of 'technicalness'.

The Army, which is almost as old as the country itself, has inherited very old traditions. In an age when society seems to want to break its ties with the past, traditions should be pruned of their 'dead wood'; some view this as a mutilation, others as an insufficient reform.

There are two large groups at the centre of the Army, differentiated by the aspirations of the individuals who form them:
— the first group comprises those persons who are attached to tradition and favour ceremony. They deplore the degradation in the nation, even in the army, of the values for which they chose to serve. They find it hard to accept current technical change and are mainly interested in classical military activities; their desire for success is located at the heart of the army, where they have their main groups of reference. However, they do not necessarily refuse everything from outside, but only refer to it as soldiers and wish to be accepted as such. Their attachment to their 'associate' group leads them to demand a better definition of its aims.
— the second group comprises persons with a professional attitude. These are increasing in number, especially among the younger and more educated. Their reference groups are mainly outside the army and they often assess themselves and appraise their current situation in comparison with these groups.

Nevertheless, both groups have a positive motivation as regards the

176

army, but for the second the greater division between reference groups and 'associate' groups is certainly proof of lower integration.

We must further mention a phenomenon encountered in the other armed forces too. It concerns the 'associate' group itself.

If the rules of the military institution are admitted to be such that this community as a whole in fact constitutes the associate group for all men in the services, we find that many see it wrongly and in fact the associate group which might be qualified as 'sentimental' is much lower down the scale and is generally formed around a particular job or mission.

In some cases an attachment to a specific specialist branch (paratrooping, mountaineering etc.) is formed at the expense of military objectives.

Thus the Army, in full technical change, one might even say in the throes of industrialisation, has been penetrated by influences from society as a whole, and its staff seek in different, individual ways, to adapt as best they can the norms of the group to which they belong to those they take as a reference in society.

In the Navy and the Air Force the essential character is technical. The men in all divisions, whether users of 'matériel' or in charge of logistic maintenance, have a direct sense of the importance of their job and their responsibilities, even if they locate their rôle at a different level from that of the mission of the entire force.

They sometimes view the bounds of their activities as antiquated and unadapted to the new norms of society as a whole, and readily reject any essentially military activity. Thus they refer continually to events outside the military environment.

And yet comparisons are not always in favour of the 'outside society', particularly if they relate to the surroundings in which the activities take place. There is a rapid attachment to this mode of life and even if an individual who changes associate group often expresses hostility towards the group he has left, this does not apply to a military man when he leaves the forces.

We must note lastly that if some traditionalists were encountered in the Navy and the Air Force similar to those in the Army, they were among the older staff who are, moreover, more attached to their particular service than to the forces in general.

CONSEQUENCES

The increasing importance of reference groups outside the Forces is the basis of a military man's attitude and behaviour.

177

References to the norms of society in general introduce some aspirations into the forces especially as regards improvement in human relations, the wish to be more widely connected with responsibilities, and even the questioning of certain vital rules which seem out-moded.

When the desire for integration into the military community is strong enough these references serve to express the wish for the forces to adopt some of these norms. If not, they serve to justify the wish to leave the community.

One must admit that at present some groups of reference are bound to be outside the associate group, but to varying degrees.

Some people, from the time they join up, have almost all the groups of reference outside. The military institution is merely a means of acquiring a professional qualification which they can use in civilian life. The final cause of the institution does not interest them.

What policy should be followed in their case? Two solutions are possible:
a. the Forces will accept this outlook and consider these men as auxiliaries outside the institution itself
b. an effort can be made to rectify this outlook and change their opinions by encouraging them to find some positive groups of reference within the institution which will counterbalance the outside groups.

In the first case, civilian status might be granted from the start to those who wish so, but with short-term engagements which cannot be renewed (i.e. asking the men to take their decision right away thus relinquishing the secure aspect of military life). The question is, would these men act in an emergency in accordance with the standards of their temporary associate group or would they overestimate their reference groups and thus be forced to withdraw even more from the rules and restrictions of the military institution.

The Army's mission requires complete involvement of the staff and this short-term service formula clearly does not favour involvement.

The second solution is in fact being applied at present, but if the Forces wish to keep their highly-qualified, arduously-trained staff as long as possible, there must be career scope almost identical to what is expected outside the Forces. In particular the advantages must increase considerably towards the end of the career. Comparisons with 'the outside world' as regards the way of life must be in the military institution's favour.

On the other hand, other men have a pronounced desire for integration from the start, and their main reference groups are within their own group. The final cause of the forces has been accepted, but it must be precise and these men are uncompromising on this matter.

If they are satisfied, there are good chances that these persons will adhere fully to this final cause. They will demand, but with a wish to improve the military institution itself, that the strong positive drifts, which mark the advance of society as a whole, be taken into consideration.

Lastly, the whole of the military staff certainly refers continually to 'outside society' these days, but in different ways.

The study of these differences, the precise determination of the way in which the comparison is made should give us an indication of the individual's integration in the military environment. This inquiry would be conducted along identical lines to the 'critical incident' study and also contribute towards more straight-forward, more complete integration.

Consequences of Specialization of Non-Commissioned Officers

J. GARCETTE*

* Centre d'Études de Sociologie Militaire, Paris.

The specialization of military men is one of the admitted facts of technical evolution in the Armed Forces.

In the French Forces, the NCO's specialization takes precedence of their multiskilled ability. Though, some aspects of the latter still exist and will always exist.

This trend, consequently, modifies the recruitment and the state of mind of the NCO. He wishes to become a specialist, which is desirable from the point of view of immediate efficiency of the Armed Forces. But specialization creates new problems for higher command: as far as relationship, management and personnel policy are concerned.

I. THE PROBLEM OF REMAINING MULTISKILLED ABILITY

The Armed Forces have entered, with the specialization of their members, the field of industrial organization. But they *cannot* accept the whole type of this organization, because of the specific character of their mission.

1. They have to insure their independent life in war-time. Their peace-time organization reflects this need in France: they provide their members with board and lodging, transport and medical care in a very large proportion. On the other hand, the Forces must keep up and watch on a heavy operational and non-operational patrimony. To do so, there are few or any convenient manpower, and this burden is on the shoulders of many NCOs who participate in '*Service Général*': officering of temporary teams for maintenance, handling, storage, watching, and so on...

2. The Armed Forces have to preserve their cohesiveness, so living in a community is compulsory. Most of NCOs have therefore to participate in officering daily-life, control of non-professional behaviour (*general discipline*) and external parade of the Services. These activities are ordered by '*Service Intérieur*' and '*Service de Garnison*', which have a permanent ritual.

All activities ordered by 's. G.', 's. I.' and 's. de G.' *have not* an operational character, and are opposed to an exact specialization of NCOs.

3. The Armed Forces are obliged to maintain combat fitness of their whole personnel, who is therefore submitted to alarms, manoeuvres, movements (*Service en Campagne*) or simply to practise shooting, marches and sports.

Those *operational* activities are carried out daily by military specialists, they are not by other specialists.

II. RECRUITMENT

1. Increasing specialization in the Services gives the character of a precise trade to each office. Recruitment is now an actual market of labour. The recruitment Office has intentionally chosen this catch-sentence 'Enlist, re-enlist, you will learn a good job'.

To learn a job in informatics or a job of helicopter-pilot is very attractive, and new men enlist, whose school-attendance is longer than in the past. School-attendance increases in the whole French society, but this trend is stronger in the French Forces.[1]

The best among the candidates are sent to military schools where they study, beyond military technics, mathematics, sciences, history, etc.[2]

These facts are very favourable to recruit good technicians who are needed by the Armed Forces. But these new NCOs have also a sharper critical faculty; and also, the training they receive allows them to pass easily from a military to a civilian employment: which results in a large turn-over in the early years of career.

2. These new NCOs often have motivations which are not military ones. It is a general trend in the society to give less importance to defence by means of weapons, or to neglect necessity for the Armed Forces to exist, and new personnel participates in the trend. 60% of old NCOs say that they have joined the Army because they liked military duty or weapon-service, active life, risk, adventures, travels, which characterize the Army; now, only 40% of new NCOs, who joined the Army after 1961 (end of Algerian war) bring up such motivations.[3]

Therefore, beside these 'military' men, the number of those whom we shall name 'professional' ones increases, whose lack of military calling also explains the turn-over.

Historical situation: the end of colonial wars, the lack of foreign threat, explains the decrease of calling of a profession which seems more and more marginal. But if it is necessary for the Armed Forces to have a staff of good technicians, the technical ability is not sufficient to accomplish all military duties: the Forces will never be large firms like others.

III. CONCEPTION OF MILITARY TRADE

Specialization takes away the traditional military mind and nearers to industrial mind.

So, in the *Air Force*, where specialization is of the longest standing and the most developed.

In the non-military specialties, any activity which jumps out of their frames is seemed strange, useless, even intolerable. In current slang all that is called 'mili' (for 'military'). Only the oldest NCOs understand the necessity to leave a tool sometimes to take a weapon, or to go out of the workshop to go the rounds.

On the other hand, their professional scrupulousness is large: they will work overtime willingly to make a scheduled flight possible; but it is not by dedication: there are only proud to carry out their professional duty. The team which bustles about a plane is tightly linked by comradeship and sense of collective responsibility. They are also proud of the achievements of their firm – the Air Force – but they do not think to give it its role in the maintenance of the defence disposition. The NCOs are conscious of industrial values and they don't shove back the idea of a representation of personnel's yearning under a trade-union form.

In the Navy, responses are close to those of the Air Force. Sorties at sea are undoubtedly operational activities, but they are considered as technical and not military ones. Fellowship is greater with foreign Navies, which practice the same technics, than with the other French Services, which carry out the same mission: this is a mark of an original character, but also a 'professional' one of the petty officers mind.

In the Army, specialization is not yet much developed. The rule is still the multiskilled ability,[4] and we can see old 'military' at the end of their career occupying administrative and sedentary posts beside young 'professional' NCOs assigned to specific military posts. Consequently the intermingling of different kinds of personnel leads to a better acceptance of operational activities; even, these are often wished by both 'professional' and 'military' personnel.

Non-operational activities remain partly integrated to the psychological field of the NCOs: it always seems normal for many of them to live a military life with a peculiar style where salute and symbolical ceremonial take place.

However, the part of time reserved to '*Service Intérieur*' and '*Service de Garnison*' seems already too large as regards specialized activities, particularly if this part is marked with a formalism which appears meaningless among social transformations.[5] As for the activities reserved to '*Service Général*' the NCOs only call 'fags' the customary servitudes which divert them too much from their specialized activities (specifically military or not). We must confess that no large firm employs a technician to participate in such works.

185

Two peculiar components of the Army illustrate the evolution of the conception of military trade.

'Troupe de Marine'[6] contrary to metropolitan troops, have not their own sophisticated logistics, with advanced equipments. Therefore they remain the nearest to Armies of the preindustrial era: they have not many specialists, combat is always their prominent function. They have also the most 'military' recruits, whose school-attendance is weak. Finally, they are the guardians of the main traditional characteristics of the old-fashioned Army.

On the other hand, the Airborne troops, either metropolitan or 'de Marine' are composed of numerous specialized personnels, perfectly disciplined, and they have a strong 'esprit de corps.' However, the parachutist specialty is liable to hide the arm-finalty, for the benefit of the individual prowess it permits, and of self brightening up it brings.

So, any specialization, even military, in the Services, leads to narrow the conception of the trade, and to lower the level of its finalties. Moreover, the more this specialty keeps off purely military activities, the more it leads to adopt the standards of the industrial society and to consider the traditional forms of military life as too heavy.

Only one of the latter is regretted by many NCOs. A consequence of atomization of work is to suppress interindividual relationship between leader and members, and even 'professional' personnels yearn to the 'large family' they think the ARMY was in the preindustrial era. Horizontal relationship is of such a good quality that many re-enlistments are motivated by it; therefore the NCOs resent the poor quality of vertical relationship more strongly.

IV. NEW PROBLEMS OF COMMAND

Therefore, specialization policy sets numerous problems to higher command. To retain the cohesiveness of units their commanding officers have to find new types of human relations, as far from paternalism and from a purely functional conception.

At management level, it is necessary to take care of the refresher training of personnel whose specialization doesn't permit to be promoted to warrant-officer's rank; to take care of resettlement into civilian life of those who have, in their whole career, practised a purely military specialty. It is also necessary to reduce the burden of non-specialized activities, the material burden of servitudes pertaining to 'Service Général,' the social burden of misfit regulations.

Lastly, at general personnel policy level, it is necessary to maintain dedication, discipline and freely accepted service, in the Armed Forces, while the natural tendency is in favour of personal blooming and measurable efficiency. It is excluded to enforce without discussion such values to personnel who are volunteers of course, but whose voluntary service can cease at short term: it is therefore necessary to permanently convince men, to sustain fighting will, to seek by all appropriate means personnel who are able to still adopt these valours.

It is not unthinkable, that to more surely reach this goal, it will be necessary to discriminate, in the Armed Forces, among those personnels who are necessary to carry out operational mission and the others. The former could be chosen, in priority, among the 'military,' 'professional' ones being assigned to other duties; a peculiar status would be granted to the latter.[7]

1. Among young men of 20, the evolution of school attendance is the following:
   More than primary school 1958   13%
                                1962   23%
                                1967   33%
   In 1967, percentages in the Army were: Sergeants   60%
                                          Warrant-officers 40%
   We must note that the present selection of NCOs is based upon a good score in cleverness-tests, cleverness and school attendance are closely related. The post selection was based upon subjective criteria of leadership aptitude.
2. In 1967 half of the new NCOs were sent to military school; 40% of all NCOs had attended these military schools, although many of them have been recently established (Army only).
3. We do not forget that they say so, and there is a good lot of rationalization in their speech. But this token is closely related to many attitudes and behaviours, and we always take care of it in our studies.
4. A recent reformation is now applied, which goes in the way of specialization.
5. For example, it doesn't seem normal to the NCOs, while nightleaves are freely conceded to privates, that regulations oblige two NCOs per unit to attend the evening call-roll.
6. Which should not be mistaken for the fusiliers in the Navy nor for U.S. Marines. 'Troupes de Marine' were born of Colonial troops the remaining missions of which they keep on overseas.
7. In the French Forces, we already have some administrative posts which can be indiscriminately given to military or civilian personnel: book-keepers, mess-directors, even technicians in Ordnance or Supply Services.
   Moreover, military tailors and shoemakers have a very peculiar military status; many present 'workers in uniform' could take advantage of a status which would be similar.

Leadership, morale, management

Do Leaders Really Learn Leadership?

F. E. FIEDLER*

* Professor of psychology and of management and organization, University of Washington.

Do Leaders Really Learn Leadership?

F. E. FIEDLER

Most military commanders as well as men in responsible business, government, or industrial positions, take it as an article of faith that leadership experience and leadership training improve leadership performance. I should like to consider in this paper some recent empirical evidence which throws serious doubt on the value of leadership experience as well as on the type of leadership training which is commonly provided. I should then like to show that these disappointing empirical data are quite consistent with some current leadership theory and research.

Let me begin by making explicit some of the key terms which I shall use in this paper.

1. By the term, *leader*, I will simply mean the person who is appointed or elected to direct, coordinate, or supervise the various functions which the assigned tasks of his group or organization require. Note that I make no distinction between the person who rises to leadership by virtue of his personal charisma or one who rises to a leadership position because his father-in-law owns 51 per cent of the stock in the organization.

2. I will confine my discussion to *task groups*. Groups which primarily serve the social or personal well-being of their members are outside the scope of this paper, as are such groups as therapy or sensitivity groups, or groups which benefit the member rather than his organization.

3. I will define an *effective leader* on the basis of how well his group performs its assigned tasks. Specifically, given a set of 20, 30, or 100 comparable groups all of which have members with the required skills and abilities, we will define the leader's effectiveness in terms of the group's performance.

Thus, we measure the effectiveness of a basketball team captain by the number of games his team wins; we define a tank crew leader's performance by how quickly his crew hits a specified target; we define the performance of an orchestra conductor by how well his orchestra plays rather than by how good a musicologist the orchestra conductor might be or by how happy his musicians might be.

One further point of importance. We distinguish between management or administration and leadership. Leadership, as it is here defined, is one part of the total management, supervisory, and administrative job. It is that particular aspect which deals with the supervision of individuals. Other aspects, e.g., writing reports, ordering supplies, negotiating with customers, suppliers, or with other supervisors in the organization, is not subsumed under leadership although it is a very important aspect of the total job a manager or military officer has to perform. I will here deal only with leadership training and not the training in administrative or managerial procedures and skills which are essential for organizational functioning.

IMPROVING LEADERSHIP PERFORMANCE

Let us now consider the question of how a man becomes an effective leader. When we think of improving leadership, we almost automatically think of training the individual. We generally mean by training that the individual is placed into a position where he is given a new perspective of his supervisory responsibilities, he may be involved in some role playing, he receives detailed instructions of how to behave in various situations, and so forth. The training program might last a few days, a few months, and leadership training as it is given in military academies or service, schools, lasts several years and is expected to remold the character of an individual.

Nevertheless, the empirical results testing the effectiveness of leadership training, and specifically, the extent to which leadership training improves organizational or group performance, have been quite disappointing. A text published in 1966 by the well-known industrial psychologist, Gilmer (1966, p. 245) stated that 'there is today not one sound study on leadership training.' This is well illustrated by Newport (1963) who surveyed 121 companies which provided middle management training for their executives. While most of these companies expressed greater or lesser satisfaction with leadership training, Newport found no objectively convincing data that training had actually benefited the managers of these various companies. Most companies evaluated the training programs by asking managers who had attended to say what they thought about it, and how well they liked it; how much they felt they had gotten from the experience. Beyond this type of 'evaluation' not one of the companies had obtained any scientifically acceptable evidence that leadership training had actually improved performance.

T-group and laboratory training, which has recently become fashionable in business and industry, has yielded similarly unsatisfactory results. Campbell and Dunnette (1968) and House (1967) recently reviewed the literature and found no convincing evidence that this type of training improved organizational performance. Fleishman, Harris and Burtt's (1961) well-known studies on the effects of supervisory training indicated that the effects of supervisory training in modifying behavior were very shortlived.

194

I would like to present the results of a number of other studies which are of particular interest in the present context. The first of these (Fiedler, 1966) was conducted at a Belgian naval training center. We chose 244 Belgian recruits and 48 petty officers from a pool of 546 men. These men were assembled into 96 groups, each consisting of three men: 48 groups had petty officers as leaders and 48 groups had recruits as leaders. The recruits ranged in age from 17 to 24 with a mean of 20, and none had been in the service longer than six weeks. The petty officers ranged in age from 19 to 45 years, with an average age of 29 years. In addition, all petty officers had received training at petty officer candidate school. This is a two-year technical and leadership training course similar in scope and design to most military colleges. During these two years the candidate is expected to pay for his own room and board and after graduation he is expected to enlist for a twenty-year hitch. Promotion from the ranks is rare. In other words, Belgian petty officers are truly motivated and committed career men; they function more like chief petty officers and warrant officers in the U. S. Navy than second, or third-class petty officers.

The petty officers were matched with the recruit leaders on intelligence and leader style scores. Each of the three-man groups worked on four tasks which were designed in cooperation with the camp's officers. One task consisted of writing a recruiting letter urging young men to join the Belgian Navy as a career; a second set of tasks required the groups to find the shortest route for a convoy first through ten and then through twelve ports; the fourth task required the leader to train his men without using verbal instructions in the disassembling and re-assembling of a .45-caliber automatic pistol. These tasks are fairly similar to group tasks which petty officers might be called upon to perform in the course of their duty. The intercorrelation among the four tasks was quite low, namely .14; and we were, therefore, dealing with four independent measures of group performance. It is important to note that these correlations show that the best leaders on one task were not necessarily good on another task. Hence, the nature of the task determined at least in part how well a man performs as a leader.

Figure 1 shows the comparative performances of groups led by recruits who had had no leadership experience or training in the Belgian Navy and of groups led by petty officers who had had two years of leadership training as well as an average of ten years of leadership experience. As can be seen, in not one of the tasks did the groups led by petty officers perform significantly better than did groups led by recruit leaders.

We recently conducted a validation experiment at a leadership training

195

workshop for 15 officers of Canadian military colleges (Fiedler & Chemers, 1968). This study compared the performance of two sets of groups, namely groups led by military academy officers with rank of captain

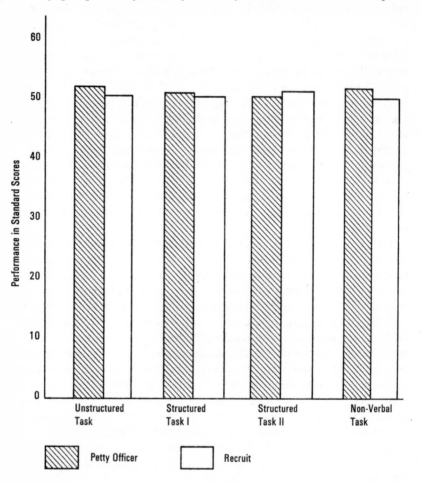

Figure 1

or major, and groups led by enlisted men who had just finished their eight weeks of basic training. All of the officers had, themselves, graduated from one of the military colleges. In addition, the officers had from 5 to 17 years of leadership experience and training after graduation. The 32 enlisted men who participated in the study were brought in under the

196

pretext that they would work with civilian instructors. The 32 men were between 19 and 22 years of age; and none, of course, had had more than basic military training. Moreover, the officers scored substantially higher than the enlisted men on verbal intelligence scales. Only one enlisted man had a verbal intelligence score which was higher than the lowest scoring officer, and this one officer was from the French-speaking part of Canada. The test, therefore, did not adequately measure his intelligence. In effect, this was a grossly unfair comparison with all the seeming advantages on the side of the officers.

We first assembled the officers and men into three-man groups and had them successively perform three tasks of varying structure. Two of the tasks were modeled after the tasks used in the Belgian Navy study. One task was to write a recruiting letter; one task involved routing a truck convoy; and one task required the groups to draw bar graphs from score distributions which then had to be converted from one scale to another. The tasks were designed so that all three group members had to participate in the work. As in the Belgian Navy study, the intercorrelations among these three tasks were again essentially zero.

Despite the advantages in training and experience which the officers enjoyed over the enlisted men, none of the comparisons in group performance was significantly different. The groups led by officers performed somewhat better than the enlisted men's groups on two tasks while the enlisted men's groups performed somewhat better than the officer's groups on one of the tasks (fig. 2). The negative results of this study were, therefore, consistent with the results obtained in the Belgian Navy study.

To check whether amount of training influenced performance in real-life situations, we conducted a study on 171 managers and supervisors of post offices (Fiedler, Nealey & Wood, 1969). The number of hours of supervisory training received by these managers was correlated with their performance as rated by two or more superiors. Amount of training ranged from zero hours of training to three years, with a median of 45 hours. Performance ratings were obtained from ratings of two to five supervisors. These ratings, adjusted for mean differences of post offices, were highly reliable. Table 1 shows the correlations with performance ratings; Table 2 shows the correlations with such objective post office performance measures as target achievement in number of first-class pieces handled. Here again, we found not one of the correlations to be statistically significant in the expected direction. In fact 12 of the 15 correlations were in the negative direction.

Neither the two controlled experiments nor the field study provides then any basis for assuming that leadership training of the type given in

197

these institutions, or in the executive training programs taken by postal managers, contributed to organizational performance.

LEADERSHIP EXPERIENCE

Let us now look at the effect of supervisory experience and the concomitant on-the-job training which this usually implies. The literature actually contains few, if any, studies which attempt to link leadership experience to performance (see Fiedler, 1970a). Yet, there seems to be a firmly held expectation that leadership experience contributes to leadership per-

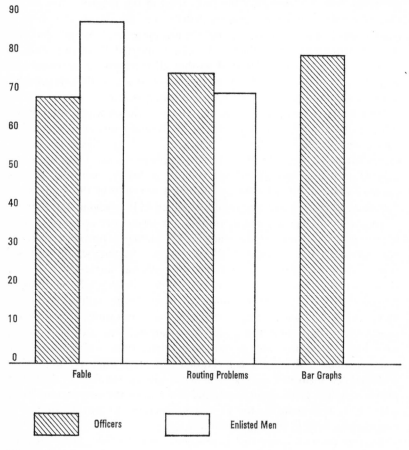

Figure 2

formance. We have more trust in experienced leaders. This can be inferred from the many regulations which require time in grade before promotion to the next higher level, as well as the many advertisements for executives which specify previous managerial experience as a prerequisite.

Table 1. Correlations of hours of training with individual performance (N = 171)

	Zero-order correlation	Partial Correlation
Post office technical training	.040	.041
Outside technical training	−.001	−.004
Outside leadership training	−.128	−.119

Table 2. Rank-order correlations between amount of training and post office productivity (N = 12)

Effectiveness criterion	Post office technical training	Outside technical training	Outside leadership training
Mail processing	−.192	.014	−.064
Mail delivery	.220	−.238	−.063
Indirect costs	−.021	−.315	−.107
First-handling pieces	−.741*	−.336	−.068
Minutes per delivery	−.056	.035	−.084

* $p < .01$.

We have already seen that the experienced petty officers and military academy officers did not perform more effectively than did the inexperienced enlisted men. A further analysis was, however, performed relating the years of experience of the petty officers, and the years of experience on the part of the military academy officers, to their groups' performance on the various tasks. Also, a second part of the military academy study utilized all 15 officers as leaders while 30 enlisted men served as group members. These two tasks involved solving cryptograms and then making scale drawings of military barracks and a military camp. Neither in the Belgian Navy study nor in the military academy study did years of experience correlate significantly with leadership performance.

In addition, we also have findings from various other groups and organizations. These include (a) directors of research and development teams at a large physical research laboratory, (b) foremen of craftshops, (c) general foremen of a heavy machinery manufacturing company, (d) managers of meat and (e) of grocery markets in a large supermarket chain, as well as (f) post office supervisors and managers at various levels. For all these managers reliable performance ratings or objective group effectiveness criteria could be obtained. As table 3 shows, none of the correlations was significant in the expected direction. The median correlation for all groups and organizations is −.12 and this is certainly not significant in the positive direction!

Table 3. Correlations between years of experience and group performance

	Correlation coefficient	N
Belgian Navy study (.08, .13, −.05, .12)	.10*	24
Military Academy study		
(.03, −.32, −.30, −.21, .42)	−.28*	16
Assistant postmasters	−.53*	19
Superintendents of mail	−.13	20
Assistant superintendents of mail	−.12	19
Second-level supervisors	.24	23
First-level supervisors	−.13	180
Research chemists	.12	18
Craftshop foremen	−.28	11
Meat department managers	.09	21
Grocery department managers	.33	24
Production department foremen	−.18	10
Median correlation	−.12	385

* Median correlations are listed since the correlations were not computed on completely independent cases.

To summarize our findings, neither leadership training nor leadership experience appear to contribute to group or organizational effectiveness. These data as well as the reviews of the literature (see Campbell & Dunnette, 1968; House, 1967) on other types of training, provide no evidence

200

that current leadership training practices in the form we know improve organizational performance. It is, therefore, obvious that we must consider alternative methods for improving leadership performance.

A THEORY OF LEADERSHIP EFFECTIVENESS

Terman wrote in 1904 that leadership performance depends on the situation as well as on the leader. Although this statement would not be questioned by anyone currently working in this area, the substance of this statement has never really been taken seriously in our training strategies. Practically all formal training programs attempt to change the individual; many of them assume explicitly or implicitly that there is one best style of leadership or one best way of acting; some others assume that the training should enable the individual to become more flexible, or more sensitive to his environment so that he can adapt himself to it. Most training programs attempt to mold the individual into a supposedly ideal pattern of personality or behavior, and this is especially true of military academies. These programs, therefore, implicitly assume that there is one best way to lead, or that there is one best type of leader personality.

I think we must reorient our thinking if we want better leadership training. We generally think of organizations and leadership jobs as fixed and rigid and we tend to think of the individual as infinitely flexible. We sometimes give the individual a course of ten lectures, or we put him into an intensive training workshop, and expect to have a changed man. As we have seen from the various studies which I have mentioned, not even two or five years of intensive training in a military school appears to change individuals so that they perform more effectively in their leadership jobs. It is difficult to see how we can do much better with these same methods in a shorter period of time.

The problem may, however, lie not so much with our training programs as with our conception of the leadership process. I would like to review very briefly a program of research carried out under the sponsorship of the u.s. Office of Naval Research and the Advanced Research Projects Agency in order to suggest a new approach to the problem of improving leadership performance.

The theory developed under these programs (Fiedler, 1967; 1970b) holds that the effectiveness of group performance is contingent upon (a) the leader's style of interacting with his subordinates, and (b) the degree to which the situation gives the leader power and influence. We have

201

worked with a leadership style measure called the 'Esteem for the Least Preferred Coworker,' or LPC for short. The subject is first asked to think of all the people with whom he has ever worked, and then to describe the one person in his life with whom he has been able to work *least well*. This 'least preferred coworker' (LPC) may be someone he knows at the time or it may be someone he has known in the past. It does not have to be a member of his present work group. In grossly oversimplified terms, the person who describes his least preferred coworker in relatively favorable terms tends to seek need gratification from attaining a position of prominence and good interpersonal relations. The person who rejects someone with whom he cannot work tends to seek need gratification from achieving on the task and from being recognized as having performed well on the task. The low LPC person thus uses the group to get the task done while the high LPC person uses the task to obtain a favorable position and good interpersonal relations.

The statement that some leaders perform better in one kind of a situation while some leaders perform better in different situations is begging a question. 'What kinds of situations are best suited for which type of a leader?' In other words, how can we best classify groups if we wish to predict leadership performance.

One way of approaching this problem is by assuming that leadership is essentially a work relationship involving power and influence. It is, therefore, not unreasonable to classify situations in terms of how much power and influence they can give the leader. One simple categorization of this type classifies leadership situations on the basis of three major dimensions.

Leader-member relations. Leaders presumably have more power and influence if they have a good relationship with their members than if they have a poor relationship with them, if they are liked, respected, trusted, than if they are not. This is by far the most important single dimension as shown by Fishbein *et al.* (1969) and Mitchell (1970).

Position power. Leaders will have more power and influence if their position is vested with such prerogatives as being able to hire and fire, being able to discipline, to reprimand, and so on. That is, a company commander has more position power than one of his men, a manager of a store or a department has more position power than the chairman of a committee.

Task structure. Tasks or assignments which are highly structured, spelled out, or programmed, give the leader more influence than tasks which are vague, nebulous and unstructured. It is easier to be a leader whose task it is to set up a sales display according to clearly spelled out steps than it is to be a chairman of a committee preparing a new sales campaign.

Using this classification method we can now order groups as being high or low on each of these three dimensions. This gives us an eight-celled cube. This scheme postulates that it is easier to be a leader in groups which fall into Cell I since you are liked, have position power, and have a structured task. It is somewhat more difficult in Cell II, since you are liked, have a structured task, but little position power, and so on to groups in Cell VIII, where the leader is not liked, has a vague, unstructured task, and little position power. An example of Cell VIII would be a disliked chairman of a volunteer committee preparing a new curriculum (fig. 3).

The critical question is, what kind of a leadership style does each of these different group situations call for? Figure 4 shows the results obtained in 63 sets of groups (a total of 454 groups are represented). The horizontal axis indicates the situational difficulty, namely, where the leader's group fell in terms of the eight-fold classification shown on the previous figure. The vertical axis shows the correlation coefficients between group performance and the leader's Least Preferred Coworker score. Note that a point on the plot is a correlation coefficient which represents not one group, but a set of groups for which a correlation was obtained between the leader's LPC score and his group's performance.

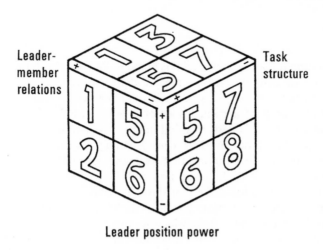

Figure 3

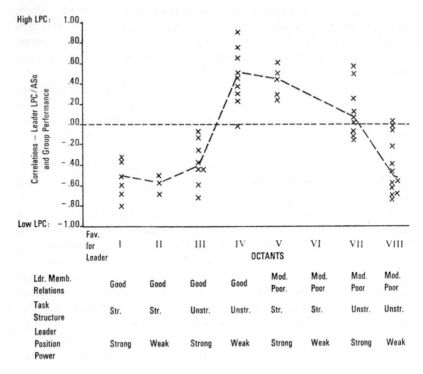

Figure 4

The important finding shown on this graph is, first, that both the relationship-oriented and the task-oriented leaders perform well under some situations but not others. Second, if our data reflect reality, it is not sensible to speak of a good leader or a poor leader – rather we must think of a leader who performs well in one situation but not in another. This is also borne out by the repeated finding, illustrated again in the Belgian and Canadian studies, that we cannot predict a leader's performance on one task by knowing how well he performed on a different kind of task. And finally, the plot shows that task-oriented leaders tend to perform better than relationship-oriented leaders in situations which are very favorable, and in those which are very unfavorable. Relationship-oriented leaders perform better than task-oriented leaders in situations which are intermediate in favorableness. This bow-shaped distribution is important and I want to return to it again.

204

Figure 5. Schematic presentation of conditions in which high or low LPC leaders are relatively most effective

| | OCTANTS | | | | | | | |
LPC	I	II	III	IV	V	VI	VII	VIII
High				Effec-tive	Effec-tive	*	*	
Low	Effec-tive	Effec-tive	Effec-tive			*	*	Effec-tive

* No prediction is possible.

Before I move on, one more important comment seems appropriate. This plot shows that the performance of a leader depends as much on the job and the organization as it does on the individual in the leadership position. Hence, the organization can change leadership performance by re-defining the leader's job, or by making certain changes in the way his position or his task is designed.

VALIDATION EVIDENCE

The critical question is, of course, how well the model predicts in new situations. There have been at least 25 studies to date which have tested the model or certain aspects of it. Let me here briefly discuss only those studies which represent exact tests of the Contingency Model. These are studies which used the LPC score of the leader as the predictor variables and which classified group situations according to the three dimensions of leader-member relations, position power, and task structure.

The studies which meet these criteria have been divided into those which were conducted in natural settings or ongoing organizations, and those which were specifically designed as laboratory or field experiments. Table 4 gives the relevant results. A detailed description of all of these studies can be found in a recent review of the literature (Fiedler, 1970b).

As can be seen, the field studies almost completely reproduce the findings obtained in the original studies (compare line 15, summarizing median correlations obtained in field studies with the median correlations obtained in the original studies on line 17). A somewhat less satisfactory

Table 4. Summary of field and laboratory studies testing the contingency model

Field studies	OCTANTS							
	I	II	III	IV	V	VI	VII	VIII
1 Hunt	−.67		−.80		.21		.30	
2	−.51						−.30	
3 Hill		−.10	−.29			−.24	.62	
4 Fiedler *et al.*		−.21		.00		.67*		−.51
5 O'Brien *et al.*		−.46		.47		−.45		.14
6 *Laboratory Experiments*								
7 Belgian Navy	−.72	.37	−.16	.08	.16	.07	.26	−.37
8	−.77	.50	−.54	.13	.03	.14	−.27	.60
9 Shima		−.26		.71*				
10 Mitchell		.24		.43				
11		.17		.38				
12 Fiedler Exec.		.34		.51				
13 West Point Cadets	−.43	−.32	.10	.35	.28	.13	.08	−.33
14 Median, all studies	−.69	.17	−.29	.38	.22	.10	.26	−.35
15 Median, Field studies	−.59	−.21	−.54	.23	.21	−.24	.30	−.19
16 Median, Laboratory Experiments	−.72	.24	−.16	.38	.16	.13	.08	−.33
17 Medians in Original Studies	−.52	−.58	−.33	.47	.42	—	.05	−.43

18 Number of correlations in the expected direction . . . . 35[1]
19 Number of correlations opposite to expected direction 9
20 *p* by binomial test 01
21 [1] exclusive of Octant VI, for which no prediction had been made.
22 * *p* < .05

outcome was obtained for the laboratory experiments, yet, even here the number of correctly predicted correlations far exceeds chance expectation (line 15). As for the entire set of correlations, 35 of the 44 were in the predicted direction, a finding which is well below the .01 level of confidence.

The only clear deviations from the predicted curve occurred in Octant II of the laboratory and field experiments. While it is too early to tell why this particular octant yielded results deviating from the prediction, it is not unlikely that certain leadership conditions are very difficult to reproduce in the laboratory or under experimental conditions.

Of particular interest to this group may be a study conducted at West Point Military Academy by Skrzypek. This study is shown on line 13 of the table and almost perfectly follows the theoretical prediction, shown on line 17.

IMPLICATIONS FOR TRAINING

What does all this mean as far as leadership training is concerned? First of all, we can see from these data that the performance of a task group depends both upon leadership style and upon the organizational factors which determine the favorableness of the leader's job. This means that a training method changing all leaders in the same way cannot be successful. On the other hand, we can modify the leader's performance by changing certain aspects of the leader's job.

The idea that we can change a leader's job in order to make him perform better is by no means new. We often hear an officer say that one of his subordinates needs to be given a free rein while another man has to be held in check; that one man can handle troublemakers while another cannot; that you have to give one man detailed direction on what to do and how to do it, while you can give another man a problem without instructions and get it done better that way.

In sum, if we want to improve leadership performance, we can either change the leader by training, or we can change his leadership situation. I would submit that it is much easier to change various aspects of a man's job than to change the man. When we talk about leadership, we are talking about fairly deep-ingrained personality factors and habits of interacting with others. These cannot be changed easily, either in a few hours, or in a few days. In fact, as we have seen, not even five years of military academy and 5 to 17 years of subsequent experience enable a leader to perform significantly better on different tasks than someone that has had neither training nor experience.

The data in this area generally do show that leadership training tends to bring about some improvements of employee job satisfaction and better interpersonal relations. Whether this alone is sufficient to warrant the high expense of current training programs is, of course, a question which must be left to administrative judgment and cost analysis. Nor do we question the value of technical training or training in administrative procedures which various leadership programs offer. But, to repeat, there is no evidence that the aspects of these programs which aim to change the individual increase organizational effectiveness.

207

A proposed training program. The training program which our research suggests would consist in grossly oversimplified form of the following steps:

First, we need to demonstrate to prospective leaders and their superiors that there are few, if any, all-around good leaders or poor leaders. A man who performs well as a leader in one situation may or may not perform well in another situation. The fact that a man fails in one situation does not, therefore, make him a poor leader; nor does a man's success in one particular task make him a good leader in others. If our data are to be believed, training must assist men in learning to recognize the types of situations in which they are likely to succeed and the situations in which they are likely to fail. Obviously, a man who avoids situations in which he is likely to fail is likely to be a success.

Second, leadership training should devote more effort to teaching leaders how to modify their environment and their own job so that it fits their style of leadership. We must get rid of the implicit assumption that the environment and the organization, or a particular leadership position, are constant and unchanging. Leaders continuously modify their leadership positions. They often speak of showing their men who is boss – presumably to assert their position power; they speak of getting to know their men – presumably to establish better relations with them; they talk of different approaches to their work; they look for certain types of assistants who complement their abilities; they demand more authority or they play down the authority they already have; they ask for certain types of assignments and try to get out of others. The theory which has here been described merely provides a basis for a more rational modification of the leadership job.

Third, it is important that we impress on managers and leaders at the second, third, or higher levels of the organization that they can directly affect the performance of their subordinate leaders by modifying various aspects of the leadership situation. A poor performance by a subordinate leader may, therefore, reflect his superior's failure to provide a leadership situation in which his subordinate can be successful.

Lastly, a word on how we can train leaders to determine the conditions under which they are most likely to succeed or fail, and how they can modify their own leadership situation. The disappointing relations between leadership experience and leader performance undoubtedly stem in part from the difficulties in obtaining feedback about one's own leadership effectiveness. Unless the group fails utterly in its task, most people are unable to say with any degree of accuracy how well their group had performed in comparison with other groups.

208

Leadership training, if our reasoning is correct, should provide the prospective leader with a wide range of leadership situations in which he can get immediate feedback on how well he has performed. On the basis of these experiences he must learn to recognize the situations which fit his particular style of leadership, and how he can best modify situations so that they will enable him to perform effectively. This requires the development of six or eight short leadership tasks and situations, or adequately measured organizational tasks, in which each trainee is required to perform. He must then be given an objective appraisal of how well his group's performance compared with the performance of others under the same conditions. Needless to say, leadership training of this type could easily be established in military institutions.

If there is such a thing as the all-around good leader, he is likely to be the individual who intuitively or through training knows how to manage his environment so that the leadership situation best matches his leadership style. It would seem that this type of training can be provided for the military leader and for the cadet in military academies.

REFERENCES

CAMPBELL, J. P., and DUNNETTE, M. D. Effectiveness of T-group experiences in managerial training and development. *Psychological Bulletin*, 1968, *70*, 73–104.
FIEDLER, F. E. The effect of leadership and cultural heterogeneity on group performance: A test of the contingency model. *Journal of Experimental Social Psychology*, 1966, *2*, 237–264.
FIEDLER, F. E. *A Theory of Leadership Effectiveness*. New York: McGraw-Hill, 1967.
FIEDLER, F. E. Leadership experience and leader performance—Another hypothesis shot to hell. *Organizational Behavior and Human Performance*, 1970a, *5*, 1–14.
FIEDLER, F. E. Validation and extension of the Contingency Model of leadership effectiveness: A review of empirical findings. *Psychological Bulletin*, 1970b.
FIEDLER, F. E., & CHEMERS, M. M. *Group performance under experienced and inexperienced leaders: A validation experiment*. Urbana Ill.: Group Effectiveness Research Laboratory, University of Illinois, 1968.
FIEDLER, F. E., NEALEY, S. M., & WOOD, M. T. *The effects of training on performance of Post Office supervisors*. Report to Postal Service Institute, Washington, D.C., 1969.
FIEDLER, F. E., O'BRIEN, G. E., & ILGEN, D. The effect of leadership style upon performance and adjustment in volunteer teams operating in a stressful foreign environment. *Human Relations*, 1969, *22*, 503–514.
FISHBEIN, M., LANDY, E., & HATCH, G. Consideration of two assumptions underlying Fiedler's Contingency Model for the prediction of leadership effectiveness. *American Journal of Psychology*, 1969, *4*, 457-473.
FLEISHMAN, E. A. *Studies in industrial and personnel psychology*. Homewood, Ill.: Dorsey Press, 1961.
GILMER, B. von HALLER. *Industrial psychology*. Second edition. New York: McGraw-Hill, 1966.
HILL, W. The validation and extension of Fiedler's theory of leadership effectiveness. *Academy of Management Journal*, 1969 (March), 33–47.
HOUSE, R. J. T-group education and leadership effectiveness: A review of the empiric literature and a critical evaluation. *Personnel Psychology*, 1967, *20*, 1–32.
HUNT, J. G. Fiedler's leadership contingency model: An empirical test in three organizations. *Organizational Behavior and Human Performance*, 1967, *2*, 290–308.
MITCHELL, T. R. Leader complexity and leadership style. *Journal of Personality and Social Psychology*, 1970.
NEWPORT, M. G. *Middle management development in industrial organizations*. Ph. D. Dissertation, University of Illinois, 1963.
O'BRIEN, G. E. Group structure and the measurement of potential leader influence. *Australian Journal of Psychology*, 1969, *21*, No. 3, 277–289.
SHIMA, H. The relationship between the leader's modes of interpersonal cognition and the performance of the group. *Japanese Psychological Research*, 1968, *10*, 13–30.
SKRZYPEK, G. J. *The relationship of leadership style to task structure, position power, and leader member relations*. West Point, New York: U.S. Military Academy, Technical Report 34, 1969.
TERMAN, L. M. A preliminary study of the psychology and pedagogy of leadership. *Pedagogical Seminary*, 1904, *11*, 413–451.

210

Some Remarks on the Construction of an Instrument for the Assessment of Cadet Behaviour

M. J. M. DANIËLS*

* Professor of Psychology, Royal Military Academy, The Netherlands.

In 1969 and in 1970 four officer-cadets* of the Royal Netherlands Military Academy have worked on assessment problems. Their work forms the basis of this paper.

No adequate computing facilities being available, much of the statistical processing had to be done 'by hand.' More sophisticated analysis could not be undertaken at all. Still, this author feels that some useful lessons may be taken from the present material.

SCOPE OF THE STUDY

An appraisal instrument was envisaged consisting of a check-list of statements devised by a representative group of the academy population. In a later phase, this instrument should be (1) used in a peer-rating process and (2) validated against the rating-scale instrument of assessment now in use. This report only covers the first steps in the construction of the instrument.

Eight cadets (3rd year) and 8 officers (lnts., Captains, Majors, all normally engaged in assessing cadets) devised 190 statements (cadets 96; officers 94). Several unsuccessful attempts were made by them to group these statements into a few broader categories. Now this is interesting. The same officers and cadets who would not have difficulty deciding whether a cadet showed 'Initiative' (or even how much), could not decide whether the item 'Always finds errors in the daily orders' had something to do with 'Initiative,' with 'Loyalty,' with 'Interest in military matters' or with 'Special skills.' Finally the statements were grouped into nine categories by the author and his staff. The few (8) statements on which less than four of the five judges could agree, were put under the heading 'Miscellaneous.'

All 190 statements ware rated for favourableness on a nine-point scale by 13 officers and 17 cadets. In this phase, it is well to remember, only *statements on possible behaviour* of cadets are being rated, *not* the *cadets themselves*. Median scale values and quartile ranges for the two judge-groups were computed for each statement.

---

* Ensigns Liefaard and Nicolai of the class of 1969, Kampman and Evers of the class of 1970, with the help of Mr. Chr. Roosen, psychologist on temporary service at the Royal Military Academy (KMA).

Table 1. Statements by categories

	1	2	3	4	5	6	7	8
				Source		Mean difference of median scale val. Officers/ Cadets	Mean quartile range	
	Category	N	%	Officers (N = 13)	Cadets (N = 17)		Officers	Cadets
1a	'Model pupil'	30	16	11	19	1.64	2.43	2.34
1b	'Manners'	16	8	7	9	0.64	1.92	2.14
		46	24	18	28	1.29	2.25	2.27
2	Sports	32	17	13	19	0.75	2.03	2.04
3	'Military Virtues'	25	13	11	14	0.50	1.77	1.74
4	Intellectual Interests	24	13	9	15	0.83	2.24	1.93
5	Consideration for Colleagues/ Subord.	20	11	11	9	0.60	1.78	1.62
6	Social Participation	11	6	3	8	0.78	1.98	2.10
7	Various Skills	11	6	11	0	0.67	2.22	1.81
8	'Show'	4	2	4	0	0.37	1.29	1.87
9	Miscellaneous	8	4	6	2	0.64	2.32	2.06
10	Items not used	9	5	8	1	—	—	—
	Totals, means	190	101%	94	96	0.82	2.00	1.94

Table 1 shows the results. Column '1' shows the behaviour categories. Typical statements would be, for

'model pupil'	(1a):	'Often stays over the weekend to study.'
'manners'	(1b):	'When in crowded train, offers his seat to elderly lady.'
'sport'	(2):	'Trains more than three hours a week.'
'military virtues'	(3):	'Regularly criticizes orders.'
'intellectual interests'	(4):	'Regards non-military courses as superfluous.'
'consideration'	(5):	'Does not ridicule subordinates.'
'social participation'	(6):	'Spends at least an hour a day in the Cadets' Club.'
'various skills'	(7):	'Is a fair cook.'
'show'	(8):	'Likes parading.'
'miscellaneous'	(9):	'Is a royalist.'

214

Columns '2' and '3' give the number and percentages of statements in each category. Columns '4' and '5' show, whether statements were devised by officers or cadets. Differences are statistically significant (10% or better) for the categories 1a, 6, 7, 8, and 10. On the whole 'officers' items tend to be of a more practical content.

Column '6' gives the mean difference between the ratings of favourableness by officers and cadets. When making up the categories, the author and his staff had felt that the distinction between categories 1a and 1b was somewhat arbitrary, although they had been able to agree. It is rather interesting therefore, to see that they show quite different statistics.

The 'model pupil' (or: general conduct) statements show both a significantly (5%) greater difference in appreciation and a significantly (10%) greater range than all other groups of statements. Thus *officers and cadets do not agree on these items, nor do they agree among themselves.* This finding shows that cadets have, on the whole, different standards of conduct from the officers, and that it makes much difference by whom one is rated on these aspects of behaviour.

On (peace-time) 'military virtues,' including living up to the cadets' code of honour, there is significantly high agreement, both among and between the two groups. The same is true for 'Consideration for peers and subordinates.'

We consider this a most important point: *There is high consensus on what should characterise the ideal officer-cadets' conduct as a colleague and as a subordinate.*

EVALUATION (SCALE VALUES) OF THE STATEMENTS

Table 2 shows how many items were rated favourable, unfavourable or indifferent by each judge-group. Officers give significantly (2%) *more extreme ratings* than cadets do. This again is an interesting finding, as it is known that when superiors assess, not statements but the behaviour of *real people*, extreme ratings are infrequently found.

We tend to think, that the officers have projected their mental image of an *'ideal cadet'* into their evaluation of the statements, whereas the cadets have based their evaluation more on what they actually see around them. The officers' 'model pupil' is more or less the cadet *who causes no trouble*. The cadets' concept more closely resembles that of their contemporaries, the university students.

From tables 3, 4 and 5 it may be seen, on which statements officers and cadets differed most. The findings are summarized in table 6.

215

Table 2. *Median scale values of statements, by source and by judge group*

Median scale values	list 1 Source: Cadets Judges: Cadets		list 2 Source: Cadets Judges: Offrs		list 3 Source: Offrs Judges: Cadets		list 4 Source: Offrs Judges: Offrs		All statements Judges: Cadets	All statements Judges: Offrs
>0–1	—		—		—		—			
1–2	7		22		5		7			
2–3	14	30 (31%)	7	40 (42%)	4	14 (15%)	5	17 (18%)	44 (23%)	57 (30%)
3–4 LOW	9		11		5		5			
4–5	18	33 (34%)	8	19 (20%)	19	36 (38%)	14	26 (28%)	69 (36%)	45 (24%)
5–6	15		11		17		12			
6–7	11		5		18		15			
7–8 HIGH	16	33 (34%)	9	37 (38%)	23	44 (47%)	15	51 (54%)	77 (41%)	88 (46%)
8–9	6		23		3		21			
Totals	96	(100%)	96	(100%)	94	(100%)	94	(100%)	190 (100%)	190 (100%)

Table 3. Statements, rated '+' by Officers, and '±' (13) or '−' (2) by Cadets

	1	2	3	4	5
	Scale value officers	Scale value cadets	(1)–(2)	Category	Content
1	8.65	5.23	3.42	1a	Seldom oversleeps
2	8.36	5.93	2.43	1a	Is never drunk
3	8.11	5.65	2.46	1a	Always behaves himself when at table
4	7.97	5.68	2.29	1a	Always has decent haircut
5	7.62	5.37	2.25	1a	Seldom uses dirty words
6	7.62	1.83	5.79	1a	Regularly stays over the weekend to study
7	7.18	5.41	1.77	1a	Shoes are well polished
8	7.01	4.94	2.07	1a	Attends to all lectures
9	6.77	5.87	0.90	7	Has some knowledge of First Aid
10	6.67	5.37	1.30	1a	Never curses
11	6.67	5.08	1.59	1a	Room and bed tidy
12	6.67	5.19	1.48	2	Wants to excel in one sport at least
13	6.50	5.12	1.38	9	Contributes well in fraternity meetings
14	6.37	5.08	1.29	7	Well readable handwriting
15	6.26	5.06	1.20	1a	Studies late, even when sleepy
$\overline{X}$	7.22	5.32	1.90		

Table 4. Statements, rated '−' by Officers, and '±' (12) or '+' by Cadets

	1	2	3	4	5
	Scale value officers	*Scale value cadets*	*(1)–(2)*	*Category*	*Content*
1	2.50	4.57	2.07	1a	Only clean tack when expecting inspection
2	2.50	4.75	2.25	1a	Clearly shows dislike for some people
3	2.67	4.39	1.72	7	Cannot write official letters
4	3.03	5.62	2.59	1a	Only studies just before examination
5	3.14	4.54	2.40	2	Does not want to participate in 'four-days-march'
6	3.34	4.67	1.33	1a	Has great liking for sex-films
7	3.50	4.57	1.07	1a	Wants to be first of his class in study
8	3.50	4.58	1.08	4	Is content with average marks
9	3.50	5.07	1.57	4	Studies for knowledge's sake
10	3.50	5.64	2.14	2	Cannot swim
11	3.83	4.35	0.52	2	Never watches sports on T.V.
12	3.92	4.58	0.64	5	At social evenings always to be found with officers
$\overline{X}$	3.24	4.78	1.61		

The large differences in scale values between officers and cadets on statements from category 1a may reflect the existence of 'two cultures.' *General conduct of a conformist nature may not be the most valued quality in a cadet, even in peace-time. But the fact remains that it is one of the aspects for which most statements were thought up by both groups; and that it is the one on which they most often and most severely disagree.*

Table 5. Statements, rated '+' by Cadets, and '±' (0) or '−' (3) by Officers

	1	2	3	4	5
	Scale value cadets	Scale value officers	(1)–(2)	Category	Content
1	6.72	4.56	2.16	1a	Attends interesting lectures only
2	6.23	5.71	0.52	1b	Goes into town with his fellow-cadets
3	6.03	5.00	1.03	5	Stands drinks when celebrating birthday
$\overline{X}$	6.34	5.09	1.25		

Table 6. Statements in each category that are rated in different classes by officers and cadets

Category	Number in category	In different class	Difference >2 scale points
1a	30	17	11
1b	16	1	—
2	32	4	2
3	25	—	—
4	24	2	—
5	20	2	—
6	11	0	—
7	11	3	—
8	4	—	—
9	9	1	—
	190	30	13

AGREEMENT WITHIN JUDGE-GROUPS

All 190 statements were rated for favourableness by both officers and cadets. Neither of the groups shows much intra-group agreement, as is shown by the quartile ranges.

Table 7. Quartile ranges of scale values on all 190 statements

Quartile range in scale points × 100	Rated by cadets	Rated by officers
001–050	2	4
051–100	21	27
101–150	40	41
151–200	52	34
201–250	29	23
251–300	19	26
301–350	13	19
351–400	13	12
401–450		1
451–500	1	2
501–550		
551–600		
601–650		1
Total	190	190

Of the 190 statements, 101 (53%) show a quartile range of 2.00 scale points or more (when rated by officers, cadets or both) and would therefore have to be rejected for practical use. If only the officers' ratings would be considered, still 77 statements (41%) would have to be rejected. Both officers and cadets found that it was far more difficult to devise meaningful and discriminating statements than they had thought before they understood the task.

CORRELATION BETWEEN VALUE AND RANGE

The question was raised, whether scale value and range would be correlated. Judges then would agree more on statements with extreme scale values than on statements from the middle ranges of the scale. This hypothesis had to be rejected. There is no connection demonstrable.

The Collective Measure of Morale: Practical and Methodological Aspects of Periodic Evaluation in Military Surroundings

J. BRÉMOND*

* Armée de l'air, Centre d'études et de recherches psychologiques 'Air,' 78 Saint-Cyr l'école.

There is no shortage of definitions of morale or of attempts to measure it in the literature on psychology. Although the meaning of the concept is generally considered as established, the proposed definitions are but of little use for forming evaluating 'tools'. The problem of gauging morale cannot be confined to finding a new definition. McNemar's advice, given in 1946, still applies: 'There are two things to be done: determine the dimensions of morale and construct and validate scales by which to measure these dimensions'.

We have taken these same steps with a view to finding a system of periodic evaluation suitable for the commanding board of the Air Force.

Once we have recalled the current theories on morale, we shall specify the relevant hypotheses and dimensions. We shall stress the methods used to demarcate the semantic content of each dimension. And then specify the use of such a system, its scope for development and its limits.

1. THEORIES ON MORALE

Most of the theories on morale are expressed as a total of factors, assumed to form the elements which determine satisfaction or dissatisfaction. These theories generally liken morale with satisfaction in one's job or work, including aspects both of the work itself and the conditions in which it is performed, and often extending to the professional framework of an individual's career.

1.1 *The existing theories*

Present-day theories on morale can be regrouped into two approaches: the 'traditional' theory and Herzberg's 'two factors' theory.

Both admit the existence of some variables relating to the work itself and to its environment. They differ essentially in the hypotheses concerning the relations between these variables and total satisfaction.

The *two-factors theory*, formulated by Herzberg in 1959, distinguishes between the factors leading to job satisfaction and better performance ('motivators', variables of content) and those preventing discontent but not contributing towards satisfaction or maintaining motivation (hygiene elements, variables of context). Herzberg stresses the semantic aspect of this distinction and underlines the fact that satisfaction and discontent are usually considered as opposites. He does not agree: the opposite of satisfaction is lack of satisfaction; of discontent, lack of discontent. He therefore makes the hypothesis of the existence of two uni-polar continuums.

The *traditional theory* however sees satisfaction and discontent at the two extremes of the same bi-polar continuum. Its hypothesis is that there are essentially linear connections between satisfaction assessed by several variables, and general satisfaction assessed as a whole. In other words, all the variables (on which matter the authors are mostly in agreement) may have a favourable or an unfavourable effect and produce satisfaction or discontent.

The polemics, which still exist, lead to controversy between the advocates of the two theories. There has been much criticism of the two-factors theory: the scope of the jobs studied is too restricted, only one attitude gauge used as regards work, no facts on validity and fidelity, no measure of total satisfaction (Ewen 1964). Research instigated by this polemic has revealed an apparent link between Herzberg's results and the methods used (Lindsay, Marks and Gorlow 1967). Works using the same methods (compilation of critical incidents) confirm the theory, partially at least (Schwarz, Jenusaitis and Stark, 1963; Saleh, 1964; Myers, 1964), whereas the writers who used methods more suited to collecting attitudes (Burke, 1966) or a statistic approach (Ewen, 1964; Friedlander, 1963 and 1964; Gordon, 1965; Halpern, 1966; Wernimont, 1966) obtained different, but convergent results. It has not been possible to confirm the hypothesis of a dimension underlying the 'motivators' and another corresponding to the hygiene elements. So Herzberg's theory appears to be an over-simplified representation of job satisfaction (Burke, 1966).

However, the distinction between content (or intrinsic) variables and those of context (or extrinsic) may be of some use, though it is hard to place certain variables, like salary and promotion, in one category or the other. If these categories are used, the variables of content would appear to contribute more towards the variance of the general unity of the satisfaction-discontent continuum than do the variables of context; this in a ratio of 3:1 (Hulin and Locke, 1966; Graen, 1966 and 1968).

1.2 *Comments*

If we examine more than twenty years' work on this subject, several comments spring to mind.

Firstly, the extension of the concept of 'morale' requires its study in several dimensions. This '*multi-dimensional*' *character* appears to be accepted these days, without further discussion. This condemns to failure every attempt to assess morale by one scale, and questions to say the least, the advisability of a sole index which can only be composite (Friedlander, 1965; Ewen, 1967; Smith and Hulin, 1968). On the other hand, this 'multi-dimensional' character makes the lack of theoretical bases particularly serious and demands the adoption of well-defined operational concepts.

Secondly, according to the approaches used, a *distinction* is made, or not made, *between dimensions and morale factors*. Confusion probably arises from numerous cases of factorial analysis being applied to many items, each considered a priori itself as a dimension, whilst in fact they might, semantically, be re-arranged, and belong to several distinct sub-groups. The first objective should therefore be to ensure that the analysis applies to uniform sub-groups; otherwise there is a risk that the results will be meaningless and the factors misinterpreted (Whitlock 1960).

Briefly, 'putting all the facts in the pot' and giving them a factorial analysis does not enable us to distinguish between dimensions and morale factors, for there should be more dimensions than factors.

The third and last comment is this: research into morale can be reduced to two main trends, neither of which is exclusive. Some research tends to expose the psycho-social factors which would correlate with specific situations of high or low productivity. Others strive, by means of polls or questionnaires, to sift out the factors which can contribute towards the worker's satisfaction and to building up good morale (Columelli and Moscovici, 1957). These two trends raise the *problem of validity*.

In the former case we are concerned with 'external validity'. Morale is viewed as something which determines output, once the influence of measurable causes has been eliminated; so it appears to be connected with set tasks. It is especially difficult to assess output in the military environment in peace-time for numerous activities. Attempts to do so in industrial surroundings by means of objective criteria have so far not proved very convincing either.

With the latter trend, the concept of external validity should be replaced by that of 'structural validity' and morale should be considered as a dependent variable. Validity is here best expressed as a stability coefficient. Only research into structural validity, therefore, can provide some theoretical basis for measuring morale.

225

2. BASIC HYPOTHESIS AND GENERAL APPROACH

With the foregoing in mind, the objective was to form a system for assessing morale periodically. This would be based on stable, differentiated measuring 'tools'.

The basic hypothesis was to consider morale as the degree of agreement between the needs of the men and of the Air Force as such.

Tensions and conflicts might be caused by needs, varying in kind and depth according to the socio-cultural sub-groups making up the Air Force, not being satisfied.

One might, for instance, draw inspiration from Maslow's motivations and needs pyramid, and formulate questions (as Porter did) corresponding with each level, then try to trace out a dimension for each. In fact the different levels of command satisfy different motivations to a varying extent. This could lead to a structural set-up to express the needs within the dimensions themselves. Guttman's hierarchical (structural) analysis enables us to test this hypothesis in particular and to trace the dimensions at the same time.

The general approach was as follows:

Firstly we had to take stock of the various aspects of morale in reference works which might apply, with or without adaptation, to Air Force Officers, NCOs and servicemen.

For each 'theme' a number of semantically uniform questions (15 to 18) was drafted, on the assumption that these embodied a dimension and might result in a Guttman scale of 6 to 7 questions.

This form of attitude questionnaire was applied to equivalent samples, representative of the staff concerned, over a period of three years.

Each time the structure (hierarchy) in the groups in question was analysed. It was possible to construct some Guttman scales, each defining an operating concept, which could be improved from one questionnaire to the next, and verified as to structural stability. At the same time new dimensions were explored which had not been tackled until then for lack of space, or which proved to be different from those explored before.

The final questionnaire will, therefore, contain some hierarchical scales and new questions can always be added if new dimensions prove necessary.

The next step will be research into a factorial structure, from which 'morale' will be defined operatively and which will aid in the choice of scales facilitating its assessment.

3. STRUCTURAL (HIERARCHICAL) ANALYSIS FOR THE DEFINITION OF THE DIMENSIONS OF MORALE

Without going into the details of the method of hierarchical analysis, we shall underline certain aspects which fit in for defining the dimensions of morale.

The fundamental principle – 'hierarchism' by inclusion – justifies its use wherever replies (to a series of dichotomized items) and respondents can be structured simultaneously, in such a way that a person rated in a particular rank 'has everything a lower-ranking individual has, and something more.' Or, in other terms, adherence to a given item includes adherence to all the less restrictive items and excludes adherence to more restrictive.

The mathematical example worked out by Guttman relates hierarchical analysis to a kind of factorial analysis adapted to the study of qualitative variables (attributes).

Items in a series of uniform content, by being structured and by satisfying the conditions for inclusion, are subjected to a veritable test of the 'unidimensionality and homogeneity hypothesis'. Not only the sample of items (or attributes) but the universe of the underlying attitude (latent variable).

Thanks to certain refinements in Guttman's original method, plus additional restraint, it can be applied to define the operating procedure.

Besides the reproducibility coefficient proposed by Guttman, the coefficients of inclusion (K in Green) and homogeneity (H in Loevinger) are used. Each scale is judged therefore from three coefficients, which separately would not guarantee unidimensionality sufficiently. Each question is followed by four possible answers, two for and two against. The only dichotomies which remain to form the scale are those described as 'logical', i.e. between the favourable and the unfavourable answers. This ensures that structuring of the items does not depend on constructional contrivances, but that the attitude attributes the various items represent fall spontaneously into the demarcated dimension, according to the same criterion. In short, intensity graphs can be drawn up, starting from each scale and allowing for any slight differences in the answers. These graphs facilitate assessment of attitude consistence in the interviewed group and divide it into favourable and unfavourable respondents.

227

4. DIMENSIONS EXAMINED

4.1 *Themes applying to personnel in regular service*

The following dimensions could be singled out from questionnaires containing about 150 questions.
a. Job satisfaction
b. Feeling of effectiveness
c. Relations with superior
d. Feeling of participation-integration
e. Attitude towards the military career
f. Adherence to objectives.

Hierarchical analysis has enabled us to draw up a 6-question scale for each theme, setting out the above characteristics. The aim was to obtain an even 'spread' of the percentages of positive answers from around 10 to 90%, as some scales do not yet have the full scope required. For this reason some questions were added each time (despite the statistical quality of the measuring 'tools' obtained), so that each dimension could be scanned by twelve questions.

The content of the dimensions is given below.

a. *Job satisfaction:* All-round satisfaction, interest, use of abilities, bringing out the best in the individual, contribution to personal education, autonomy, pride, feeling of usefulness, right amount of work.

b. *Feeling of effectiveness:* Effectiveness of working methods and of job description; difficulties arising from organisation, possibility of reorganisation to make some duties less urgent and to gain time; co-ordination of work at the heart of the unit, division of duties; information available on the job to be done.

c. *Relations with the superior* (a dimension recognised by all authors as being particularly important): Attitude towards the subordinate; understanding of difficulties; bringing out the best in the subordinate as regards his superiors; acknowledgement of ability; superior's arbitration sought in conflicts; superior informed of subordinate's activities; superior's readiness to listen; wish to defend superior if criticised; responsibility assumed by superior for decisions taken in his absence; wish to establish 'extra-professional' relations.

d. *Feeling of participation* (*and of integration*)*:* Encouragement to take initiative; effort by superiors to develop team-spirit, to comment on orders, to listen to ideas or suggestions about work; participation in the unit's mission, wish to have a more important part in this; consultation of subordinates about taking decisions; pride in belonging to the unit; feeling of being affected by events concerning the unit; feeling of solidarity.

e. *Attitude towards the military career:* All-round satisfaction; requirements of the ideal are met; opportunities to obtain high qualifications; social success represented by the highest grade one can aspire to; acceptation of some self-sacrifice; security of this employment; preference for a military career to others with better salaries and material conditions.

f. *Adherence to objectives:* Feeling of being affected personally by the objectives of the Air Force; agreement with personal aspirations; useful purpose of the task accomplished for one's country; place of personal interests; acceptance of a possible increase in responsibilities and military obligations; acceptance of inconveniences in private life; conviction of serving a common cause; belief in the value of the Air Force objectives.

These are the dimensions whose content can be defined and specified. Many other questions relate to other elements of satisfaction or dissatisfaction: material working conditions, assignment at that particular time, living and leisure conditions, possibility of resettlement, systems of reward or punishment, etc. Some of these elements viewed in great detail produce classifications along Thurstone 'interval method' lines. Others, considered alone, might be included in the final plan if they prove to be correlated with the nucleus which the scales already make up. They might eventually give rise to clusters, even scales.

4.2 *Themes relating to conscripts*

All the foregoing themes, except for adherence to objectives and the attitude towards a military career also apply to national servicemen. However, two more dimensions were examined in their respect: attitude towards national service as an institution and satisfaction in actual service. These two dimensions also resulted in satisfactory scales.

a. *Attitude towards the national service as an institution:* Usefulness for the country's defence; usefulness for moral and civil training of young men, for acquiring the sense of group life; democratic aspect of national service; possibility of abolishing national service without reducing the efficiency of the Forces; opinion on censure of national service.

b. *Satisfaction in actual service:* All-round satisfaction; feeling of wasting time; opportunity to pursue general education or professional training; conditions under which service is carried out; acceptance of military obligations and the limitation of individual freedom; feeling of being considered as an individual.

5. RESULTS AND USE

There have been three annual questionnaires so far; the most noteworthy results follow below.

The most important sampling variables are rank and mission defined by the Command to which the individual belongs. The effect of rank on all previously defined attitudes has been revealed clearly: the military chain of command is reflected almost fully in the answers to the questions. Generally speaking, the higher the rank, the greater the likelihood of a favourable attitude.

As far as morale is concerned, the members of the Air Force can be divided into two sub-groups. Regulars on the one hand, conscripts on the other. The differences arise primarily from the dimensions themselves. Four are met in both groups, two among regulars and two among conscripts.

But other differences are found at the very heart of identical dimensions, in that the content of one and the same dimension may be slightly different for regular staff and for conscripts. This will lead to two separate assessments of morale, despite the interest and wish to compare them on certain points.

In practice, a single index for the morale for each sub-group cannot be located for the time being. How, then, can a system with various measuring 'tools' be used?

Different scales enable us to compare the different sociological groups determined by variables like rank, mission, corps, origins, in order to discover the extent to which one group is more or less satisfied than another, for each dimension.

In view of the preponderant influence of rank on all attitudes, all comparisons are made within each rank category. Some tables have been drawn up with the dimensions of morale on the Y axis and for example the different mission on the X axis. The significant differences, if there are any, within each rank for a given dimension or rank are entered in the squares of the table. A table can be made along the same lines for the different corps.

If, for example, we take a look at the table for attitude according to mission, each high command is characterised by the dimensions which differentiate it from another (rank by rank) at some stage. The total development of the attitudes can also be noted from one inquiry to another. The system can be used as a 'differential detector' and to determine whether to launch a more thorough opinion survey for some categories or for specific problems within a high command.

Another aspect of the methods used can also be turned to account. As we have seen, a given sub-group can be divided into those favourable or unfavourable as regards a particular attitude. Take the national servicemen for example, and their attitude towards national service as an institution. The amendments which Parliament adopted recently concerning the length and terms of national service will certainly make an impact on young conscripts. By means of 'intensity graphs' we can observe where and how the gap between those in favour and those against moves. In other words, we can judge whether the measures have resulted in the expected effect in this dimension. The same applies for any measure aimed at improving the stay of conscripts in the Air Force evaluating the changes in attitude towards actual service.

Moreover, annual inquiries will supply a wealth of data which could lead to studies – reviewing particular categories of personnel, simulation of changes in attitude...

6. CONCLUSIONS

This system has not been completed yet, nor have all the problems, especially those concerning method, been solved. However, the problem of morale in the military environment could be posed operatively. The basic dimensions are uniform operative concepts with corresponding stable, differentiating scales: thus reconciling as much as possible two contradictory requirements.

The system can be developed, in that new dimensions can be explored, but only accepted if they make an appreciable contribution to the system as a whole. Hierarchical analysis is intended to prove uniformity of the dimensions and specify their semantic content. The various dimensions will be examined as one structure by factorial analysis, resulting perhaps in a final choice.

Though this system supplies high command with valuable information, it has decided limitations. Obviously as regards method and deontology, the results of each inquiry cannot attain assessment of the morale in a specific unit. Another limitation is the relative 'cost' of the methods used: the themes of the questions should be fairly general to achieve valid measures; each scale comprises 6 to 7 questions, so half the questionnaire should be reserved for assessment proper. This restricts the number of other questions.

As such this system is more of an organisational psychology level than of a mere opinion survey. So it will constitute an increasingly useful source of information for the Command. Since the results must be used at the right level, authors of reports will have to try to translate the statistical data into clear terms.

BIBLIOGRAPHY

BURKE, Ronald J., 'Are Herzberg's Motivators and Hygienes Unidimensional?', *J. App. Psy.*, 1966, *50*, 4.

COLUMELLI, F. et MOSCOVICI, S., Le moral de l'entreprise, *Bulletin du CERP.*, 1957–VI–no. 2.

EWEN, Robert B., 'Weighting Components of Job Satisfaction', *J. App. Psy.*, 1967, *51*, 1.

EWEN, Robert B., 'Some Determinants of Job Satisfaction', *J. App. Psy.*, 1964, *48*, 3.

FRIEDLANDER, Frank, 'Relationships between the importance and the satisfaction of various environmental factors', *J. App. Psy.*, 1965, *49*, 3.

FRIEDLANDER, Frank, 'Job characteristics as satisfiers and dissatisfiers', *J. App. Psy.*, 1964, *48*, 6.

GORDON, G. G., 'The relationship of 'satisfiers' and 'dissatisfiers' to productivity, turnover, and morale', *American Psychologist*, 1965, *50* (Abstract).

GRAEN, George B., 'Testing traditional and two-factors hypotheses concerning job satisfaction', *J. App. Psy.*, 1968, *52*, 5.

HALPERN, Gerald, 'Relative contributions of motivator and hygiene factors to overall job satisfaction', *J. App. Psy*, 1966, *50*, 3.

KATZELL, R. A., 'Industrial Psychology'. In P. R. FARNSWORTH (Ed.), *Annual review of psychology*, Palo Alto California: Annual reviews, Inc. 1957.

LINDSAY, Carl A., MARKS, Edmond and GORLOW, Leon, 'The Herzberg Theory: A critique and reformulation', *J. App. Psy.*, 1967, *51*, 4.

MCNEMAR, Q., 'Opinion-attitude methodology', *Psycho. Bull.*, 1946, *43*.

MARCH, J. G. et SIMON, H. A., *Les organisations – Problèmes psychosociologiques*, Dunod, Paris, 1964.

MASLOW, A. H. M., *Motivation and Personality*, Harper and brothers, New York, 1954.

MULLER, Philippe et SILBERER, Paul, *L'homme en situation industrielle*, Payot, Paris, 1968.

PORTER, L. W., 'Job attitudes in management', *J. App. Psy.*, 1962, *46* and *J. App. Psy.*, 1963, *47*.

SALEH, S. D., 'A study of attitude change in the preretirement period', *J. App. Psy.*, 1964, *48*, 5.

SMITH-MIKES, Patricia and HULIN, Charles L., 'Use of importance as a weighting component of job satisfaction', *J. App. Psy.*, 1968, *52*, 5.

WERNIMONT, Paul F., 'Intrinsic and Extrinsic factors in job satisfaction', *J. App. Psy.*, 1966, *50*, 1.

WHITLOCK, Gerald H., 'The status of morale measurement, 1959', *Tech. Rep.*, WADD-TN-60-136, May 1960.

Military Management:
A Fantasm or a Necessity?

J. P. MOREIGNE*

* Maître de recherche de psychologie clinique du Service de Santé des Armées, France.

A nation's military defence organization formed into armies constitutes, from a sociological point of view, a human collectivity which is structured into a society by the ends of which it has to serve.

We shall consider this partial society from a restricted point of view, when it does not include the entire population mobilized for the same purpose of defence. We shall be concerned only with the category of people whose present social condition is the military status.

The specificity and grouping of such individuals assume a finality, as they do of every group of people which tries to find the conditions necessary for its survival. The very fact that this collectivity has an intentional structure warrants it being called 'enterprise,' lending this word a wider meaning than it has in political economy.

If one takes into account what people undertake, the people who undertake, and the social context in which this collective action is performed, can it be said that there is at present a style of conduct better than any other? That is the question we shall try to elucidate.

To simplify matters, we shall consider successively two different perspectives: the collectivity and the individuals, without overlooking the fact that the problem arises from the conjunction of these two perspectives.

MANAGEMENT AND THE MILITARY COLLECTIVITY

For the last ten years the analysis of the concept of management has been a matter of reflection for all those who are concerned with organizing. But management and organizing are not to be confused. The field of the organization is easier of access, easier to master than the field of authority, and reducing the authority to the organization would be only a manner of evading the very problem of human management.

The expression 'management' possibly owes its undeniable success to its ambiguity. Let us point to the pretension of the different definitions found in the literature, in contrast with its modest etymological origin. For instance, Gelinier defines management as 'the dynamics of the higher human energy' while Ardoino traces back the origins of the word both in Italian 'manegiarre', which means to manoeuvre, and in common Latin 'mansio': house. From the good control of the household to the incitement of a purpose of action, the gap is too wide to include only complementary conceptions and to avoid contradictory representations.

For this reason, we shall not yield to this fashion, which already contains the germs of future disappointments, and instead of studying the military 'management,' which would be a revolutionary substitution for the traditional command, we shall try to find in the contemporary analyses of management the elements which would probably facilitate regeneration of the function of authority by emphasizing the present deficiencies of its applications.

Let us specify what, in this function, has deteriorated through history, and what has become irrelevant because of the evolution of the context in which it is exercised.

FROM COMMAND TO MANAGEMENT OR VICE-VERSA ?

Even at the risk of being criticized, both by 'radicals' and 'conservatives,' we shall assert that the command, in its essence, was an appeal for participation (cum-mandare), the correlative notions of ascendancy and personal authority making implicit the obligation of assuming controversy; the function of the person who commanded was to develop the initiative of his subordinates to the extent where they helped to achieve the aims to which he had successfully made them adhere.

Are we so far removed from a 'management by participation' in accordance with the contemporary ideal of management in the big enterprises?

We shall not deny that this representation of command has lost its original characteristics through the security of unchangeable status, and through a timorous practice of responsibilities derived from the growing and ponderous bureaucracy, and that this evolution has weakened human relations until they have been completely excluded. But from our point of view, it is more a question of restoring things than innovating.

Let us remember that the concept of authority takes its roots in the idea of procreation, conception, that it refers to the fact of giving birth, that is to advance in risky, uncertain and hazardous conditions, and not to stick excessively to the tradition.

As to the human relations within the military collectivity, we think that the six following items would be sufficient to restore to the command its original meaning, while becoming consistent with the management approach:
— To restore the initiative at every level.
— To create a general commitment towards the aims by informing and discussing freely.
— To combine the dynamics of all the individuals within the functioning of the collectivity.
— To prefer the agreement of individuals to a collective conditioning, leading to a decay in human relations.

238

— To decentralize partial powers.
— To replace the list of rules, which make certain conduct compulsory, by the general directives indicating the aims.

Evidently, it is very easy to state general principles; we have now to explain the difficulties to which their application will give rise.

The sociological structure of authority to which such principles refer is based on the one hand on a humanist ethic, and on the other hand on a clear representation of the finality which is expressed in the missions which have been partitioned into objectives and functions.

This paper is not concerned with the concept of defence, but a psycho-sociological approach to the concept of authority inevitably raises the problem of the definition of the missions.

Let us consider the missions of 'intervention', 'dissuasion', and 'operational defence of the territory' on the one hand, and the functions of civic formation or social promotion on the other. Does that constitute a consistent and homogeneous set, or are there distinct aims? They might be compatible, but this compatibility has to be analyzed so that congruous human structures can be created for each type of mission.

Let us consider a second contribution of management to the military affairs.

MANAGEMENT: INTEGRATING NEW RESOURCES TO SOLVE A PROBLEM

Whatever the meaning of an action as a function of the political options, the results of the action being estimated by reference to these options, an action always has a precise and limited *aim*, is performed within a defined *situation* and by defined *means*.

We are faced with some new characteristics (at least three) of the context in which the action is performed:
— The aim changes increasingly, within the constancy of the mission.
— The situation itself evolves more and more rapidly, and furthermore there are a lot of methods which increase the amount of information given on its evolution.
— The means which are used are more and more expensive and require careful management.

To these three characteristics, the management seems to have found satisfying answers:
— Modular functional structures which allow flexible junctions between functions, and a plasticity which organizes the changes.

— The answer to the constant increase in information is evidently the development of information processing.
— Models of budget prognoses, mathematical methods in the study of the ratio between costs and efficiency are a useful contribution by management.

We shall not discuss the preceding points, but they had to be mentioned.

Our first conclusion is that the military organization has to take into account the contributions by the management as far as organizing and administering are concerned; on the level of human relations, the management refers simply to a reflection on the nature and the characteristics of command.

MANAGEMENT AND THE MILITARY

What has been said before concerned individuals belonging to the military community. For them, it means a behavior, a state of mind, a way of life, a method of reflection and of decision making that are recommended. But if they are constituted in a military society, they are not separated from the global society. They come from it, they partly live in it, and one day they will have to find their role in it.

Presently, in this global society, there are some new models that one has to take into account if a disastrous separation is to be avoided.

The future military managers generally receive the same education as the middle or top managers in public administrations or in firms. During this period they acquire knowledge, the use of which is determined, whether it is mathematics, economics, group working methods, it is a personal investment that has to yield, for oneself as well as for the collectivity, some profit. They are specified less early in their interest in a military career. The analogy with the managers should not be overlooked.

Another striking contemporary change in the social dimension of life is the social mobility.

Such notions as short career, three careers, third-age career, or as shift in professional activity, permanent education, such facts as the suppression of fields of activity, as the gigantic growth of others make it hazardous to define one's career. The risk is that of being stopped too early, if there are not ways of modifying one's orientation.

It has to be accepted that general culture is not a sufficient guarantee for a rapid change in profession.

Management requires a certain plasticity.

240

More precisely, if young officers should at any time think that they might find a quick way of learning the methods used in business, they would consider the peculiarities of their work with less anxiety.

It seems fundamental to suppress the discontinuity between the military career, whatever its length, and the civil career, which inevitably follows it. The solution offered by a few associations anticipates the institutional solution which will be necessary.

In this perspective, management might fill the gap between the military and the civil professions. Since the armies are preoccupied with the legitimate interests of their employees, it appears necessary to recognize institutionally the fact that the military career is only one part of man's life. Hence, the possibility of *adaptation* to other ways of life is to be encouraged within the army.

Military management, a fantasm or a necessity? Shall we answer that question?

The management cannot be reduced to a set of methods, to a technique of directing. It has not to be considered as a social philosophy. Why not keep it as a necessary fantasm?

Note: In this paper the author was deliberately indulged in a certain level of generalization because he wanted to promote a general discussion.

The Military and the Political Order: An Evaluation from a Civil-Military Relations Point of View

Professionalization, Politicization and Civil-Military Relations

R. D. McKINLAY*

* Lecturer, University of Lancaster, England.

The two major vehicles of approach to the perennial problem of civil-military relations in the twentieth century have been professionalization and politicization.[1] It is the primary aim of this paper to clarify the dynamics of the political dimension of civil-military relations in the modern nation state.[2] This exercise involves three tasks:

1. An elucidation of the several dimensions of civil-military relations;
2. An examination of the nature of professionalization and its relation to these dimensions;
3. An examination of the nature of politicization, its relation to professionalization, and its relation to the dimensions of civil-military relations.

CIVIL-MILITARY RELATIONS

Since we shall be interested in the political aspects of civil-military relations, it has proved useful to delineate three major dimensions to define such relations: the means of control or restraint on military political activity, the mode or level of such activity, and the motivational orientation of that activity.

The Means of Control

The means of control or restraint of military political activity fall into three main categories.

The first category is composed of both formal and informal controls. The formal may include military prescriptive specifications on the role and sphere of military political activities, and of punishments, e.g. loss of rank, expulsion etc., for any deviation. The informal controls are more important and relate to the internalization and socialization of non-political values by the military. The acquisition of such a set of values may be precipitated either on account of the development of a specific normative code of conduct, or on account of occupational specialization and the division of labour. The normative code of conduct would lead the military to eschew spontaneously certain forms of action. The division of labour means that occupational specialization has reached such a stage that only one range of activities can be adequately satisfied at any one time, and that to engage in a broader sphere could only lead to the debilitation of the major activity.

As opposed to these voluntary restraints, the second type of control,

247

i.e. civilian imposed controls, embraces two very distinct types: insulation and infiltration. The process of insulation involves specific action by the civilian polity to isolate or insulate the military from the polity. This may include attempts to disperse military training centres and bases, and to locate them away from centres of political power; or to forbid the military from joining political parties or voting or standing as candidates; or of a more indirect but nonetheless effective nature to control the size of the military budget.

Infiltration must in turn be divided into two distinct forms: implicit and explicit. The former relates to the situation where the civilian polity can maintain control of the military by virtue of the coincidence of interests based on the overlap of personnel in the top military and civilian political ranks. The coincidence of interests must be a more positive bond than the simple division of labour as found in internalization, and is usually based on common class or ideological base. The explicit type relates to the formal attempts by the polity to penetrate army ranks to ensure loyalty. This may include the use of commissars, control of training and education, the development of a control mechanism parallel to the army hierarchy or of rival forces, such as specialized branches, police or peoples militia.

The third situation relates to the condition where both military and civilian controls fail. The most exaggerated form was found in the caudillo tradition in Latin America, where small armed groups could unite around a local leader and usurp government by force. Although such complete erosion of both civilian and military controls is not a feature of the nation state, the category is included and has relevance in that at varying times civilian and/or military controls have waned to a low ebb. The Tanzanian Mutiny represents a dual failure, whereas the French army Algerian crisis represents a partial breakdown in military controls.

These forms of control are not mutually exclusive and any one case of control may combine elements from each major type.

The Mode or Level of Military Political Behaviour

The second dimension of civil-military relations, the mode or level of military political activity, may be represented in terms of a continuum, on which three major points may be located. The first relates to a pressure group role. In this capacity, the military engages in political activity in a lobbying capacity in an attempt to influence the policy formation of the major governmental bodies. The second level may be termed conjunction. At this level the military exceeds the pressure group role in that it actively

248

participates in governmental policy decision making in conjunction or coordination with the civilian polity. For such a role to be identifiable, it is necessary that the range of decisions exceeds the norm of the military's immediate sphere of occupational competence. The degree of conjunction may range from a more limited position, i.e. including fringe areas of military concern in a situation where civilian forces are clearly dominant, to a more inclusive level, in which the scope of military policy decision making expands and the dominance of the civilian element concomitantly declines. The third level is total intervention. This involves the explicit assumption and direction of major governmental offices by the military and the expulsion of the civilian occupants of these posts. At its lower level, total intervention merges with a high level of conjunction, while in its most marked form it entails the occupation of all top civil governmental posts by the military. Total intervention may be said to persist so long as the military occupies top political office (P. M. or President), that major governmental posts if not actually occupied by the military are held by military appointees, and that major governmental functions remain under military direction.[3]

The Factors Motivating the Military's Orientation to Political Action

The third dimension of civil-military relations involves the factors which motivate the military's political action. The first complex may be designated as personal or individual. In this context the military resources would be mobilized for the furtherance of the interests of only a limited number of persons.[4] The second complex is organizational. This means that the military's orientation to political action is derived in terms of the interests of the organization as a whole. At a point which approximates the personal complex, such an orientation may be for a simple pay increase, i.e having relevance only for the personal benefit of those within the military organization. At a broader level, the motivation for political action may be oriented towards influencing policy decisions which, though having immediate relevance for the military, do have repercussions for groups or interests outside the military. Thus, for example, the campaign for a certain type of defence system has immediate reference to the military but also broader consequences for national security.

The third and fourth types of motivational complex, the national and national sectional, are not as easily defined. Of the many definitional features of the nation state, one is of particular import for our purposes, namely the rise of a national authority structure based on mass popular resources and supports and acting with reference to mass popular demands. If a military motivational orientation is national, two ingredients are essential: first, the object and end of the activity must lie outside the military's own occupational sphere of reference, and second, this activity must be in consonance with the interests and demands of the mass populace. National sectional activity differs in that although the orientation is towards actions having direct relevance for the total populace, those deriving immediate benefit from such action are only a small sectional group of the population, such as a class, a region, or a tribe.[5] National or national sectional motivation necessitates a willingness on the part of the military to enter politics at least at the level of conjunction, for to play such a role the military must affect policy beyond its own sphere of competence.

We may now turn to examine two of the major approaches to civil-military relations and to analyse how they bear on the three main dimensions of these relations.

Although consensus on a definition of professionalization has not been established, a sufficient number of dimensions constantly reappear to make such a consensus a near likelihood. We shall employ five main dimensions.

The first criterion of professionalization relates to the development of a high degree of generalized and systematic knowledge based on a complex of intellectual advancements. Furthermore, this expert body of knowledge must encompass formalized means for technical training including methods of validating both the level of training and the means of training. This dimension may be assessed in terms of the type of training and the level of technical knowledge.

The second dimension relates to the development of institutional autonomy. As an occupational organization becomes a profession, it is necessary that it develops a high degree of autonomy within its own sphere of activity or competence. Furthermore, this autonomy must be accompanied by permanence and continuity of occupation, and by formal institutional means validating this autonomy. This dimension is manifested and may be examined in terms of the development of formal demarcation, i.e. formal legal documents specifying the nature of the profession and its sphere of competence, in terms of the non-infringement of this sphere of competence, and in terms of the formalization of tenure of employment and of payment.

250

The third dimension is corporateness. This involves the development of a collective sense of unity and the collective recognition of the clear differentiation of that body from other organizations. Corporateness is manifested and may be measured in terms of the loyalty of the members of the profession to each other, the development of egalitarian means of interaction, and the absence of any conflicts and cleavages.

The fourth dimension refers to the development of internal controls and internal affective neutrality. The development of internal controls entails the development of self-controls of behaviour, which become internalized in the process of training or occupational socialization. The emergence of affective neutrality relates to the impartial application of the major norms of the organization whether these apply to recruitment, promotion, modes of conduct and interaction. These features may be assessed in terms of the establishment of a body of rules governing controls and punishments, the consolidation of achievement norms for recruitment and promotion, and the impartial application of such controls and norms.

The final dimension relates to the development of a professional social ethic and of affective external neutrality. It is evident that the high development of a branch of technical knowledge and skill provides those possessing such knowledge with powerful tools for the control of nature or society. This final dimension of professionalization requires that this body of knowledge be applied and harnessed to socially responsible uses. Thus, the orientation of the application of this knowledge must be to community rather than personal, group or organizational interests. It is the social responsibility which distinguishes the professional man from other experts. External affective neutrality simply means the impartial external orientation of the profession, i.e. toward societal goals and organizations as opposed to their own more specific ones. This dimension may be assessed in terms of the non-personal activity and societal orientation of responsibility of that organization in the field within which it is an expert.

The Relation of Professionalization to Civil-Military Relations

The major problem now is to examine the relation of professionalization to the three dimensions of civil-military relations.

The most obvious result of professionalization for the means of control is the development of spontaneous internal controls. Thus, the development of technical expertise means that military functions become a full-time occupation and the military man occupies the position of an expert.

The development of institutional autonomy and corporateness means that the military is clearly demarcated and differentiated from the major complex of political roles, and is willing to act only within its own sphere of competence and expertise. Finally, the development of a professional ethic and social responsibility means that the military sees its own task as insuring national security, and to the extent that the major locus of popular demands and authority lies within the polity and that the major body for the formulation of national goals and policies is the polity, then the military must accept the directives of the polity. Therefore, both the organizational, i.e. the division of labour and expertise, and attitudinal, i.e. the professional ethic, drives of professionalization lead the military to develop its own internalized loyalty and subservience to the polity.

The development of internalized professionalization by the military is the most effective way of minimizing civil-military conflict. It is most effective in that a clear division of labour between the polity and the military emerges, and in that the polity does not have to employ elaborate or expensive means to ensure the loyalty and achieve control of the military.

It has frequently been assumed that the spontaneous developments of military controls mean that the military completely withdraws itself from politics. However, this assumption is largely fallacious, for not only does professionalization not exclude a political role but it may also precipitate such a role.

The first level at which the military may act is the pressure group. All professions are composed of individuals and all professions have a particular location in society, and may be expected to hold and express political views concerning their nature and place in society. The major areas of military pressure group activity concern the size of the armed forces and the size of the budgetary allocation and the nature of the defence system. Not only is it perfectly legitimate for the military to play a pressure group role (note many professions have become fully unionized) but it is also in an excellent position to do so (by virtue of access to Defence Ministry).

Several factors are of interest with respect to potential strife with the polity at this level. In the first place, any conflict is limited and constrained, and due to security reasons often concealed. In the second place, two factors derived from the professional complex have consequences for the polity. Thus the military tends to favour unity and efficiency and derides the conflict and fragmentation among politicians and particularly oscillations in the policies between various governments. Further, the focus of the military on national security leads it to develop a more conservative

252

outlook and a greater degree of sympathy with such a type of government.

The second level of political action by a professional military is balance or conjunction. Such activity is in consonance with military professionalism in conditions of national crisis or war. Given that guardianship of national security is the primary function of the military, whenever such security is in jeopardy either from internal or external sources, the military is legitimately obliged to take action. Where the security threat is sufficiently grave, corrective action may involve not only the utilization of physical force but also the mobilization and deployment of other domestic resources to enable a more optimal use of force, i.e. conscription, rationing, control and direction of economic production, distribution of economic resources. At this level the military is clearly involved in policy making, which, though of relevance to its activities, lies outside the direct sphere of military competence. Nevertheless, to the extent that the military is acting with reference to its major function, such political activity is quite in consonance with professionalization. It follows that the more localized or the less enduring the threat, the less salient the military political role.

It is at this level that several interesting points emerge. In the first place, given the proposition that the greater the security threat the more dominant the military conjunctive role, there seems to be a wide range of variation. Thus, Bismarck never permitted his generals even to play a role in treaty making, whereas after World War 2 the American generals not only played a major role in treaty making but also in the subsequent rehabilitation programme, cf. the Marshall Plan, and indeed in American politics generally. Within the frame of this proposition, the main factors which determine the relative balance of power between the military and the polity seem to be the calculation of the strength of the two sides in terms of personalities, unity and the immediate availability of resources.

In the second place, the ambiguity in the definition of national security threat by the military and by the civilian polity becomes of great importance. The major points of conflict centre in a situation of crisis on the object of corrective action, its duration, the proposed outcome and on the attempts to calibrate military and political victories; in a situation of pre- or post-crisis, the major conflict usually centres on the division of labour with respect to the identification and estimation of security threat and the extent of necessary preventive action.[6]

In the third place, although the military generally favours the expansion of military operations as a security guarantee, the position can be reversed. The most common occurrence is the juxtaposition of a professional military and an expansionist polity, e.g. there was some opposition from Hitler's troops to his expansion of the War or, again, the Egyptian army opposed the commitment to war with Israel by Farouk.

The third level of possible military political action involves the complete take-over of government by the military. Two conditions exist when even this dramatic type of political action is consonant with military professionalism.

The first relates to the situation where the civilian polity infringes the professionalization of the military. Such infringement may involve the use of the military as an internal police-force, attempts to interfere with military training, attempts to control recruitment and promotion, attempts to interfere with military organization and the execution of its duties. To the extent that any of these actions infringe the military's professionalism and are therefore perceived by the military as being a threat to its efficiency and therefore to the security of the national defence, it is quite legitimate to take the necessary corrective action.

The second condition for professional take-over relates to the situation where the civilian polity is unable to constitute the source of social responsibility for the military's professional allegiance. This category is more important than the first, by which it is frequently accompanied. It is derived from the situation where it is difficult to identify what exactly constitutes the centre of nation state authority. This situation may be summarized under political instability. Political instability represents that condition where the polity for a wide variety of reasons is unable to satisfy its major functions. This decline may be due to four main factors. First, there may be an obstruction or stagnation of the decision making process which results in the polity being unable to achieve one of its major goals, namely policy formation. Secondly, the polity may develop a high degree of corruption and patronage and may deviate from its own constitutional code of conduct. Thirdly, the polity may lose support, but be unwilling to transfer power. Finally, the polity may prove simply incapable of dealing with the demands and loads made upon it. Political instability may vary from a high degree of conflict where opposing groups are polarized, to a situation of stagnation where there is a simple loss of resource and capacity for action. However, in either case the end result is the same, namely that no responsible central authority exists, and to this extent national security may be endangered and the military may legitimately intervene.[7]

The third dimension of civil-military relations relates to the complex of factors which motivate military political performance. Professionalization inhibits any personal political action as this is quite clearly contrary to the development of social responsibility. However, the professional military may act politically on an organizational basis to the extent that it plays a pressure group role. Any activity beyond this level, i.e. more direct influence on policy decisions motivated purely for organizational benefits, represents a contradiction in professionalization. Furthermore the professional military may not act in terms of national sectional interests as again the sectional element represents a contradiction in the development of a national social ethic. Finally, the national motivation is in consonance with professional military political activity at the conjunction and take-over levels.

POLITICIZATION

Although the rise of professionalization represents the dominant organizational and attitudinal form of the military in the nation state, not all armies have developed all the indices and dimensions to the same degree. The most important summary concept covering a degree of variation from professionalization for civil-military relations is politicization.

Politicization is the process involving either the inculcation of values and opinions or the expression of action towards the polity based on such values, which lies outside the political frame of reference dictated by the functional sphere of competence of any organization. Politicization is of two very different types: induced and overt. Overt politicization represents the deliberate or overt drive by the polity to inculcate extra-military political values into the armed forces.[8] Induced politicization has the same end product as overt, i.e. the acquisition of an enlarged sphere of political reference, but differs in the process of the acquisition of the political values. Thus, as opposed to being deliberately imposed by the polity, they are acquired or induced more spontaneously through the general process of interaction between the military and polity. These types vary to such a degree that it is necessary to consider individually their repercussions for civil-military relations.

Overt Politicization

Overt politicization is primarily the product of the rise of the one party state. The essential features of this type of state are first that only one party is legitimate, and second that the function of the party extends beyond simple support mobilization and the recruitment of leaders to include major governmental and control functions, i.e. party and state authority merge. Overt politicization is partly an ideological phenomenon in that in the one party system all organizations in society are seen as part of an organic whole and must belong to the main-stream of that whole (i.e. the party), and partly the consequence of the development of the control function. Not only are one party states generally committed to enforced growth and development engendering increased centralization and direction, but any opposition to the one party is regarded as anathema and a threat to its existence – a powerful military is one obvious source of opposition.[9]

Overt politicization is manifested in several manners. First, recruitments and promotions may be made in terms of party affiliation. Thus the achievement norm of professionalization either becomes eroded or supplemented by party loyalty as the dimension for the evaluation of personnel. Secondly, the party can attempt to recruit or distribute party cards among the military in order to build up a core of loyalty. Thirdly, the polity may delegate government posts to top military leaders thereby involving the army in the general policy making process. Fourthly, the party may utilize political commissars both to encourage the military to become party members and also to propagate and supervise. Finally, the polity can engage in political education and indoctrination through special ideological schools. In general, these last two factors indicate a higher degree of politicization. Armies may vary widely in their degree of politicization, for example the Tanzanian military after 1961 began a mild programme of politicization, whereas the Chinese military manifests a much higher level.

The Relation of Overt Politicization to Professionalization

It is necessary to note that overt politicization is not antithetical to the development of professionalization. Although it does represent some points of conflict, it does not constitute a complete negation. Thus, we noted that the major indices of professionalization were a technical body of knowledge and the development of social responsibility. To the extent that a one party state constitutes the nation state authority and to the extent that it is publically accepted as such, then there is no reason why politicization should affect social responsibility. (For example, there is no reason to suggest that Soviet or Algerian military are any the less socially responsible than the British.) Unless politicization has any marked effect on promotion and training, it need have no adverse bearing on technical knowledge. The Soviet armed force is highly sophisticated and manifests a higher skill level than several professional armies. (It may be recalled that immediately prior to World War 2, however, the Stalin purges in the army severely hampered its capabilities.)

256

Although politicization does not represent a negation of professionalization, it obviously does represent some deviation. The major dimension of variation is the development of institutional autonomy. It may be noted by way of qualification that all major professions in the nation state are never completely autonomous and could never be unless existing in a vacuum. Thus many are subject to government inspection, or are tied to the government through salaries, or have government defined spheres of autonomy. Overt politicization represents a direct attack on institutional autonomy in order to prevent the military from developing its own independent resources and orientations. The polity clearly invades the minimum or unambiguous sphere of competence of the military.[10]

The Relation of Overt Politicization to Civil-Military Relations

With respect to the means of control, the development of overt politicization has direct relevance to the establishment of infiltration. Indeed one of the primary motivating factors for politicization on the part of the polity is precisely to establish control over the military both in terms of supervising the military and in terms of integrating it into the party mechanism. In this respect, it will be recalled that many one party regimes arise from conflict situations and are geared to rapid development.

The development of a high degree of politicization as evidenced in Communist countries has proved a most effective insurance against an internal military coup. In no Communist country has there been an internal domestic coup and, although other one party states have experienced coups, the rate is lower than for otherwise similar two- or multi-party states.

However, where the one party system is not strong, the attempt to politicize the army may well prove to have deleterious effects. This is because politicization heightens the military's political sensitivity, increases its awareness of the weaknesses of the polity, induces party conflicts and cleavages into the army and embroils the army in party politics (especially salient since many formal institutional mechanisms, such as transfer of power, are lacking). There have been indications of such problems in Communist countries (see for example the role of the army in Kruschev's succession struggle), but these are much more likely to prove problematic in the weaker non-Communist one party states.

Finally, it is interesting to note the conflict between politicization and professionalization as a means of control. All Communist states have embarked upon a programme of overt politicization, but in all cases a

257

professional hierarchical army has begun to emerge. Some resistance from the army has been manifest against a high degree of politicization. This has been evidenced in the USSR in a contained fashion, and in a more open manner in China.[11] Furthermore, overt politicization can lead to a higher degree of conflict when it is introduced into an army which is already developing along professional lines. One of the reasons for the Ghanain coup of 1966 was the army's resentment of Nkrumah's attempts at politicization.

The primary effect of politicization on the level of military political activity is either to involve the army in some kind of conjunctive role, with the army in a clearly subordinate position, or to give the army a pressure group role. In general terms a conjunctive role is more likely when politicization leads to implicit infiltration, for in this situation the military and political interests merge to a higher degree on account of the interchange of personnel. For example, a significant percentage of the Chinese cabinet is composed of army leaders, whereas in the USSR where implicit infiltration is not as evident military leaders are not so salient. It is important to note that the conjunctive role of the politicized military is much more permanent than the conjunctive role of the professional military, as it is not contingent on the incidence of a national crisis. Where take-over does occur there follows only a minor change in the political structure involving usually a change in personnel and a modified change of policy. Thus the Algerian coup led to only a small number of cabinet changes and a slight modification of policy.

Concerning the motivational complex, the development of overt politicization inhibits the army from acting on a personal basis. Furthermore, to the extent that overt politicization involves implicit infiltration, a clear-cut organizational orientation for a pressure group role does not emerge. As overt politicization involves moderate explicit infiltration, then a more clearly defined organizational orientation may crystallize. Any national sectional activity is clearly excluded. National motivation is manifest to the extent that the military plays a conjunctive or take-over role.

Induced Politicization

As opposed to the specific inculcation of political values and roles of overt politicization, the induced variety is the more spontaneous product of the dual natures of the military and the polity and their interaction. As such, the conditions under which induced politicization develops are much more complex than the unilateral action of a one party system. In general

258

terms this type of politicization may be the product of three main classes of factors: those pertaining to the nature of the military organization, to the type of polity, and to the nature of the interaction between the military and the polity. These factors are too extensive to be covered fully in the scope of this paper, but examples of each category may be given.

One of the precipitating factors of induced politicization, related to the internal organization of the military, concerns the degree to which the military reflects the social structure of the society of which it is a part. To the extent that all armies are part of a social system, they obviously must manifest some reflection of the social structure of that system. One of the primary features of professionalization is that such reflection becomes minimized, i.e. the professional military man sees himself primarily as a military representative rather than a product of that part of the social structure from which he is drawn. Given a society in which there exists a marked degree of cleavage conflict, e.g. class, tribal or regional conflict, and given a situation where the army reflects this cleavage strife in some manner and still identifies with the sectional groups from which it is recruited, then politicization is a likely consequence. Thus in several Latin American nations where class differences are very salient and the military is drawn from one specific class, it is likely to act in the interests of that class. Or again, in Nigeria the army became a reflection of the tribal division within Nigeria itself. The first military coup was a partly abortive attempt by the military officers of the East to rectify their grievances, while the second was largely a Northern response to this.

The main factor, related to the polity, which tends to precipitate induced politicization is a mild version of the overt form. It involves the attempt by the polity to induce military members to join or back certain government groups, or the attempt to effect a number of political promotions, or to distribute a number of political rewards to the military. This is clearly differentiated from overt politicization by virtue of being considerably less organized or pervasive and being considerably more conciliatory. Such attempts by the polity to induce politicization usually arise where there exists a weak polity which is unable to rely on the loyalty of the army, or where, lacking a popular base, it seeks to maintain itself in power by relying on the tacit support of the army. Indonesia represents a good example of an army which largely resisted such attempts at politicization, whereas Syria represents the opposite case.

Two examples of the nature of military political interaction as precipitants of politicization may be given. The first relates to the role which the military plays in the achievement of independence. Where indepen-

259

dence is not a constitutional transfer and the military becomes involved in an armed struggle, the military is pushed into a central political role. The best examples may be seen in Latin America. The second and more important precipitant of politicization relates to the past role of the military in assuming total governmental controls. The assumption of total government power by the military is likely to lead to politicization on a number of grounds. First, the military is actively obliged to make policy decisions and to cooperate with the major civilian political groups. Even though the military may unmistakably remain the executive, it is by necessity transformed into a political group. Secondly, the process of political rule by the military means that the top leaders are divorced from the army and this may lead over time to an internal cleavage. Thirdly, once the army has assumed power it becomes particularly prone to the development of divisions on how or on what policies ought to be executed. Even a professional army is subject to these strains: thus there is the problem of when to intervene and, second, the problem of when power ought to be returned to civilians and the conditions under which such a return may be effected. If military rule may threaten to politicize a professional army where the range of choice is relatively limited, the strains on a low professionalized or politicized military are considerably greater. Finally, even the process of transfer of power back to civilians is likely to lead to politicization, since the military are likely to take a number of actions to ensure that the conditions which led to its intervention are not likely to recur. This frequently takes the form of some supervisory allocation to the military.

The Relation of Induced Politicization to Professionalization

In considering the relation of induced politicization to professionalization, two factors must be taken into account: first the degree of politicization, and second the uniformity of politicized groups within the military, i.e. whether all the politicized members belong to the same political faction.

Two general points may be made. Firstly, it must be noted that, like overt politicization, the induced type does not represent a complete negation of professionalization. However, it does have negative consequences for dimensions of professionalization which differ from the ones affected by overt politicization. The direct repercussions of induced politicization on professionalization relate to the development of the affective neutrality both concerning internal controls and external responsibility. Political promotions and recruitment tend to erode the development of neutral achievement internal norms while the increased political sensitivity of the army inhibits neutral impartial external interaction. In the second place, although induced politicization only necessarily affects these two dimensions, it can generalize to other types more easily than the overt form.

Beyond these two general points, account must be taken of the variables mentioned above. Politicization can vary enormously in degree and it follows, of course, that the lower the degree the less serious the consequences for professionalization. In this context it must be noted that a very mild form of politicization is found in many professional armies. Of equal importance to the degree of politicization is the nature of its uniformity within the army. Where the army's politicization is uniform, there need be no major consequences either for the skill level, autonomy or corporateness. Where the army has two or more rival politicized groups within its ranks, the consequences for other dimensions of professionalization become very serious. Corporateness obviously becomes an impossibility, and skill level and efficiency equally suffer. The Syrian army represents a classic case of an army completely divided by rival socialist and conservative factions, although in recent years a degree of uniformity has been established by the general dominance of one particular political faction.

The Relation of Induced Politicization to Civil-Military Relations

In attempting to examine the relation of induced politicization to the main dimensions of civil-military relations, it is necessary to consider both the degree of unity of the politicized military and the strength of the polity.

The main consequence of politicization for the establishment of controls over military political activity is the fluidity and lack of development of such controls. The development of internal controls is uncommon, but is more likely to take place when politicization in the military is uniform and does not encompass rival political groups. The establishment of insulation is equally difficult to achieve as the level of political interest of the military is likely to lead to strong resistance to any attempts by the polity to divorce it from its source of political rewards. Insulation is more likely to be achieved when the polity can strengthen itself and rely on sources of support extraneous to the military, while the military remains divided. A more common form of control relates to implicit infiltration. This is possible to achieve when the political interests of the military and the politicians overlap, due to their common origin. A very moderate form of explicit infiltration as a means of control may be found, but this never approximates the level or intensity found in one party states.

261

Where the political interests of the military coincide with those of the political leaders, a considerable degree of harmony may develop between the military and the polity. Thus many Latin American nations have passed through periods of civil-military coalition due to the common class and therefore political background of the respective leaders. Where the civil polity was able to establish itself more strongly it could gradually begin to embark on a process of insulation, e.g. Chile or Uruguay. In other nations, diversification of the recruitment of military leaders (usually to include more middle class) has led both to increased politicization and to increased disharmony with the polity when its diversification has proved faster or slower than the polity's. In this context, Argentina after 1930 has an interesting sequence of alternating progressive and reactionary coups. The most heightened situations of conflict emerge either when politicization of the military is very much out of tune with the civilian polity yet the military wishes to continue its political role, e.g. the Spanish civil war, or when the factionalization of politicization within the military mirrors an equivalent factionalization in the polity, e.g. Nigeria.

Given our previous discussion of the growth of professionalization and its relation to the nation state, we may expect under continuous nation state development the gradual erosion of politicization. Indeed politicization is only found in those nations where the military has played a long political role, e.g. Latin America, or where the polity has persistently proved weak, as in Syria. As the polity begins to develop, there begins to emerge insulation (Turkey under Ataturk represents a good example), or as army recruitment, training, or international exposure change, then there begins to emerge internalized control, e.g. Indonesia or Peru.

The consequences of induced politicization for the level of military political behaviour are largely contingent on the discussion of the means of control. A politicized military is unlikely to content itself with a pressure group role but will most frequently be found playing a conjunctive role punctuated by periods of take-over. The relative weight of the military is directly dependent on the unity and strength of the polity, the unity of the military, and the degree to which the polity is manifesting the interests of the military. Much of the history of many of the more advanced Latin American nations from 1880–1950 (approximately) could be written in terms of such oscillations. The conjunctive role which the military may play, unlike the professional military role, is not limited of course to times of national crisis.

With reference to the occasions of total intervention, several factors are of interest. Firstly, where nation state development is low, the politicized military may easily make a coup. Secondly, where politicization in the military leads to fragmentation, a bewildering series of military coups and counter-coups develops, cf. post World War 2 history of Syria. Thirdly, unlike the professionalized military, the politicized one is under no obligation, having made a coup, to attempt to return power to civilians as soon as possible, nor to restrict itself to removing the causes of the coup. Fourthly, as nation state development advances, although the politicized military may continue to make coups, it must begin to prove willing to adapt itself to nation state demands. The main way in which this has been established is for the military to transform itself into a quasi political party. In this respect, it is interesting to note how willingly and easily the Latin American military has achieved this. Such a development has proved the transition whereby the military has legitimized itself as a quasi civilian political force. The guardian role of the military in some of the more advanced Latin American nations supports this. Finally, it is interesting to note that the joint civil-military coup is almost totally restricted to politicized coups and is rarely found in the more autonomous professionalized military.

With reference to the third dimension of civil-military relations, we find again a more fluid picture. The personal motivational complex is not generally found in the politicized military of the nation state, but is restricted to the caudilly-type of activity of pre- or threshold nation state societies. It is interesting to note that such activity was found in several central American states until recently. Organized motivation is of course found but, unlike organized motivation in the professional army, is not limited to the pressure group level of political activity but may prove the motivating factor for conjunction or take-over. The most common motivational complex (particularly under nation state development) is the national sectional. In Latin America the most common sectional bond has been that of class and, to a lesser degree, region, whereas outside Latin America the ethnic group or regional bonds have been more common. National motivation is consonant with political action by a politicized army at the conjunctive level in times of national crisis, but otherwise is incompatible with the political action of the politicized military.

It would be redundant in conclusion to reiterate the many specific observations concerning the relation between professionalization, politicization and civil-military relations. Rather it is hoped that this paper has made some contribution to clarifying the dynamics of the political dimension of civil-military relations in the modern nation state.

1. The discussion of professionalization has developed primarily from Huntington's classical work (cf. S. P. HUNTINGTON, *The Soldier and the State*, Harvard U.P., 1964). However, the discussion of professionalization has atrophied somewhat given an active political role on the part of the military. Furthermore, politicization has been used rather as a catch-all concept to salvage any case of a military organization not conforming either to professionalization or to harmonious civil-military relations, and as such has been devoid of rigorous analytic content.

2. It must be pointed out that, in the broadest sense, civil-military relations include that complex of behaviour in which civilian and military interaction takes place and, as such, may encompass political, economic or cultural interaction. The general discussion of the political dimension of civil-military relations has generally been inhibited through being cast in terms of civilian control of the military. Such an approach has been derived from the Western liberal-democratic tradition (being based on ideological grounds rather than on empirical investigation). As we shall show, civil-military relations have connotations beyond the simple notion of control.

3. A corollary to the level at which the military may act involves the manner in which such activity takes place. Again, a continuum may be established ranging from peaceful constitutional action, to the threat of withdrawal of services, to the threat of the use of the means of violence, to actual deployment of the means of violence. Pressure group activity normally involves a peaceful means of action but may involve the threat of withdrawal of services, i.e. equivalent to strike action. The conjunctive role may involve any of the four manners. Total intervention invariably involves the deployment of the means of violence, although the deployment may be a bloodless one.

4. The best examples are found, outside our immediate frame of reference, in caudillismo. Nonetheless, a strong personal element lay behind the first Dahomeyan coup.

5. Latin America represents the best examples of national sectional political activity. After the decline of caudillismo and the military dictator, a common pattern to emerge was the national sectional coup. Nation state developments were underway, and then national sectional activity represented the activity of the military to prop up the ruling oligarchy. In the more advanced nations, the sectional bias has been increasingly less evident and the national more prominent, e.g. Argentine, whereas in the central American states the sectional bias still outweighs the national one.

6. Numerous examples may be cited: the Truman-MacArthur struggle, or the amount of resources to be mobilized for Vietnam, or, in the less sophisticated but nonetheless professional armies, the resentment of the Pakistani army at the cessation of hostilities by Liaquat Ali Khan.

7. We may illustrate with some of many possible examples. Thus in 1960 the Turkish army made a coup in keeping with professionalization. The government under Menderes was increasingly deviating from constitutional norms in its actions against the main opposition party, while at the same time attempting to use the military as an internal police force to further its own political ends. Or again in 1959 the Pakistan political system had become completely bankrupt. No advance was being made on major political policies, and the polity itself was increasingly racked with open strife. Further, the military was being increasingly used to put down

264

riots. Or again, in Egypt it was the very development of professionalization after 1936 which led the military to look to the international context and realize the backward position of the polity. All these cases have in common the fact that it was the military's professionalism which precipitated the extreme level of intervention.

8. The overt inculcation of extra-military political values by the polity must be clearly differentiated from the simple infusion of political values. To some degree all polities attempt to infuse various values of patriotism or national loyalty in varying degrees. In this respect, Israel represents a more overt case than Britain. However, this type of inculcation of political values differs radically from politicization in that it concerns only political values related to national security and which are therefore consonant with the role of the military; politicization involves the inculcation of values on a much broader front.

9. Overt politicization, though mainly the product of the actions of the polity, may also be stimulated to some extent by the army itself. This is usually found where a national hierarchical army develops from a former guerilla army, cf. China.

10. It may be noted that some degree of politicization is found even in many professional armies but usually only in the most minor form, i.e. a certain degree of nepotism or political favouritism in promotions. In fact, this may be openly sanctioned by the polity in such forms as the civilian executive control over the appointment of generals.

11. See R. KOLKOWICZ in J. VAN DOORN (ed.), *Armed Forces and Society*, Mouton, the Hague, 1968; and C. JOFFE, *Party and Army: Professionalization v. Political Control in the Chinese Army*, Harvard U.P., 1965.

Professionalism and Politicalization: Notes on the Military and Civilian Control

M. D. FELD*

* Center for International Affairs, Harvard University, Cambridge, Massachusetts.

I. The general topic 'Military values in a Democratic Society' should be approached with caution; not because of its novelty, but rather because of the fact that the assumed conflict is a somewhat conventional and over-worked one. It certainly does exist, but there is not much agreement as to what it involves and what it means.

To begin with, the existence of any particular group within the general society – from the family on upwards – poses problems of conflict. The conventional democratic attitude seems to be that these can almost always be resolved with mutual benefit. Indeed, it can be argued that this process of conflict and agreement is what the term society actually stands for. If a group doesn't raise such problems, e.g., interstate pen pals, it isn't really very social.

Between armed forces and a society considering itself democratic, on the other hand, this assumption is considered to be somewhat shaky. A widely spread sentiment holds that armed forces are at least a necessary evil and at worst a social menace. The prospects for mutual benefit are, in fact, held to be exceptionally limited. In case of conflict, it is felt, someone has to give in and the party that gives in loses: if the military, its effectiveness; if society, its democratic values. Similar situations, moreover, are not assumed to apply to other general social systems: monarchic, aristocratic, oligarchic, traditional, totalitarian, etc. There it is assumed that the process of negotiation can take place without either side's running prohibitive risks, mainly because the process of negotiation is controlled by an ultimate authority which can be depended upon to resolve all quandaries in terms of what it considers to be its own benefit. In democracy, however, the process of negotiation is assumed to be an open-ended one. If there is an irreconcilable conflict, therefore, it is because of the belief that the two concepts 'democracy' and 'military' are unnatural partners, and the job in order is to find out why this belief should exist.

What, first of all, do we mean by the term 'military'? A profession? A branch of the political order? A social class? A conglomerate of all three? Mostly the first, to judge by current usage. But if a profession, why the concern with social compatibility? We have recently come to hear a good deal about the social responsibilities of doctors, lawyers, academics and clergymen. But that is not the same as questioning the social utility of their calling. The assumption remains that they perform a valuable social role. With the military, however, we cannot ignore the persistent and widespread belief that their professional attitudes and skills are socially both useless and destructive, and that their failure to subvert democratic values is attributable only to political weakness on their part and the determined vigilance of their opponents.

269

It can be argued that it is the peculiar nature of military professionalism that causes the trouble. An armed force can be defined as a group trained and disciplined with the aim of its being an instrument for the systematic manipulation of violence. As such, it is clearly a threat to everyone else. But, by analogy, we could define lawyers as a group trained and disciplined as an instrument for the systematic manipulation of property transactions and official procedures, and doctors as a group designed for the systematic manipulation of bodily processes, academics of thought processes and clergymen of individual consciences and moral codes. All implicitly threatening preoccupations. So, where's the difference?

Medicine, law, education, and religion are professions which appear to pose less of a threat or which seem to be more controllable. Perhaps because a democratic society harbors the assumption that there is a basic equality when contacts can be negotiated on the basis of personal choice and when the layman is free to shop among a range of particular skills and outlooks. Moreover, in most cases the professionals we deal with are primarily members of our particular community and only secondarily members of an exclusive class. We are dealing with individuals, in a series of discrete acts. The power we give them may affect our own particular welfare, but it has virtually no effect on the basic social structure. Whereas, in the case of the military we are always dealing with a monolithic system and cannot bargain on an individual basis. Indeed, in an analogous case that where religion is so organized that society can only deal with its professional members as part of an organization and where no differences are recognizable or permitted among individual clerics, the church has generally been regarded as a threat to democratic values. It can be argued, therefore, that when we speak of democratic values, we mean pluralistic as opposed to totalitarian democracy, and that opposition to the military as a component of society is based on the belief that essentially and unalterably it is a monopolistic and monolithic structure. It is the nature of the system rather than its function that raises difficulties.

There is, as a matter of fact, a traditional ideological allegiance between non-professional, i.e., militia-type military organizations and societies more or less democratic and pluralistic in nature. Such societies held that armed forces whose officers are primarily members of some secular body and only subordinately soldiers posed no threat to civilian control. The assumed danger of military intervention comes only with the advent of professionalism; the existence of a body of officers exclusively devoted to a military life.

It is not that democratic-pluralistic type societies are opposed to violence. There is no firm ground for holding them to be either more or

270

less pacific in nature than societies of any other kind. There is, moreover, not much evidence that in societies of this kind military organizations – professional or otherwise – are more inclined than other groups to subvert the normal processes of government. The influence of big business and of professional political associations is, it can be argued, much greater and much more adept at thwarting and distorting expressions of the general will. What is really held against the professional military, it seems to me, is the belief that they are a more or less alien body, unwilling and unable to play the social game as others feel it should be played.

II. What kind of game do they play? Is it the systematic manipulation of force in an incoherently violent society that puts us off? But then how much violence is there in a military career? Consider the hypothetical case of a professional American officer born in the early 1890's. He would have gotten his commission in time for a year's combat in World War I, seen, at most, four years of action in World War II, three years battle in Korea, and then retired in the middle or late fifties; a maximum of eight years of war in a forty-odd professional career. Compare this to the career of a doctor or lawyer and the suspicion emerges that war may not be the working context of military life.

This contrast is indeed enlightening in more ways than one. Professionalism in one case limits access to society, in the other broadens it. The doctor or the lawyer, for example, may have worked during his career span as a private practitioner, for some official agency, in business or for some non-profit institution. The professional soldier, on the other hand, will have worked only in the context of an armed force, and there exclusively in the service of the state. The connection seems invariable: no political system, no armed forces; no armed forces, no military career.

Military experience then is time spent within a peculiar system. Military careers are determined almost entirely by that system's values. The professional prospects of a soldier are determined by the grades he receives in the performance of his particular assignment, be it P.X. commander or Kamikazi pilot. If his superiors give him a favorable judgment, he moves on to higher and greater responsibilities. If not, he stays where he is or drops out.

The professionalism of the military is, therefore, radically different in nature from the other social instances of this concept. There is no 'free-floating' element in its application. Lawyers, doctors and Ph. Ds may lose the approbation of their peers and still gain a satisfactory degree of personal satisfaction working for some other non-professionally oriented social institution, if society is such as to allow a sufficient degree of pluralistic differentiation. Soldiers can find professional satisfaction only within the context of an armed force.

A realistic analysis of the relationship between an armed force and its society must, therefore, concentrate on the problems which the factors of internal control and external self-sufficiency pose for a massive bureaucratic system. In doing so, it is advisable to concentrate on the routine rather than the extraordinary circumstances of military life. Combat accordingly should be seen in proper perspective. It is abnormal insofar as it subjects military operations to factors falling outside the control of the system. Its conduct exposes the 'natural' network of communication and authority to unforeseeable and often unmanageable disruptions. It forces the system to accept as members, individuals whom it would otherwise judge to be unqualified and undesirable. It exposes its operations to the judgments of uncommitted and unsympathetic outsiders. If the organization survives and prospers, it is in spite of and not because of such experiences. The strength and wellbeing of a military organization is to be measured not in terms of its relationships with actual or potential allies and opponents, but rather by its capacity to mobilize and manipulate its own internal resources.

III. In its way, all this reduces itself to the old chestnut of the armed forces being a 'state within the state.' There is, however, a vital difference. The ostensible objective of the conventional state is that of coordinating the activities of the various social groups so that they work towards some general end or set of ends. The ostensible objective of a professional armed force is to plan and carry out its operations with a minimum of interference from outside forces. This objective reflects another peculiar aspect of military professionalism, what might be called its intransitive nature, that is to say, its reluctance to act outside the organizational framework. Let me be more specific: the primary target of other professional activity is the uninitiate, laymen who are devoid of the skills in question. Normatively speaking, it is more meritorious and more rewarding to serve the ignorant rather than the informed. Among the military, on the other hand, professional reputation increases proportionately with the professional level of those who are the object of one's skills; leading a commando unit is preferable to serving with the militia, staff appointments preferable to line appointments, regular opponents preferable to guerrillas, etc. The organization not only dictates the standards of proper and improper behavior, it also sets itself up as a working model of the social system within which such conduct is to be carried out. The ultimate goal of a military career is an appointment in an organization where every individual present has attain-

272

ed the highest possible level of experience and authority, e.g., the U.S. Joint Chiefs of Staff.

Another way of phrasing this is to say that the values of military professionalism are upwardly mobile. Far from seeking to increase his circle of inferior and dependent laymen, the individual officer charts a career whose success is measured by the degree to which his associates are equal or superior in rank to him; if not in rank then at least in some quasi-ideological equivalent, valor, social caste, race or doctrinal purity. In this again, it can be contrasted with other professions whose social values are downwardly mobile, i.e., their proficiency is measured by the degree to which untrained individuals are brought under their influence and control.

As an individual operating within a social system, therefore, the professional soldier's major objective is that of closing the circle of his social contacts, so that his activities take place in a context where everyone involved is not only a member in good standing of his own organization, but also someone whose future prospects are better than average. His own professional standing is a direct reflection of the aggregate rank of his associates. In planning and evaluating his own career he accordingly has an intense interest in prescribing and maintaining the standards and practices of his peers. We can contrast this with other professions where prestige and success are measured by the nature and the number of the laymen served.

A soldier trained and indoctrinated according to a certain pattern has then a vested interest in the maintenance of that formula. It guarantees the professional value of his own skills and it provides him with a scale for measuring the status of his associates. More significantly, he will see in his associates' standing a reflection of his own. In an army where horsemanship is the measure of merit, assignment to a mule train may well be regarded as a dead end. In a system where staff planning is stressed, an unbroken succession of field and combat assignments might, even if honorific, be considered a prelude to an early retirement. Not because the skills involved are lacking in complexity or that they are unimportant, but because it is a matter of common observation and general knowledge that officers given such assignments are being denied the company and the experience of their more promising colleagues.

IV. What I have been describing are the mechanisms whereby a profession is transformed into a caste; in this particular case, the armed forces from an agency of public service into an exclusive social system. But even in the context of this admittedly hypothetical transformation, the fact remains that armed forces cannot exist in isolated form. They

273

are by necessity attached to the outside world; but their inward orientation makes this attachment fundamentally simple. In simple logical terms,
their external relations can be described as falling into two general classes:
relations with individuals who are not members of any armed force, and
relations with individuals who are members of another armed force (in the
interests of simplification, let us assume that within any given society all
soldiers are members of a single armed force.) The former class are, of
course, civilians, the latter opponents, actual or potential.

Under the conditions of pluralistic democracy, the relations between
the armed forces and civilians are, at least theoretically, quite straight-
forward. Soldiers are public officials. They are not the embodiment of
any particular set of values. They are not the chosen defenders of any
specific social or political institution. They hold public office on the
assumption that they will provide society with a specific set of services
whenever society considers itself in the need of having such services
performed.

The formal contacts of soldiers and civilians are therefore political in
nature; that is to say, they focus on the problem of the acquisition and
retention of public office. The medium of civil society provides the soldier
with a background from which he emerges and a standard by which the
social importance of his services may be measured. If soldiers need other
soldiers in order to give themselves the sense of belonging to a profession,
they need civilians in order to persuade themselves that the profession they
belong to operates in the real world, and that its criteria are objectively
imposed and officially accepted. Without the civilian alternative, military
rank would be a natural not an elective state. Without the notion of
political accountability military status would be a caste function rather
than a token of efficiency. Under these latter circumstances armed forces
could certainly exist, but they would not be professional in the generally
accepted sense. The existence of an active public permits the military
assumption that rank confers responsibility and that professional advancement is a form of compensation for personal sacrifices in the general
interest.

Relations with opponents, according to the same formal system, can be
described as being economical in nature. They provide a framework for
the allocation of resources. The existence of an active public gives the
armed forces a claim to reality; they are doing something for someone
and not merely serving themselves. The existence of opponents gives a
formal structure to the military world. It links their activities to the
material and ideological conditions of the society they serve. Enemies,
real or hypothetical, provide the professional system with a rational

outlook. They are the basis for describing the missions armed forces are expected to perform. They measure the relative utility and scarcity of available resources and provide a spectrum of competing ends and means according to which the maximum degree of security is to be attained.

Civilian control has, even in the best of circumstances, been a chancy thing; under ordinary conditions a convention, and in critical times an unwarranted luxury. As a general rule, it appears that the need society assumes it has for an armed force is inversely related to the degree of control it can exercise over the latter's operations; the greater the dependence, the lesser the controls. It may be that this is the case because of the three functions involved, only the political (that of granting commissions and subsidizing rewards) is under the direct influence of popular judgment. The other vastly more critical functions (the determination of professional standards and the formulation of operational values) are conventionally treated as a matter of caste expertise.

Assuming that a democratic society is willing to sponsor an armed force, and that it wants to have a professional one, there are three general areas in which the issue of political control must be extended: the recruitment and indoctrination of officers, the allocation of status, the determination of goals. In the matter of recruitment and indoctrination, the major concern is that of the degree to which the officer corps is, at least in origins, expected to mirror the general composition and beliefs of their society as a whole. The democratic principle would hold that the more a professional body approaches the condition of a self-perpetuating caste, the more remote it is from the values of the society it professes to serve. Conversely, an officer corps could be considered attuned to the operating consensus to the degree that its origins presented a social profile approximating the social composition of the politically active public, e.g., parliament or a national convention.

In the allocation of status the general principle should be one of bureaucratic control; namely that of the accountability of officers in terms of debatable and reviewable standards of public service. Here the assumption would be that the prime value for military responsibility is the maintenance and promulgation of egalitarian values. This, of course, runs somewhat counter to the notion of professionalism.

The third point – the determination of goals – now seems to present the broadest range of problems. It covers not only the decision to go to war and who makes it, but also the description of the hypothetical range of possible conflicts and the instruments and methods with which they are to be conducted. In essence it poses the problems of what sort of wars are rational for a given society, how the decision to undertake them is to be made, and what sort of behavior is permissible in their name. It is this point that has really upset the balance. There was a time when the choice was limited by the boundaries of the state and the conventions of warfare. Modern technology has, however, given advanced societies the capacity to determine in arbitrary fashion where their frontiers are, and to devise in equally determined and arbitrary fashion the methods and instruments for 'defending' them. An advanced armed force does not solve problems so much as it creates them. Once in existence, it embarks upon a race to anticipate the reactions its simple presence will logically elicit from any presumably hostile power. The very anticipation creates a spiralling process.

Ultimate control then would depend upon the existence of a general public with a belief in its own rational understanding of military problems as firm as that of the professional body with whom they are to debate them, and with that, the belief that military expertise is more public than it has been and less professional than it seems.

Models of Civil-Military Relationships at the Elite Level

D. R. SEGAL*
M. W. SEGAL**

* University of Michigan.
** Eastern Michigan University.

Discourse on the quality of civil-military relations in the United States has focused on the possible existence of an unholy alliance between military organization and industrial bureaucracy, dating back to C. Wright Mills' (1956) warning us of *the power elite* and Dwight D. Eisenhower's warning us of *the military-industrial complex* (see for example Pilisuk and Hayden, 1965). It is our thesis that differences in the nature of interpersonal networks between military and civilian arenas and differences between military and civilian organizational structure preclude the development of a power elite as Mills saw it. These same factors make military organization in the United States unresponsive to public opinion. If relations between the military and civilian sectors of American society are indeed unholy, they are unholy in ways not anticipated by critics of the military-industrial complex.

THE POWER ELITE MODEL

The basic assumption underlying Mills' formulation was that a high degree of interpersonal contact takes place among corporation executives, military leaders and elected public officials in both formal and informal settings. These three groups of people were purported to come from similar social backgrounds, to travel in the same social circles and to take each other's interests into account in the process of making decisions within their own organizational spheres.

Similarity of background would certainly expedite sociability among these three groups. From what we know of their backgrounds, they are not all that similar.

American business leaders tend to be the sons of business leaders, and in general are recruited from the higher strata of society. They tend to come from the Middle Atlantic, New England, and Pacific Coast States, and are likely to have been born in large urban areas. Most tend to be college educated (Warner and Abegglen, 1955). Military leaders also tend to come from high status backgrounds, with over half their fathers having been in business and the professions (Warner *et al.*, 1963). Military leaders, however, are far more likely than corporation officials to come from rural areas, and to overrepresent the southern states (Janowitz, 1960). In addition, of course, military leaders and corporation executives receive their higher educations at different institutions, the former being preponderantly military academy graduates. Thus, the ranking officers of the American armed forces differ from their industrial counterparts in terms of urbanization, regionalism, and ties to institutions of higher education.

Although we are not concerned here with differences among the civilian elements of the power elite, let us note that such differences exist. Hacker (1961), in a comparative study of u.s. Senators and corporation presidents, noted that while both groups were roughly geographically representative, senators tended to have been raised in rural areas, while corporation presidents came from urban centers. Similarly, although both groups were college educated, the corporation executives were more likely to have gone to Ivy League schools, while senators were more likely to have attended state universities. Hacker argues that these background differences lead to disparate images of society and a lack of communication between these groups.

THE QUALITY OF INTERPERSONAL RELATIONS

Beyond the differences in social background that exist among the groups that are postulated to comprise the power elite, our knowledge of human sociability in modern society would lead us to question the existence of a military-industrial clique as described by Mills.

In the ideal-typical simple society, individuals do not have highly differentiated role sets, and they relate to each other as total personalities rather than in the context of specific social or economic exchanges. Such societies are characterized by high levels of affective investment in one's interpersonal relations (Tönnies, 1957). In complex modern societies, by contrast, individuals have highly differentiated role sets and relate to others in the context of these roles rather than as total personalities. Such relationships tend to be constrained by the temporal and spatial limits associated with specific roles. They are functionally related to the roles being played, and are characterized by relatively low levels of intimacy and affect. Such affective neutrality is one of the hallmarks of ideal-typical bureaucratic organization. Contemporary organization theory suggests that such alienation from one's social contacts is even more characteristic of post-bureaucratic society (Bennis and Slater, 1969; Riesman, Potter and Watson, 1960).

There are, of course, arenas of modern life that may be characterized by intense primordial affective ties, rather than by secondary relationships. The most common of these is defined by life-cycle phase. During childhood, roles are not highly differentiated. The child has the same persons as friends, neighbors and school-mates, and develops deep attachments to them. The ties that are developed later in life with associates who are either neighbors or work-mates or fellow club members do not seem to be as intensive, due in all likelihood to the differentiation and compartmentalization of these roles (Granovetter, 1969). The weakening of social ties with age is reflected in sociometric studies, which indicate that friendship choices are less likely to be reciprocal in older than in younger groups (Laumann, 1969).

Some sectors of modern adult life are constrained by occupational or institutional boundaries in such a way that people either do not have highly differentiated role sets, or the other people with whom they come into contact tend to comprise a constant set regardless of what roles they are playing. The former may be exemplified by the total institution – the institution that circumscribes the totality of the lives of its inhabitants (Goffman, 1961). Both the boundary conditions and the low level of social differentiation in the total institutions discussed by Goffman are reminiscent of simple societies and childhood peer groups. Were it not for the tendency of their inmates to be characterized by affective disorders, we would anticipate close primary ties among them.

Certain occupations place similar although less compulsory constraints on their members, in that they define the set of individuals with whom a member is likely to associate both on and off the job. Thus, at the very least, the roles of friend and workmate are superimposed. Lipset, Trow and Coleman (1956) demonstrate that this is the case among typographers.

Among the occupational groups that expedite and encourage primary relationships, the military profession ranks high. Having discovered that it is group cohesion rather than ideological commitment that makes effective fighting men (Shils and Janowitz, 1948), the American military services have explicitly set out to build cohesive organizational units (cf. Shils, 1950).

Again, sociometric data are useful in demonstrating differences in group cohesion. Davis and Leinhardt (1967) analyzed the structure of 30 adult groups and 30 student groups selected randomly from an archive of sociograms, in an effort to test seven predictions regarding group structure based upon Homans' (1950) propositions. Their data indicate that among the military adult groups, an average of 1.2 of the 7 predictions per group were unsupported by the data. The corresponding figures for the student samples and for the adult non-military samples were 2.03 and 2.24 respectively. That is, the military groups formed more solidary subgroups on bases anticipated by Homans than even the student groups did, age differences notwithstanding.

281

An additional indicator of the degree to which military structure is based on primary relations and thus differentiated from civilian life is the establishment of 'traditions' of military careers within families. Warner *et al.* (1963) report that 9 per cent of the military leaders they studied had fathers in the armed forces at the time they themselves entered military service. While only a minority of military officers seem to be recruited through such ascriptive in-breeding, there is clearly a higher rate of occupational immobility with regard to the military than is the case for other sectors of the American labor force.

In brief, then, we suggest that styles of interpersonal life differ between the civilian and military arenas. The military is characterized by strong affective ties to one's fellow-workers, supported in some cases by affective ties to the military profession as a family tradition. The modern civilian administrator, on the other hand, is not strongly tied to his fellow-workers on affective grounds, and has only moderately stronger ties to friends and neighbors who, unlike the case of the military, are unlikely to be fellow-workers.

The civilian administrator either in the governmental or corporate sphere is unlikely to involve himself in a highly cohesive power-elite. Such a degree of cohesion is foreign to his interpersonal style. The military leader, for his part, is unlikely to invest a great deal of affect in such compartmentalized contacts. His affective ties are elsewhere.

THE BUREAUCRAT VERSUS THE POST-BUREAUCRAT

Another aspect of the power-elite model is the interchangeability of personnel between military and civilian organization. Clearly, there is no lateral entry of members of the political or corporate elites to the upper reaches of the military hierarchy. There is some flow of personnel in the other direction, but its magnitude is not great. Biderman and Sharp (1968) point out that fewer than 30 per cent of retired officers work for large business establishments, and defence industries make up only one sub-group of such establishments. Moreover, less than 30 per cent of retired officers are in business and managerial positions. It is unlikely that these two sets are totally overlapping. Therefore, the number of retired officers who assume high level positions in defence industries cannot be great. Further, those that do move into the industrial structure are unlikely to have the necessary skills to reach the highest strata of that structure.

Segal (1970) has suggested a structural explanation for the low level of civil-military managerial interchangeability. On the basis of recent theories of formal organization, he suggests that management in the civilian context has come to be increasingly professionalized. Large corporations have come to be run not by personnel who have demonstrated competence with regard to the specific product or service that the organization provides, but rather by professional administrators. These men may have very little familiarity with the specific production processes within their organizations. Rather, they have the ability to establish organizational climates within which coordination and collaboration are expedited, so that 'technocrats' can deal with specific operational problems. These organizational skills are postulated to be transferable among corporate enterprises (Bennis and Slater, 1969).

Military organization, on the other hand, is thought to approach more and more closely the bureaucratic model (Grusky, 1964). Bureaucratic careers are characterized by upward mobility within the organizational structure on the basis of demonstrated competence in the provision of the product or service that the organization supplies. In the case of the military this service is combat, and several studies have shown that it is the combat specialists who ascend to the top strata of the American military hierarchy (Van Riper and Unwalla, 1965). Indeed, if military organization in fact requires 'generalist' administrative skills at the top level as civilian bureaucracies are purported to, then the promotion of officers to general and admiral grade on the basis of combat specialist skills may be seen as a special case of the Peter Principle, viz., military officers are promoted to their own levels of incompetence because the skills on the basis of which they are evaluated has nothing to do with the job they are expected to perform at the highest levels of the structure (cf. Peter and Hull, 1970).

MODELS OF MILITARY STRUCTURE AND CIVIL-MILITARY
RELATIONS

We have suggested three different models of elite social structure in military organization. Each of these models has different implications for the structure of civil-military relations at the elite level. The first, which we may call the pre-bureaucratic model, suggests traditionalistic recruitment bases, and intense affective ties among military personnel. We would anticipate that careers in such an organization would be based on ascriptive non-rational criteria. We would expect such a structure to be associated with a military ideology that viewed the military as an active and largely autonomous force in the political system (Derthick, 1962).

283

The second model is the bureaucratic model, which is characterized by a broadened recruitment base, and by careers oriented toward promotion based upon achievement with regard to rational criteria of evaluation. These criteria, in turn, are postulated to reflect the mission of the organization: in the case of the military, combat expertise. The ideological stance of the ideal-typical bureaucratic military organization is one of affective neutrality. We would expect such an organization not to be involved in the formulation of political decisions, but rather to implement decisions involving military activity made within the civilian governmental structure.

Finally, we have suggested a post-bureaucratic model of organization in which people would be expected to reach the top levels of military structure on the basis of organizational and administrative skills, rather than combat skills. Because of isomorphism with civilian corporate structure, we suggest that the military leader qua professional manager would be most comfortable in the company of professional colleagues who manage corporations in the civilian sector, and would therefore be the most likely type to participate in a military-industrial directorate.

THE UNITED STATES NAVY AS A CASE IN POINT

Segal (1970) has elsewhere presented data on the United States Air Force. Since the Air Force is the newest branch of the American armed forces and has the most complex technology of the armed services, it was expected that it would have a highly rationalized structure. It was indeed drawn to approximate the bureaucratic model, but combat rather than administrative skills were shown to be the criteria on which promotion to general officer grade and assignment to principal command and staff positions were based.

Previous research suggests that the bureaucratic model is a poor one for the United States Navy. Davis (1948) suggests that although the Navy aspires to a bureaucratic structure, it is characterized by buck-passing, excessive legalism, insulation from civilian life, and ceremonialism. All of these factors mitigate against organizational rationality. Similarly, Turner (1947) sees conflicts between orders from superiors, on the one hand, and regulations on the other, as well as the underlying structure of the Navy both in terms of the juxtaposition of rank and role and the network of informal relationships as mitigating against efficient bureaucratic functioning. Indeed, we can conclude from these studies that the Navy is at the very least less bureaucratized than the Air Force, and therefore less similar in structure to civilian corporate organization. The Navy might best be characterized as a 'mock bureaucracy' (cf. Gouldner, 1954: 182 ff.).

There is another sense, however, in which the Navy is worthy of our consideration. The Navy is the ranking service in terms of the social background of its officers (Janowitz, 1960: 81). Therefore, if any branch of service is likely to have social networks that extend into the civilian elite, and to promote officers through its hierarchy on the basis of their positions in this network, the Navy is likely to be that branch.

DATA

The homogeneity of the Navy elite in terms of educational background, as well as the incidence of managerial as against combat skills in this elite is indicated by data in the Navy Register. Segal's (1967) data on the Navy indicated that in 1951 and 1964, all vice-admirals, admirals, and fleet admirals of the United States Navy were naval academy graduates. Some non-academy officers did attain rear admiral rank. As Table 1 demonstrates, our analysis of the educational backgrounds of u.s. Navy

Table 1. Per cent of U.S. Navy admirals with academy degrees: 1958, 1962, 1968

Officer rank	1958		1962		1968	
	% academy	N	% academy	N	% academy	N
Fleet Admiral	100	2	100	1	—	—
Admiral	100	7	100	7	100	9
Vice Admiral	100	30	100	32	100	35
Rear Admiral	99	206	98	207	92	212

Source: *United States Navy Register*, Adjutant General's Office, 1958; *Register of Commissioned Officers of the United States Navy and Marine Corps and Reserve Officers on Active Duty*, Adjutant General's Office, 1962 and 1968.

admirals in 1958, 1962 and 1968 confirms this finding. In all three years, all admirals in the top three grades were academy graduates. While there is increasing representation of non-academy officers at rear admiral grade, this representation is still minuscule. It is clear that no old school tie links the Navy elite to the political or economic directorate.

285

Table 2. *Per cent of U.S. Navy admirals with management* or combat** training: 1952, 1958, 1962, 1968*

Rank	1952			1958			1962			1968		
	mngt.	cmbt.	n	mngt.	cmbt.	n	mngt.	cmbt.	n	mngt.	cmbt.	n
Fleet Admiral	—	67	3	—	50	2	—	100	1	—	—	—
Admiral	—	60	5	—	43	7	—	100	7	—	100	9
Vice Admiral	—	70	23	—	80	30	3	100	32	—	100	35
Rear Admiral	—	67	193	6	76	206	6	92	207	5	95	214

* Management training: post-graduate training in business administration, management, industrial engineering, industrial management, naval administration, island government, personnel administration financial management, public administration, police administration, advertising, commerce, comptrollership, computer systems management, economics and systems analysis, foreign trade, hospital administration, hotel administration, logistics management, petroleum management, procurement management, systems inventory management, transportation administration.

** Combat training: destroyer command, naval aviation, submarine duty, submarine command, Air Command and Staff School, Air War College, Armed Forces Staff College, Army War College, Command and General Staff College, General Line School, Imperial Defence College, National War College, Naval War College, Amphibious Warfare School, Canadian Defence College, NATO Defence College, United Kingdom Joint Services Staff College, French Naval War College, Spanish Naval War College, Inter-American Defence College, Marine Corps Command and Staff College, Royal Naval Staff College, Royal Air Force Staff College, German General Staff College, Indian National Defence Service Staff College, post-graduate study in weapons systems, nautical science, naval science, merchant marine.

Source: *United States Navy Register*, Adjutant General's Office, 1952, 1958; *Register of Commissioned Officers of the United States Navy and Marine Corps and Reserve Officers on Active Duty*, Adjutant General's Office, 1962, 1968.

These figures include all line officers at flag rank for 1952 and 1958. The figures for 1962 and 1968 include all unrestricted line flag officers. In addition, the following designated categories formerly included in general line listings are retained for comparability: (for 1962) engineering duty, aeronautical engineering, SDO cryptology, SDO law, SDO intelligence, (for 1968) engineering duty, aeronautical engineering, SDO cryptology, naval intelligence, judge advocate general's corps. The services not included for any year are: supply corps, corps of civil engineers, TAR, medical service, dental service, chaplain service, nurse corps.

As a test of the bureaucratic versus professional management models of elite ascent, we coded the training experience of U.S. Navy admirals on the basis of whether they were geared toward administrative or combat training. Our results are presented in Table 2. The most dramatic datum in this table is the dearth of managerial training among the men who run the Navy. No admirals or fleet-admirals in any of the four years studied had such training. By 1958, a small percentage of rear admirals had received such training, and the percentage has remained relatively constant since, with little indication that rear admirals so trained will be promoted to higher flag ranks.

With regard to advanced training in combat skills, on the other hand, there is an upward trend at all grades, reaching unanimity at all grades above rear admiral by 1968.

While not all rear admirals have received in-service combat training, the trend is clear at this grade. Sixty-seven per cent of the 1952 cohort of rear admirals had received such training. By 1968 the figure was up to 95 per cent. Moreover, given the unanimity of combat training at the top three flag grades, it would be reasonable to anticipate that only rear admirals with such training will be promoted to those grades in the future. The fact that the skills of the ranking admirals of the Navy differ from those of the captains of industry both in their lack of training in administrative matters and in their explicit training in activities that are overtly disvalued (if covertly cherished) by a civil society where the value of human life is sacred, suggests further barriers to civil-military elite integration.

Table 3. Per cent of U.S. Navy admirals with aviation training: 1952, 1958, 1962, 1968

	1952		1958		1962		1968	
Officer rank	% aviator	N	% aviator	N	% aviator	N	% aviator	N
Fleet Admiral	—	3	—	2	—	1	—	—
Admiral	40	5	43	7	57	7	33	9
Vice Admiral	35	23	47	30	44	32	43	35
Rear Admiral	35	193	36	206	39	207	40	212

Source: *United States Navy Register,* 1952 and 1958; *Register of Commissioned Officers of the United States Navy and Marine Corps, and Reserve Officers on Active Duty,* 1962 and 1968.

The importance of combat skills for advancement in the Navy may be seen more specifically with regard to adaptations to aviation technology at flag grade. These data are presented in Table 3. While we are dealing here with only one particular kind of combat skill, note that by 1968, 40 per cent of the rear admirals had aviation training.

Implicit in our earlier discussion was an expectation that the Navy would be characterized by a traditionalistic pre-bureaucratic command structure. Our data, however, suggest that the Navy might be described by the same model that fits the non-traditional and highly technologized u.s. Air Force: a bureaucratic model in which promotion to the top strata of the hierarchy is based upon mission-oriented skills.

DISCUSSION

We have suggested three ideal-typical models of structural modernity for military organizations. Each model is characterized by skill distributions and styles of interpersonal relations that have implications for the development of a military-industrial power elite.

We had anticipated finding the pre-bureaucratic model to most closely describe the structure of the u.s. Navy. Our analysis of the formal training experiences associated with mobility through the Navy hierarchy to flag grade, however, suggests that the bureaucratic model may fit best. Military family traditionalism, of course, is likely to create deviations in a pre-bureaucratic direction.

The bureaucratic structure of military organization poses two major obstacles to the formation of a military-industrial cabal. First, the academy-trained and combat oriented military bureaucrat has little in common with the professional civilian executive, in terms of either background or interest. Second, one of the characteristics of bureaucratic organization is the maintenance of a posture of ethical neutrality.

The assumption of ethical neutrality does not preclude the military officer from valuing military activity positively, or from viewing warfare as a reasonable way to conduct foreign affairs. It should prevent the military from being the strongest pro-war lobby, while contributing to the development of a political environment that nurtures sentiments of belligerence originating in other quarters.

Our basic position is in agreement with that of Admiral Hyman Rickover, who feels that the military isn't a contributing partner to a 'military-industrial complex', but rather is an agency that is used to the economic advantage of certain sectors of American industry. We similarly agree (if not sympathize) with corporation executives who feel that they should get top billing, viz., that social scientists and journalists should speak about the industrial-military complex, although they are probably overstating the role of the military.

We concur with Fusfeld's (1968) analysis, which traces America's willingness to engage in foreign wars to the corporations that profit from those wars. The magnitude of federal monies spent on the military is frequently cited as evidence of the existence of a military-industrial complex. If indeed military expenditures represent 15 per cent of American GNP, as Fusfeld estimates, we view this as the best evidence that it is private corporations, rather than the military, that reap the spoils of war.

This is not a uniform indictment of the American corporate structure. We know that some industries, notably ordnance, aerospace, primary metals and marine transportation stand to lose the most if peace breaks out (see Leontief and Hoffenberg, 1961). Others, such as construction, stand to gain. In the aggregate, however, the costs of war seem to be carried most by the consumer, who has trouble buying butter when the government is buying guns, and only secondarily by the butter-producing industries (cf. Russett, 1969).

Another bit of evidence frequently cited for the existence of a military-industrial complex is that some high ranking military officers do indeed move into corporate positions after retirement. We have argued above that the magnitude of such mobility is small, and that the officers who make such moves are unlikely to have the necessary skills to reach the top of the corporate hierarchy. There are other points to consider as well.

Perhaps most often overlooked is the fact that the earlier an officer terminates his military career to enter civilian industry, the lower his military rank when he leaves. Even those officers who leave after 20 or 25 years of service are far more likely to be colonels or brigadier generals than they are to be major generals or generals. Thus, such mobility does not move military elites into civilian industry, although it may provide linkages between civilian and military elites to the extent that the colonels who enter industry were academy class-mates and friends of the generals and admirals who remain in the military. The crucial point, however, is that it is *not* the military elites who are moving into civilian industry.

A second point is that the concentration of economic power in the United States has been attributed largely to interlocking directorates among banks and large corporations. The military is not directly involved in these networks of interlocks. While occasionally retired high ranking military officers may be appointed to the boards of directors of large corporations and may use friendships with the 'military directorate' in the interest of their corporations, what is important here is that such activity takes place *after* the completion of the military career of the person involved. Thus, military participation is through cooptation, not cooperation.

These structural factors notwithstanding, the military has been identified by the antiwar movement in the United States as the primary evil in the military-industrial complex. Far more of the movements' resources have been aimed at severing university relations with the Reserved Officers Training Corps (ROTC), preventing universities from accepting Department of Defence research contracts and grants, interfering with military recruiting, demonstrating in and around armed forces installations, and harassing the Selective Service than with protesting the role of private corporations in the war effort. While such protests have occurred (as in the case of Dow stockholders who objected to the manufacture of napalm or the relatively isolated instances of harassment of industrial recruiters), demonstrations against private corporations in the United States are far more likely to be rooted in policies regarding pollution or discrimination against minority group members and women in employment than they are to confront the issue of war profiteering.

This focus on the military has at least two important consequences for American society. First, by channeling the resources of the antiwar movement away from what we see as the true economic impetus of American military activity, it probably extends the life of military operations, rather than hastening their demise.

Secondly, the success that the antiwar movement has experienced in moving ROTC units off campuses and in opposing conscription has placed restrictions in the input of civilian sensitivities into the armed forces. We concur with Moscos' (1970) observation that as the military becomes increasingly separated from civilian society, greater latitude for international irresponsibility on the part of civilian leaders is a consequence that may be anticipated.

REFERENCES

BENNIS, Warren G. and Philip E. SLATER, *The Temporary Society*. New York: Harper, 1969.
BIDERMAN, Albert D. and Laure M. SHARP, 'The convergence of military and civilian occupational structures.' *American Journal of Sociology*, 73 (January): 381–399, 1968.
DAVIS, Arthur K., 'Bureaucratic patterns in the Navy officers corps.' *Social Forces*, 27: 143–153, 1948.
DAVIS, James A. and Samuel LEINHARDT, 'The structure of positive interpersonal relations in small groups.' Dartmouth College, mimeo, 1967.
DERTHICK, Martha, 'Militia lobby in the missile age,' pp. 190–234 in Samuel P. HUNTINGTON, ed., *Changing Patterns of Military Politics*. New York: Free Press, 1962.
FUSFELD, Daniel R., *Fascist Democracy in the United States*. Paper presented to the University of Michigan-Western Electric Symposium on the Corporation at Mid-Century. Ann Arbor, Sept. 21, 1968.
GOFFMAN, Erving, *Asylums*. Doubleday: Garden City, 1961.
GOULDNER, Alvin W., *Patterns of Industrial Bureaucracy*. Glencoe: Free Press, 1954.
GRANOVETTER, Mark, 'Alienation reconsidered: the strength of weak ties.' Department of Social Relations, Harvard University, mimeo, 1969.
GRUSKY, Oscar, 'The effects of succession,' pp. 83–111 in Morris JANOWITZ (ed.), *The New Military*. New York: Russell Sage Foundation, 1964.
HACKER, Andrew, 'The elected and the anointed: two American elites.' *American Political Science Review*, 55 (Sept.): 539–549, 1961.
HOMANS, George C., *The Human Group*. New York: Harcourt Brace, 1950.
JANOWITZ, Morris, *The Professional Soldier*. Glencoe: Free Press, 1960.
LAUMANN, Edward O., 'Friends of urban men.' *Sociometry*, 32 (March): 54–69, 1969.
LEONTIEF, Wassily and Marvin HOFFENBERG, 'The economic effects of disarmament.' *Scientific American*, 204 (April): 47–55, 1951.
LIPSET, Seymour Martin, Martin TROW, James COLEMAN, *Union Democracy*. Glencoe: Free Press, 1956.
MILLS, C. Wright, *The Power Elite*. New York: Oxford University Press, 1956.
MOSCOS, Charles C., *The American Enlisted Man*. New York: Russell Sage, 1970.
PETER, Laurence J. and Raymond HULL, *The Peter Principle*. New York: Bantam, 1970.
PILISUK, Marc and Thomas HAYDEN, 'Is there a military-industrial complex which prevents peace?' *Journal of Social Issues*, 21: 67–117, 1965.
RIESMAN, David, Robert J. POTTER and Jeanne WATSON, 'Sociability, permissiveness and equality.' *Psychiatry*, 23 (November): 323–340, 1960.
RUSSETT, Bruce M., 'The price of war.' *Transaction*, 6 (October): 28–35, 1969.
SEGAL, David R., 'Selective promotion in officer cohorts.' *Sociological Quarterly*, 8 (Spring): 199–206, 1967.
SEGAL, David R., *Civil-Military Differentiation in the New Industrial State*. Paper presented to the Working Group on Armed Forces and Society, VIIth World Congress of Sociology. Varna, Bulgaria, September, 1970.
SHILS, Edward A., 'Primary groups in the American army,' pp. 16–39 in Robert K. MERTON and Paul F. LAZARSFELD (eds.), *Continuities in Social Research: Studies in the Scope and Method of 'The American Soldier.'* New York: Free Press of Glencoe, 1950.
SHILS, Edward A. and Morris JANOWITZ, 'Cohesion and disintegration in the Wehrmacht in World War II.' *Public Opinion Quarterly*, 12 (Summer): 280–315, 1948.
TÖNNIES, Ferdinand, *Community and Society*. Ed. and trans. by Charles P. Loomis. East Lansing: Michigan State University Press, 1957.

TURNER, Ralph H. 'The Navy disbursing officer as a bureaucrat.' *American Sociological Review*, 12: 342–348, 1947.

VAN RIPER, Paul P. and Darab B. UNWALLA, 'Military careers at the executive level.' *Administrative Science Quarterly*, 9: 421–436, 1965.

WARNER, W. L. and J. ABEGGLEN, *Big Business Leaders in America*. New York: Harper, 1955.

WARNER, W. Lloyd, Paul P. VAN RIPER, Norman H. MARTIN, Orvis F. COLLINS, *The American Federal Executive*. New Haven: Yale University Press, 1963.

Adaptive Politics, Social Learning, and Military Institutions

D. B. BOBROW*

* Professor of Political Science and Public Affairs and Director, Quigley Center of International Studies, University of Minnesota; the views expressed in this paper are solely those of the author.

Rates and forms of change in post-industrial societies will increasingly test the viability of democratic political systems. Social learning must become faster and more powerful as the deadline on political demands becomes shorter and the complexity and variety of demands become greater. The military can play an almost uniquely helpful role in social learning. Social scientists have the qualifications and much of the responsibility for use of the military as a national resource for the testing and evaluation of social inventions.

These views imply significant changes in military institutions. However, changes of one kind or another will occur whether or not we adopt the social learning perspective. The other major possibilities for post-industrial societies in the next decade involve: virtual elimination of military establishments; severe deterioration in military command and control; or the emergence of politically coercive and socially homogeneous armed forces. Each of these alternatives seems markedly unattractive compared with the social learning option.

The purpose of this paper is to summarize the rationale for the assertions in the first paragraph and to indicate the content of a social learning role for the military. Accordingly, the first part of the paper suggests alternative views of (a) key relationships between the political order and the military, and (b) how social scientists can relate to problems of the military role. Those distinctions help clarify the starting points for the analysis and recommendations contained in the rest of the paper. In the second section, I review a number of historically familiar prescriptions for the role of the military vis-à-vis the political order and point out their shortcomings relative to my view of key political processes and collective welfare. The last two sections are more concerned with the future and less with intellectual history. One asserts a set of normative goals for the political process and parameters which affect their pursuit. The parameters are provided by domestic social trends and military developments. The other and final section develops the social learning role as a means to achieve political process goals within the constraints of the parameters mentioned earlier.

I do not mean to contend that the approach taken here is the only or the most valuable way to conceive of the role of the military. It does seem to me to be an important and relatively unattended point of view. Parenthetically, given increased NATO interest in social as distinct from military problems, it suggests a way of combining reassessment of member country priorities with previously established organizational patterns focused on the armed forces.

The main purpose of the following paragraphs is to clarify the different subjects which we may refer to under the general labels of military-polity relations and the contributions of social scientists to the role of the military. I will distinguish a variety of perspectives and indicate which ones govern the rest of this essay.

Central Processes in the Political Order

Any discussion about the role of the military in politics must begin with some assumptions about what are the central processes in the political order. In fact, there is no consensus on what are the key political processes and thus no agreement on what matters most for describing and prescribing the military role. It seems useful to summarize four major formulations and their implications for assessing the role of the military.

1. *Participation through Office-holding.* The central process of politics is gaining and holding offices in public organizations. Accordingly, the military role consists of active-duty, reserve, or veteran presence in government positions. For descriptive purposes, this view leads to tabulations of military vs. civilian office-holding; for prescriptive purposes, it leads to formal rules about eligibility for office. A variety of elite studies rest on the participation perspective.[1]

2. *Control.* The central process of politics is the authority to make others follow one's preference when they hold a different preference. In this perspective of who does what to whom, the military role consists of the ability to impose its preferences on civilians. The control perspective leads analysts to describe the independence and cohesion of military command and control chains relative to those manned by civilians, and the extent to which civilians require military support or at least acquiescence. For prescriptive purposes, it leads to efforts to divide those who control instruments of coercion (e.g., service rivalry), to penetrate military hierarchy (e.g., political commissars), and to create consensus among civilians on what are legitimate limits of military concerns.[2]

3. *Resource Allocation.* The central process of politics is the allocation of utilities (Lasswell's Who Gets What, When and How).[3] Accordingly, the military role is in effect that portion of the utilities, e.g., money or deference, in the public sector allocated to military matters. A minimal description consists of that portion of government budgets allocated to

military purposes. These include relevant technological, industrial, and intellectual activities by civilians as well as direct allocations to the uniformed services. A more comprehensive description also includes the ability of the military and its associates to generate expenditure opportunities, the society's acceptance of opportunity costs in domestic sectors, and the degree to which citizens agree that military resources are public goods. Prescriptions about how to constrain the military role tend to emphasize cutting military budgets, restricting the development of new weapons systems, calling attention to the costs in lost domestic programs of military expenditures, and demonstrating how the burdens and rewards from military resources are distributed inequitably.[4]

4. *Steering*. The central process of politics consists of setting goals and modifying strategies and tactics to achieve them in the light of feedback, that is, of subsequent information about internal and external situations. If we begin from the steering perspective formulated by Karl Deutsch,[5] we treat the military role as equivalent to the weight of military issues in national goals and of military considerations and organizations in feedback. Descriptively, we assess to what extent national goals stress military threat and force posture. We also estimate to what extent intelligence about foreign and domestic developments, first, stresses capabilities and intentions for violence, and, second, reaches political leaders through military organizations. Prescriptively, the steering approach leads us to concentrate on: (*a*) conceiving and making salient other goals; (*b*) intelligence about factors other than order of battle, military technology, and industrial base; and (*c*) curtailing the role of the defence establishments in appraising foreign and domestic developments.

My view is that the steering process is central and that the others primarily have importance as they affect it. Accordingly, it becomes appropriate to evaluate and design the role of the military in terms of that process. It also becomes appropriate to treat the military not as a 'concrete structure' whose members are identified by organizational affiliation, but as an 'analytic structure' whose members have that status as they are primarily concerned with external coercive threats and coercive instruments to handle them.[6]

Social Science and the Role of the Military

As the introduction indicated, this paper intends not only to suggest a role for the military in economically advanced societies, but also to

297

suggest a role for social scientists in achieving it. Accordingly, it seems useful to engage in a similar exercise as that in the preceding section. This time, however, our focus is the role of the social scientist. I will distinguish five possibilities.

1. *Theory*. The social science contribution is an ahistorical deductive apparatus which yields important and testable derivations. Efforts to build theory about the military have not been particularly successful.[7] The phenomena at hand are complex and difficult to test. Although theories about the behavior of large organizations are relatively applicable and advanced, however, they deal primarily with their internal behavior and not with their relations to other organized and unorganized elements in a social system. Military-polity issues primarily involve such relations. Even if we are successful, theory has few direct implications for policy.

2. *Understanding Historical Instances*. Here the social scientist dissects specific cases and relates them to general perspectives. This has been done for a variety of military institutions in particular countries at particular points in time.[8] These inquiries can be suggestive; they do not provide us with answers or a mechanism for arriving at answers to the questions: what will bring the military to behave in a particular way, or how ought it to behave if we desire a particular social outcome.

3. *Warning*. The social scientist alerts us to probable undesirable future states of affairs. For warnings about the military to be reliable, we need to have time-series observations on military attributes and actions which feed into models of the military role. Unfortunately we have such data for very few military institutions and for very few of their relationships with civilian society. Even when we do, such analyses point out problems but do not provide even partial solutions.

4. *Institutional Improvement*. Social science can design procedures to improve internal military performances. There is a long and notable list of accomplishments of this engineering kind, particularly with regard to personnel management. However, such work begins by assuming that assisting the military to improve its own performance goals is equivalent to improving the social utility of the military.

5. *Public Policy*. In a public policy role, social scientists seek to improve the contribution of social resources to particular goals for the political system rather than for a particular bureaucracy. Military budgets,

298

personnel skills, equipment, and facilities are such resources. The initial analytic problem consists of locating points of leverage on the realization of political goals, i.e., points where particular amounts and types or resources and information or particular structures for handling resources and information impact strongly on political system outcomes. With that knowledge, social scientists then proceed to design and evaluate programs to use the leverage points. In contrast to the institutional improvement role, the public policy mode assumes no necessary relationship between collective wellbeing and improved military performance.

This paper deals with the role of the military as it affects the steering performance of the political system, and approaches that problem from a public policy perspective.

PRESCRIPTIONS AND DILEMMAS

The problems posed by the relationships between the military and the political order have led in the past to a small number of rather general prescribed solutions. It seems useful to summarize these and point out the probable negative implications associated with them for the quality of the political steering process. Many of the disadvantages noted below would not be important were we to concentrate instead on office-holding, control, or resource consumption by the military.

1. *Neutrality and Obedience.* The military obeys instructions from a civilian government no matter how unrepresentative or ill-advised those instructions may be. The military also views its mission narrowly, that is, as the use of coercion. However, obedience to a ruling elite is not in fact political neutrality. Civilian ruling groups frequently are not neutral in their ties to diverse elements in the population and often are not adaptive to domestic and international realities. Coercive threats and actions by the military as authorized by a ruling group frequently do not benefit all citizens equally. In sum, the prescription is conducive to adaptive politics if the government meets certain conditions; it is inimical to that end otherwise.[9]

2. *Civilian Control.* Members of the uniformed services come under the direction of civilian participants in the military institution, for example, as in the United States Department of Defence. The solution assumes that civilians inherently will have significantly less parochial views on the needs of the political system than the military. Accordingly, civilian controllers will not bias the steering mechanism of the polity as the

299

military would. In practice, there is reason to doubt the validity of the assumption. It requires that the civilians in question differ with the uniformed military more than they differ with civilians outside the defence establishment. A more likely situation is that the civilian regulators become absorbed in a community with the regulated of relatively shared priorities and beliefs about what are reasonable national interest requirements. The regulated military and not the general population becomes the client. A similar sort of implicit symbiosis characterizes most regulatory agencies in the United States and Great Britain and those whom they are supposed to constrain. Why should relationships between uniformed and civilian members of defence establishments be an exception?

3. *Broadening the Military Mind.* Military contributions to public policy are less biased when military men are aware of relevant non-military considerations. The principle leads to emphasis on broadening the minds of military men through training in a host of natural and social science disciplines, and by detailing them for periods of service in other parts of the foreign policy community. Such steps may achieve broadening; they carry no necessary implication for subordinating the classic priorities of the military to other concerns. Instead, broadly educated military men may simply be able to frame their preferences more persuasively or enter into more extensive coalitions, e.g., a military-industrial-academic complex. The garrison state does not occur when military men are narrow but when they have much in common with other elites and organize together around salient external security threats.[10]

4. *Professionalism.* Military professionalism has been suggested as a device for restricting military impact on political systems. Yet this form of focused commitment need not have that effect. Military professionals, like any body of professionals, tend to make resource demands with reference to other groups in the profession and not to other groups in a social system. Resource demands and resource consumption impose opportunity costs on the political order. Narrow professionals are relatively insensitive to those costs and are very sensitive to the level of resources secured by foreign armed forces or by other branches in their own defence establishment.

5. *Social Management.* The military will contribute to political systems in a less skewed way if it is given a major role in managing social problem-solving. This prescription is the opposite of professionalism. It calls for

300

the military institution to take a leading role in coping with a wide variety of social needs. However, the social management remedy can also lead to distortions in the political order. Two possibilities in particular should be noted. The military may in enlarging its sphere of authority increasingly weaken the representation and influence of other groups, especially of civilian experts on domestic problems. The military may also convey the notion that its activities suffice when in fact they are secondary to and shaped to conform with more customary military concerns. The military can act as social manager without being socially effective or socially dedicated.

6. *Isolated Backwater.* The final suggestion I wish to note is that the military be put off in a distant corner by limiting its resources severely and depriving it of high status. Clearly, this course lessens the possibilities that the military will actively distort public policy. However, it does not insure that political adaptiveness will be unconstrained on another dimension. If the political system must adapt to coercive threats at home or abroad, an insignificant military establishment limits the possibilities of adaptation by denying options to political leaders.

To summarize, we find none of the more familiar prescriptions for military-polity relationships comfortable. Some are unrealistic; others have important negative second-order effects on the key political processes of resource allocation and steering. We are well-advised to modify our pursuit of these prescriptions as solutions. More positively, we need to seek a role for the military institution in the context of the state of other elements in the political system. No military role exists independent of certain required traits of other institutions. Accordingly, we should estimate probabilities of military behavior in the polity as a function of the differences or disparities between the military and other groups. Relevant types of disparity include status, skill, cohesion, resources, and values. We should also entertain the view that the military role is most effectively shaped in a two-step rather than a direct fashion. That is, we can do more to share the role of the military by providing other social units with particular profiles than we can by direct actions on the military institution.[11]

POLITICAL ORDER AND THE MILITARY IN THE FUTURE

The assumption which underlies this paper is that we are not indifferent to the nature of the political order of our countries. Strategy and tactics about the role of the military follow from our preferences for the political order. In addition, strategy and tactics contribute to realizing our preferences as they take into account the constraints of probable situations. This section states one preference for the political order and probable constraints in the post-industrial societies which make up most of the membership of NATO.

Desired Political Order

Let us assume we desire a political order with the following characteristics. There are numerous possible and legitimate coalitions which have the opportunity of winning power. All population groups including members of the military have the opportunity to be members of more than one of these coalitions. No single population group must belong to a coalition for that coalition to gain power. That is, no subset of society has veto power over all others. Transfer of power from a previously successful coalition to its successor is willing and orderly.

Certain requirements must be present for these preferences to prevail. There must be widespread satisfaction with the prospects for realizing personal and group hopes through the existing political order. This does not mean satisfaction with the status quo; it does mean satisfaction with possible futures. Such satisfaction or optimism in turn requires basic trust in the general intentions of non-preferred winning coalitions. That is, population groups must believe that even when their favorites do not hold power, those who do are not evil, or dangerously incompetent, or committed to retaining power indefinitely.

Social Constraints

Social trends in post-industrial societies make our desires for the political order increasingly difficult to attain. Demands tend to emerge and to escalate to a politically salient position more quickly. At the same time, willingness to accept delay in the gratification of demands seems to be declining sharply. The strain these phenomena place on public satisfaction and trust multiplies because of other trends. Awareness of the demands of other population groups and governmental compliance with those demands make all population groups increasingly prone to see distributive inequities. The quality of life even of those who are materially comfortable is seen as slipping and in danger of decaying badly. The aggregate effects are to produce rates of growth in demand higher than rates of growth in public resources. The only possible remedies involve

302

resource reallocation and/or increased mobilization of social resources. However, the latter course of action becomes increasingly difficult as persons and groups demand autonomy in defining and pursuing their desires.

To cope with this set of pressures, democratic political systems will need to take special steps to accomplish three improvements. First, they will have to improve their anticipation of popular demands and the readiness of quick response programs. Second, trial and error procedures in response to new types of demands will have to be replaced in large part by complex experimentation ahead of demand deadlines. This means substantial changes in the scale and sophistication of public policy experiments and their evaluation. Third, particular efforts will be required if public expenditures for particular programs are to be seen as public goods. One major possibility is to shape new and existing organizations increasingly into institutions which serve multiple population groups by pursuing a host of different objectives.

Military Institutions

In the context of the domestic constraints summarized above, the military policy and military institutions of the North Atlantic post-industrial democracies will have the following attributes. Most of the military establishments will not be at war at any one point in time. Even when a nation's armed forces are involved in a war, most military personnel will not be in combat. Expensive, technologically complex weapons systems (nuclear and non-nuclear) will still be in national inventories; however, they will seldom be used and the credibility of pleas to augment them will suffer accordingly. Finally, most foreign involvements by the military will commit the least costly elements of the force structure. Conventional ground units with modest logistic support will be used to interpose a barrier between disputants. Since prolonged foreign involvement is feared not desired, the emphasis will be on neutrality and minimizing violence. This emphasis implies new formulations of success and of courage, formulations which are inherently less suited to mobilizing popular sentiment at home.

For the military establishment, the combined effects of the trends discussed in this section will operate to limit the military in several important ways. First, cost-benefit analyses of military resource requests will center on the criterion of domestic contributions and not on ratio relationships with foreign armed forces. Second, military consumption of resources increasingly will be perceived as a drain from the resources

303

to meet social needs, as actively hostile to those ends. This perception will not be balanced by perceptions that members of the armed forces incur great risks or make vital contributions to national survival. Third, the able and energetic will be less attracted to and retained in military institutions. In part, this personnel problem will follow from declines in military resources, prestige and a sense of being 'where the action is.' In part, it will follow from the decline in opportunity for uniquely important and heroic action which the limited use of military forces abroad implies.

These developments may lessen the extent to which the military obstructs the adaptive politics democratic systems must become better at. They do not provide for a constructive contribution by the military to that adaptativeness. Nor do they warrant confidence that North Atlantic post-industrial societies will maintain an adequate military capability.

SOCIAL LEARNING

In our earlier discussion of the needs of the democratic political order in the future, we stress the need for public policy experimentation. I suggest that the military can provide civilians with a uniquely helpful 'test-bed' for social change. The 'total institution' aspects of the military allow for the trying out and evaluating of social inventions in ways which are less feasible in civilian arenas. Use of the military for social learning can secure public satisfaction payoffs from resources allocated to the military.

It is important to distinguish the social learning role proposed here from the social management role discussed previously. In the latter case, the military largely determines social problems for attention and directs and participates in production programs to deal with those problems. In contrast, for social learning civilians outside the defence establishment select the problems, design trial projects to discover solutions widely applicable to the civil society, and direct military personnel who play subordinate roles in the test activities. When test-bed results warrant, the learning can then be applied by civilian organizations to populations outside of the military. Parenthetically, given the underemployment which persistently characterizes peacetime military establishments and the military situation projected earlier, there is no obvious reason why the social learning role should impair combat effectiveness. Indeed, one can reasonably argue that without developments along social learning lines, the military is unlikely to be able to attract and retain substantial numbers of highly capable personnel committed to democratic politics.

It seems useful to conclude with some examples of social learning problems to be addressed through military test-beds.

1. *Group Relations.* Military personnel are drawn from major ethnic, racial, and religious groups in the civil society. Military organization assumes that men from different groups do not regard others as enemies. This is the case even though the group members in the military are drawn from the young male segment of the national population most likely to express group enmity directly. Accordingly, the military can well serve as a site to learn how to induce cooperation on joint problems without denying group autonomy. Innovations can vary from, on the one hand, procedures to insure equitable behavior by authorities drawn primarily from one group toward subordinates from another to, on the other, penetrating experiences which bring equals to treat each other as human beings with a rationale for their actions.

2. *Upgrading Skills.* May persons enter the military without the skills to secure more than dead-end jobs in the civilian economy and perhaps not even those. Accordingly, the military population provides a suitable vehicle to demonstrate the efficacy of alternative methods for vocational education, methods which do not require a lengthy list of formal accomplishments unrelated to the technical specialty involved. The very size of the military and the fact that its members have work to perform while learning strengthen the analogy with the education of civilians who have left full-time student status.

3. *Systems Innovation.* The military is for many purposes a total institution with one authority structure over both its mechanical and social components. Accordingly, it provides a relatively unique situation for blending the technological and human components of systems, and for doing so in innovative ways free of the constraints which are often present in the civilian sector. Examples from the American experience include hospital design and mass-produced housing. Other possibilities include elementary schools and new communities. In all these cases, the military test-bed is relatively free of the constraints of local ordinances, trade union regulations, and professional stakes which characterize the civilian sector.

4. *New Forms of Social Organization.* As a large organization in modern society, the military exhibits increasingly familiar stresses between authoritarian customs and democratic norms of new members. It also

manifests recurrent problems in large organizations, for example, those of fidelity in transmitting adverse information to higher levels. Given the variety of missions and personnel composition of military elements, it should be possible to determine the feasibility of democratic decision-making procedures. It should be equally possible to develop practices which get bad news to central decision-makers.

5. *Restraint of Violence.* Military personnel are at the same time taught how to use violence and subjected to a command and control structure so that coercion is not used unless sanctioned. Accordingly, another use of the military test-bed can be to try out and evaluate training and command programs to insure that those trained and equipped for violence restrain themselves in most situations. The implications for civilian police behavior are obvious.

6. *Multiple Careers.* Military service may be viewed as one career among many during the life span. Reasons for this include: (*a*) the physical youth required for some military roles; (*b*) the need to avoid a distinct military caste as reliance on compulsory service systems declines; and (*c*) the need to weed out less outstanding personnel. Accordingly, the military can be used to evolve processes of education and experience which make transition from one career to another feasible and comfortable.

REFERENCES

1. For example, see: D. WRIGHT MILLS, *The Power Elite*. New York: Oxford University Press, 1957; and Harold D. LASSWELL and Daniel LERNER (eds.), *World Revolutionary Elites*. Cambridge, Massachusetts: The M.I.T. Press, 1965.
2. For examples, see: D. FEDOTOFF WHITE, *The Growth of the Red Army*. Princeton, New Jersey: Princeton University Press, 1944; David B. BOBROW, *The Political and Economic Role of the Military in the Chinese Communist Movement*. Unpublished Ph. D. dissertation, Department of Political Science, Massachusetts Institute of Technology, June, 1962.
3. Harold D. LASSWELL, *Politics*. New York: Whittlesey House, 1936.
4. For data, see: Bruce M. RUSSETT, *What Price Vigilance?* New Haven, Connecticut, Yale University Press, 1970.
5. Karl W. DEUTSCH, *The Nerves of Government*. New York: The Free Press, 1963.
6. On the distinction between concrete and analytic units, see: Marion J. LEVY, Jr. *The Structure of Society*. Princeton, New Jersey: Princeton University Press, 1952, pp. 199–207.
7. Perhaps the most wide-ranging attempt has been that of Stanislaw ANDRZJEWSKI, *Military Organization and Society*. London: Routledge, Kegan & Paul, 1954. See also the anthology edited by Samuel P. HUNTINGTON, *Changing Patterns of Military Politics*. New York: The Free Press, 1962.
8. For example, see: John P. LOVELL, ed. *The Military and Politics in Five Developing Nations*. Kensington, Maryland: Center for Research in Social Systems, March, 1970.
9. For example, see: Michalina CLIFFORD-VAUGHAN. 'Changing Attitudes to the Army's Role in French Society', *British Journal of Sociology*, 15 (1964), pp. 338–349.
10. Harold D. LASSWELL, 'The Garrison State', *American Journal of Sociology*, XLVI (1941), pp. 455-68.
11. For empirical analysis, see: Robert D. PUTMAN, 'Toward Explaining Military Intervention in Latin American Politics', *World Politics*, XX (1967), pp. 83–110; and Roger W. BENJAMIN and Lewis J. EDINGER. 'Conditions for Military Control', *Journal of Conflict Resolution* (forthcoming).

Non-Conventional Educational Requirements for the Military

M. D. HAVRON*

* President Human Sciences Research, Inc., USA.

To say how the military should be educated requires some forecast of future missions – what the military will do to serve a national purpose. And forecasting requires some degree of prescience, a talent which is in great demand but short supply. Accepting uncertainties, I feel that extrapolation of post World War II trends uncovers certain future missions and directions which have not been sufficiently well recognized as requirements of military forces of technologically advanced nations. Pursuit of technological advances can blind us to their significance and importance. Hence the educational base for such missions have not yet been well defined, nor implemented.

The key mission of the military is to defend its country against external aggressors. But, in addition, I suggest that missions wherein national objectives cannot be attained solely by use of military forces in a destructive capacity are becoming more important. These missions being heterogeneous, are not as sharply defined as the conventional military mission. Most would prevent war rather than win it in a conventional sense; most, but not all, would use military forces in a constructive capacity. A contrast between educational requirements for traditional missions and those I will talk about will help better to define the latter.

For conventional missions the objective of education is to teach leaders the strategic and tactical use of military forces. The officer-manager is educated to coordinate major military elements to destroy an enemy who fights battles in much the same way; the interface of concern is that between our own military forces and those of an enemy. A second set of missions for which education is needed are those involving use of military forces at a different interface – that between the military force and the civilian population and its leadership. I will mention how capabilities for these latter missions may be imbedded in the military, and give examples of supporting educational requirements.

Requirements for this type of mission which I shall call non-conventional stem from developments that started prior to World War II and continue. Most of you have read or written of these trends. I summarize here[1]: *First*, for centuries nations could follow the dictum that military might was to be exercised to the utmost, as Clausewitz said. Not that politicians always pushed to final victory, but they could without risk of international holocaust. Nuclear weaponry has changed this. The existence of nuclear capacities and the threat of escalation does much to shape the decisions of politicians responsible for the use of military power. Use of military forces is hedged by many constraints. Our military com-

311

manders in Vietnam and the Dominican Republic complained, but with these encounters ended, many governing political constraints are here to stay. *Second*, products of communications technology have spread around the globe. Any peasant who cannot buy a radio can listen to his neighbors'. Thus, almost any military confrontation occurs in a goldfish bowl and among civilian populations with the world looking over the shoulders of the contestants. *Third*, subversives have learned to make civilians a source of recruits, intelligence, logistical support and battlefield assistance. The traditional military force with superior firepower, logistical support and mobility – the great triumvirate of conventional military ideology – has no valid answer for this tactic. It cannot be countered by conventional doctrine. The military force must learn to gain the support of the citizenry. *Fourth*, the military as a disciplined force has the capabilities and, often when it isn't fighting, the time for constructive activities. Our first engineers were trained at West Point – they built the railroads to the West; military initiative gave rise to the principle of interchangeable parts; military research eliminated yellow fever.[2] Military research sponsored by our military has contributed many technological developments to our civilian society and continues to do so.

But the ability of the military to serve constructive purposes is more important to undeveloped nations than to NATO countries. Here political and public service organizations are less well articulated and integrated. Here it can serve as the cutting edge for political, technical and economic modernization. Membership in military forces can engender a sense of national identity. Men educated in the military, when discharged from the service, can serve as teachers and community leaders. The technical skills learned in the military can be of use to the civilian economy. Of course, the military is not the only institution that can, or should, do these things. But in most developing countries with a limited number of educated people, limited managerial capabilities, and limited resources, it is cost-effective to put the military and its managerial skills to work for constructive purposes.

It has been argued that getting the military of developing nations involved in constructive tasks dulls its fighting ability. I suspect it does. But what it loses in this respect, it gains in its ability to gain the support and respect of the people. Its ability to defend borders may be degraded, but the respect it can gain in its work with and for the people can strengthen the military as a counterforce against subversion. For most developing nations, the threat is internal.[3] A major role of the military of *modern* nations can then be to help the military of *underdeveloped* nations become an instrument for modernization. This is not easy, but I believe it possible.

312

While the complexity of this task should not be underestimated, it offers exciting possibilities.

These are arguments for educating a military force to deal with people and their leadership. But the education and the ideology underlying non-conventional uses of military forces differ markedly from those needed for conventional warfare. The basic assumptions as to objectives of employment and the meaning of victory differ.[4] Winning for a traditional military involves killing or incapacitating the enemy. Winning in the low-level spectrum involves helping develop rapport between the indigenous government and its own people. The approach and strategies differ. Conventional operations involve massing forces to overcome an objective. Non-conventional operations require understanding people, and use of persuasion to obtain popular support and, from this, the intelligence that allows a stronger force to prevail. We want the traditional warrior to regard the enemy as a cipher; humanitarian sentiments are suppressed. Operations at the civil interface require consideration of people – their culture, habits, and values. Finally, the underlying technological base for traditional forces derives from physics, ballistics, engineering, electronics, and the physical sciences. Operations at the civil interface call for principles and concepts available from areas such as political science, sociology, psychology, anthropology and economics. Thus, educational requirements for these non-conventional missions differ greatly from those needed to support conventional military operations.

APPLICATION OF NON-CONVENTIONAL CONCEPTS

If the philosophy and approach of non-conventional uses of military forces differ from those used to employ forces in a conventional manner, how is this non-conventional approach introduced into the military? What are examples of supporting educational requirements? Different ways by which the philosophy and concepts can be represented in the military are cited in the foregoing, along with examples of educational requirements. There is substantial overlap among these areas; often they amount to different views into the same peep box.

Emphatically, I refer to education, not training. While the demarcation between the two is not distinct, by education I refer to providing general concepts applicable to a broad spectrum of situations, concepts that would allow an officer to determine what he and his staff needs to learn, to be trained in, if you will. This contrasts with training which would

313

increase proficiency in tasks which, even though complex, have been rather well reduced to standard and contingent routines. I might add that the conventional warrior also needs this education, if in lesser depth, than the officer who conducts, or advises the command in the non-conventional spectrum.

CIVIL AFFAIRS

Civil affairs – recognized as a military function – is the management of military-civilian relationships to the interest of the military and its mission.[5,6] In limited conflict situations certainly, there should be a civil affairs officer on the command staff from battalion upward. A civil affairs element such as a company may also be available.

The area of civil affairs is broad in scope and a broad education is required. Civil affairs officers need concepts and frames that would allow them, at least in certain key areas, to analyze a culture. They need, quickly, to be able to identify sources of authority and leadership among the population wherever military units are stationed.[7] The importance of knowing where the power lies and what authorities the people consider to be legitimate is nowhere better illustrated than in Vietnam. There, at various places, groups of Cao Dai, Hao Hoa and Catholics have frequently formed more or less spontaneously for self-defence. In most instances they have been more effective as a deterrent to insurgents than the physical defence means that circle villages with barbed wire and rifle pits. A combination of means, i.e. building around true local authorities and beliefs and supporting them by physical means, works best. But this is subtle business which takes time. It requires the military that would provide assistance to learn locally accepted role relationships, and to respect and work with indigenous leadership.

Economics can provide concepts which civil affairs officers need to strengthen the local economy. Unfortunately, many of the economic principles that have evolved in the North Atlantic community do not apply well to the local scene in most of the underdeveloped countries. An obvious example of the use of economic concepts is recognition of the need to cushion the economic impact that a large modern military contingent will have on an underdeveloped economy. Frequently, large military contingents have moved in without adequate planning to dampen their inflationary impact.[8] The seriousness of the situation is only recognized after inflation is rampant. I am reminded of the notice a Marine sergeant in Vietnam placed on the company bulletin board, 'Marines

314

will not pay more than $ 3.00 for female entertainment in Hue.' But however well intended, such isolated efforts are not enough. Sensitivity to the need for controls in prior plans and in their implementation in operations would pay for the effort many times over.

And inflation brings other problems in tow. With the influx of a large military force, people in society normally low on the social ladder – the cab driver, the pimp, the prostitute, the bartender – suddenly acquire wealth and affluence. This is resented by the civil servants and others in the middle classes, whose wages lag behind inflation. Loss of confidence in their own government and resentment of foreign presence can readily follow. Knowledge of indigenous power structures and the need to foresee inflationary impacts are but two examples of concepts for the civil affairs officers.

Returning now to the role of the civil affairs officer in the command staff: in low-intensity conflict – in situations that are basically political in nature – the Civil affairs officer should be viewed as a second operations officer. He should have as much influence as the traditional operations officer in helping the commander to define the mission. As the G-3 is responsible for the interface between the military element and the enemy planning missions *vis-à-vis* the enemy, the G-5 helps articulate military missions at the interface between the military element and the civilian population. Both are operations officers; as such their functions differ from those of the other staff members (the G-1, G-2, and G-4) whose jobs are to support the mission rather than to define it. This is the concept; in practice it has not been implemented in the American Army. Nor, would I recommend it at this time. Educational requirements which would allow the civil affairs officer to play this role have not been clearly enough defined. Civil affairs concepts and practices need to be further developed for low-intensity conflict situations, both for ourselves, and to help local forces develop their own Civil affairs capabilities. Recent developments in the u.s. Army such as the initiation of the Military Assistance Officer Program will help.

MILITARY ASSISTANCE

A second recognized area requiring a new kind of education is that of military assistance operations. The u.s. has military assistance contingents in many countries who would help modernize foreign military forces. Most military assistance has involved training indigenous military in the use and maintenance of modern weapons. This seems appropriate if the threat to the nation being assisted comes from beyond its borders. If the threat is internal, as is more frequently the case, training indigenous military to look to weaponry for their security may be counterproductive. Further, in a developing nation having few educated and skilled personnel, to use these scarce personnel resources to maintain and operate complex weaponry may not be directing assets to the best ends.

Here again, the military assistance officer needs a broadly based education – an education that would enable him to be a diagnostician, a manager, and a respected advisor. Working with the local military, he needs to be able to evaluate the relative seriousness of external and internal threats so that the orientation of military assistance is geared to the threat.

This in turn requires education in foreign relations adapted to the country in question, and in concepts of politico-social processes that would permit definition and interpretation of indicators of internal stability. Obviously, a rather broad education is required.

So much for diagnosis. Problems of implementation have substantial educational prerequisites. A good deal of research supported by the American military has looked into requirements for effective advisor-advisee relationships. Much less attention has been given to the dynamics of the interchange between an American advisory staff at several echelons and considered as a single unit and the indigenous military organization it would assist. Here we need further knowledge of processes and interrelationships to provide an educational base.[9]

A broad educational background is needed by the advisory staff in-country both for diagnosis and treatment. Any large bureaucracy – the u.s. military in this case – sets certain goals and policies which maintain direction by a sort of bureaucratic momentum. This can occur without adequate regard for local needs as well as changes in the situation. u.s. military assistance, often by a sort of autonomic response, has handed out aircraft, tanks, electronic equipment – items designed essentially for defence of the United States. This u.s. inclination is often reinforced on the indigenous side, where a destroyer or a few F-4s serve as visible symbols of power even if they cannot be kept in operating condition. An educated military assistance contingent is needed to adapt assistance to needs and to give our bureaucratic thrust an appropriate metamorphological vector.

316

The constabulary, as another form of capability, can serve both to prevent and engage in low-intensity conflict. On several occasions the U.S. military has sent contingents abroad to develop indigenous constabularies.

A constabulary in its mission and *modus operandi* represents a blend of responsibilities and duties of police with those of a military fighting force. It has a greater range of operations than does a police force; company size elements can work and fight as teams. But it draws its strength from the respect it earns from the civilian population. And its responsibilities are rooted in civilian custom and law. A soldier who kills an enemy in battle has no responsibility for the victim. But if a constabulary member captures a bandit or insurgent, his action must be justified by civil law, and the victim is entitled to the protection of the courts.

The typical constabulary operation involves a sponsoring nation going into a troubled situation and providing initially the leadership, all or part of the manpower, and logistical support. In a successful operation, the sponsoring nation trains the indigenous force then gradually withdraws so that the constabulary becomes completely indigenous.

HSR scientists have recently studied U.S. constabulary operations in five different countries occurring over a time span of some 70 years.[10,11] In spite of this time span and great differences in local cultures, general principles emerge which should be part of the intellectual armamentarium of officers who would establish and train an indigenous constabulary, or who are involved in counterinsurgency operations. Perhaps the most striking principle was that U.S. successes occurred when we took pains to learn the language and culture and to stimulate local initiative. Our unsuccessful experiences were characterized not by any lack of activity, but by deficiencies in perspective. We did not sufficiently well appreciate that we needed to develop knowledge of people, customs and motivations as a basis for enhancing the culture's ability to integrate innovations. This all seems obvious. But the too frequent problem is that goals get expressed in terms of easily countable things – schools built, wells dug, etc. and placed on a tight time schedule. Field managers are then faced with a dilemma. The time required to develop local initiative and skills is too great to permit attainment of goals on that schedule. On the other hand, bypassing local people fails to develop worker and managerial skills and loses an essential ingredient – local psychological involvement. The social sciences do not yet provide an adequate way to define and

317

apply indicators of societal growth and health, or to estimate for particular cultures the proper pace at which desired change can be absorbed. Here research is needed to develop the basic concepts that would support an education.

Perhaps the most successful U.S. constabulary experience was in development of the *Fita Fita* Guard in Samoa. The Guard became a respected symbol in the eyes of the people. The Guard organization became a conduit for broadening the leadership base – a medium by which able youngsters were recruited, trained and prepared for positions of responsibility in the Samoan society. The Guard remained intact for some 50 years, benefitting the Samoan people at a minimal cost to the U.S.

In passing, I salute the British Colonial Police. Educated and trained in the local culture, they were always respected. Long before Secretary of Defence McNamara emphasized cost/effectiveness concepts, the British had the saying, 'We have troubles; send us an infantry battalion or one Colonial Police Officer'. The Colonial Police helped to maintain social stability for centuries with minimal forces. And, equally significant, often they were able to leave a stabilizing force behind. This story should be part of an officer's education for low-level conflict situations of the future.

Concepts that should be part of an education for constabulary operations include:

1. General principles as to how needed technology can be harmoniously syncretized with indigenous ways. This, in turn, requires knowledge of people and the wellsprings of their motivation.
2. The significance of the knowledge local people have about one another, and of their surroundings. Frequently, conventional military forces have failed to draw from locals knowledge that was readily and abundantly available. The conventional approach to intelligence – wherein the enemy rather than the people is the referent – falls short.
3. How 'good' social changes – the constabulary itself and its works – can be stabilized so that they continue after the sponsoring force has departed. Here is an area in which many of the basic concepts for an education are still lacking.

PSYCHOLOGICAL OPERATIONS

Perhaps the most complex capability needed in this field wherein the mission of the military cannot be achieved by force alone is psychological operations. You are familiar with psychological warfare – communica-

318

tions to the enemy. Psychological operations as American doctrine defines them, embrace psywar but include communications to neutral and friendly audiences as well. They involve communications by words and acts to enemy, neutral and friendly that would forward the missions of military forces.

Psyop takes many forms and directions. I take an example which departs from my earlier definition of missions having to do with the interface between the military and the populace. The example illustrates the significance of communications by actions, and the fact that psyop is not landbound.

Tacit negotiations with evident force may continue in the future. The world looked on with awe when in 1962 President Kennedy placed a quarantine around Cuba to prevent further import of Russian missiles. Professional pacifists were quick to criticize the U.S. U.S. ships never fired a shot. But they represented a symbol of intent, and the determination to back it up.[12] Actions communicate!

This confrontation also illustrates the need for changes in weights of the command decision matrix as we have emerged from a pre-nuclear to a nuclear international environment. U.S. naval officers wanted to engage Russian ships at sufficient distance from Cuba that land-based MIGs in Cuba could not interfere. From a strictly military view, this made sense. President Kennedy, advised by Ambassador Ormsby Gore, drew the ring of ships in closer to Cuba, running this tactical risk in order to give the Russians more time to think.[13] An excellent example of the need for an appreciation of the factors that must govern employment of the military in a nuclear age.

Again, the presence of the 6th Fleet here in the Mediterranean – a fleet which in almost a quarter century has not fired in anger – constitutes an important communication. I understand recently that citizens of certain nations along the littoral areas – Turkey and Malta were mentioned – need to be convinced, or perhaps reconvinced, of the need for the 6th Fleet. The essential influence tool to improve this situation would be psychological operations.

In land operations of the future, I believe that psyop will take on additional importance. In low-intensity conflict situations a psyop capability is a must. Psyops may be represented by a staff officer from battalion level up, and added groups are required who have psyop as a sole mission.

Where the struggle is essentially political, a sophisticated communication capability is needed to decide how issues are to be presented.[14] The communicator determines what patterns of logic and the ethical considerations can be brought to bear on interpretation of issues and events

319

that have political overtones. The ability to identify the allied government with these issues in a favorable way, with the aspirations and needs of the people, and to destroy the credibility of the claims of the other side decides the winner. Perhaps most important of all, these issues need to be framed in terms of the habits of thought and values of the audience – not those of the communicator.[15]

If we are to conduct effective psychological operations, operators and managers require an education. (That some of the best communicators have operated from an intuitive feel for the audience and lacked formal education in the culture does not contradict this.) This education should start with the commander who needs to know how to use psyop. For the psyop staff officer who needs knowledge in depth and detail, here are examples of areas key to his role and function:

1. Knowledge of values and beliefs of indigenous groups which determine how communications are interpreted.
2. Recognition of the need for pre- and post-test of programs, themes, and messages so that audience responses can be gauged and communications efforts adjusted.
3. Realization that actions of allied indigenous forces speak louder and more credibly to the population than words; this in turn requires psyop assistance in planning operations of the military element.
4. Recognition that for allies in a foreign country, a major mission is to develop an indigenous psyop capability.

HIGH LEVEL SUPPORT AND DIRECTION OF MISSIONS THAT CANNOT BE ACCOMPLISHED BY USE OF MILITARY FORCES ALONE

The above four examples of ways in which non-traditional thinking can contribute to operations refer to operations in foreign countries. To provide policy guidance and to support these operations, there is a need for officers at the highest levels in the Department of Defence to understand their nature, and to provide needed guiding concepts. These officers in the Department of the Army and at theater command levels need to exercise surveillance so that guiding concepts are translated adequately in field.[16]

Providing policy guidance alone is not adequate. When a conventional military organization is given the task of implementing a conventional mission, plans and activities can be expected to follow pretty much the intent of the guiding strategy. However, when a conventional military organization attempts to implement missions at the civil interface the purpose and intent of the mission can get lost during the translation. If leaders do not understand the mission, their implementation reverts to something they can understand. Two examples:

1. Psychological operations typically entail producing a desired audience impact. A very intensive audience study is required to develop programs, themes, and messages that will be credible and produce this impact. This is a complex and continuous task. It will not come off well unless both high level policy-makers and senior commanders appreciate its complexity, and take steps to provide in the field the expertise it requires. Lacking this, psyop gets translated into leafleteering. Elements are tasked and their success measured in terms of number of leaflets produced and dropped. Too often continuous checks are not made on their legibility, on the compatibility between the implicit assumptions of the text and the beliefs and values of intended audiences, or on whether leaflets as a medium constitute a sufficiently credible means of communication. Thus, measures of effort become the criteria; objectives of achieving impact, and the need to collect impact indicators so as to provide feedback to the communicator to enhance impact, are easily lost sight of.

2. In the area of civil affairs and military assistance, materiel assistance is a means only, not an end. Among its objectives are to build skills, to strengthen the society, and to enhance a sense of national identity. Given these objectives, there is a maximum rate at which assistance can be absorbed by its recipients. Also the type of assistance and the manner in which it is provided should stimulate the social processes necessary to achieve the above objectives. Unless the administrator takes these factors into consideration, means become ends and success of a military assistance program is evaluated in terms of amount of materiel distributed and/or how much is done for the recipients. Our studies as well as a more sophisticated view of the process and objectives show this not to be the case. But the tendency to do more, and to equate the amount done by the sponsor with degree of success is strong.

The high level decision-maker in the Department of Defence must not only set policy; he must exercise surveillance so that policy is properly implemented. Presently he is handicapped. Indicators are needed that focus on social and political processes – the heartbeat of societies. These are needed along with counts of physical structures and battle statistics. Such indicators would allow assessment of the effectiveness of field

321

programs and operations. But as indicated earlier, sufficiently valid indicators adapted to specific countries and their cultural nuances are not available. Research is needed to develop concepts and social indicators for the benefit of high level Department of Defence officials.

CONCLUSION

I have cited evidence for the growing importance of a diverse set of military missions that have at least this in common: use of destructive means alone cannot accomplish the national objectives from which the mission of the military force is derived. A number of ways in which military organizations may incorporate this thinking have been described. For each, examples of organizational requirements have been cited. While the military has been late to recognize the importance of these missions and the need for supporting educational backup, a number of moves initiated by the u.s. Army should help to provide necessary capabilities. I refer to the establishment of the Military Assistance Officer Program at John F. Kennedy Center at Fort Bragg, North Carolina, to the development of a curriculum for advisors to be taught at Fort Leavenworth, and to continued Army sponsorship of the research that will provide needed concepts and principles – the educational base for these types of missions. These efforts represent a significant beginning. Their extension and expansion will help provide the education to better prepare the military for the challenges of the future.

NOTES

1. James M. Dodson, William W. Chenault, M. Dean Havron, *The Role of Psychological Operations in Naval Missions: An Appraisal and Recommendations* (McLean, Va.: Human Sciences Research, Inc., June 1968).
2. Secretary John W. Weeks, 'Other Things the Army Does Besides Fight'. Address presented at Los Angeles Chamber of Commerce Banquet, Los Angeles, California, May 1923.
3. From interviews with officers responsible for plans and policy in the U.S. Department of Defence, 1969–1970.
4. M. Dean Havron, 'Military Employment in Counterinsurgency: A Conceptual Problem', an unpublished working paper (1969).
5. M. Dean Havron, Randolph C. Berkeley, Jr., *The Role of Civil Affairs in Marine Corps Operations* (McLean, Va.: Human Sciences Research, 1966).
6. James E. King, Jr., *Civil Affairs: The Future Prospects of a Military Responsibility*, CAMG Paper No. 3 Bethesda, Maryland: Operations Research Office, June 1958 (Staff Paper ORO-SP-55).
7. William W. Chenault, M. Dean Havron, *Pilot Study of SAF Afloat Requirements for Operations Against Incipient Insurgency* (McLean, Va.: Human Sciences Research, 1969).
8. The impact has been amply documented, of course, for South Vietnam in the mid–1960s. See, for example, Harvey H. Smith, *et al.*, *Area Handbook for South Vietnam*, DA Pam No. 550–55 (Washington, D.C.: Government Printing Office, April 1967), pp. 309–310.
9. Human Sciences Research, Inc., *Planned Social Change (U)*, 2 Volumes (McLean, Va.: Human Sciences Research, Inc., 1969).
10. M. Dean Havron, William W. Chenault, James M. Dodson, A. Terry Rambo, *Constabulary Capabilities for Low-Level Conflict* (McLean, Va.: Human Sciences Research, Inc., April 1969).
11. Bruce C. Allnutt, *Marine Combined Action Capabilities: The Vietnam Experience* (McLean, Va.: Human Sciences Research, Inc., December 1969).
12. Dodson, *op. cit.*
13. Arthur M. Schlesinger, Jr., *A Thousand Days: John F. Kennedy in the White House* (Boston, Mass.: Houghton Mifflin Co.; Cambridge, Mass.: The Riverside Press, 1965).
14. Lucian W. Pye, *Guerrilla Communism in Malaya* (Princeton, N.J.: Princeton University Press, 1956).
15. Peter G. Nordlie, 'The Role of Values in Psychological Operations' in *HSR Conference on Psychological Operations and Communications With Foreign Nationals* (McLean, Va.: Human Sciences Research, Inc., 1968).
16. Recently the Department of Army has recognized this need explicitly and sought to fulfil it in the promulgation of AR614-134 which establishes the Military Assistance Officers Program (MAOP). MAOP provides a career pattern and organization for high level politico-military specialists charged with implementing U.S. military policy with political implications in the field and monitoring the implementation and its effect at headquarters organizations. Over the past year HSR has been engaged in research to identify and support the operations and training requirements of members of the program.

The Israel Defence Forces as an Agent of Socialization and Education: a Research in Role-Expansion in a Democratic Society

M. LISSAK*

* The Hebrew University, Department of Sociology, Israel.

On examining the contemporary role of the armed forces both in the developed and the developing world, one cannot but conclude that its classical definition of being exclusively confined to the security-military sphere is rather obsolete. Today, more than ever before, the military – under a variety of circumstances – is fulfilling new functions which often have nothing to do with security in the narrow sense of the word. Not only is there a growing involvement in political affairs – but many armies are also engaged in a variety of projects for the development of their countries' economic infrastructure, physical communications, telecommunications and health services. Some armies are engaged, with varying degrees of intensity, in the operation of education facilities at various levels as well.[1]

The wide spectrum of educational activities can be classified according to two criteria which can in turn be sub-divided into two categories. The main two criteria are:

a. *The identity of the client-consumer:* Generally two distinct categories may be distinguished – the civilian sector on the one hand and the military establishment (or groups of various types of soldiers within it) on the other.

b. *The contents of the educational services provided by the military:* Here again a general distinction may be made between two types of services: professional-military instruction designed to impart to the soldier and the officer in the most direct manner specific knowledge essential for promoting the professional standards of the military system on the one hand and on the other hand educational services of a more diffuse nature.

By combining these criteria four main types are obtained which are, however, not mutually exclusive. One type or several types may predominate or appear simultaneously or else one type may be exclusively represented, all according to the conditions under which the military operates.

Type A

The first type consists of limited professional facilities in a strictly military context, whose purpose is to enhance the consumer's mastery of the art of war, the consumer himself constituting an integral part of the military system. Nevertheless some of the knowledge acquired in this way can

327

also be converted and adapted to civilian uses (driving, mechanics, etc.). Many armies of the Western democracies, and their auxiliary forces in their former colonies have been giving decisive if not exclusive priority to projects of this type, which also exist, however, in countries that are not necessarily democratic, such as in part of the Latin American states.

The Identity of the Client

		The soldier as individual or the military establishment as a whole	The civilian sector
The content of the educational services	Limited Professional Services	A	B
	Comprehensive Educational Services	C	D

Type B

Here direct military, pre- or para-military training is given by the army to certain civilian groups other than army reserves. This may take the form of military training for youngsters prior to their enlistment in a premilitary setting, or of the establishment of various para-military bodies (civil guards and the like).

Type C

The third type of training and education takes the form of special army programs, in addition to the projects of the first and possibly of the second type, designed to raise the general non-military standard of education or of vocational skill of soldiers and officers.

Type D

This comprises the same kind of activities as were included in the previous category except that they are not exclusively designed for the military but are, in a fairly regular and institutionalized manner, carried

328

on also in civilian settings and on behalf of the civilian sector. Non-military vocational training given to servicemen prior to their release is also included under this heading.

In the absence of statistical and other data it is, of course, difficult to estimate the extent of the educational activities carried on by various armies in each of these prototypes. Nevertheless, from the piecemeal information at hand it appears that while in the not too distant past only few armies in the world engaged in extensive educational programs and usually confined themselves almost exclusively to projects of the first type, the situation has changed considerably. Armies are increasingly taking upon themselves a greater variety of educational-socializing tasks. At least part of the civilian sector is becoming a consumer of military services initiated and provided by the army.[2]

The case study of the Israel Army presented below is not merely another example of educational programs and projects of this type or the other. It is one of the few armies whose educational-vocational training functions have reached within the framework of all the four prototypes mentioned a considerable degree of institutionalization.[3] The main purpose of this paper is to show some typical examples of types of educational services it provides.

a. Technical-vocational training in the army

For most of the trades the Israel Army needs it must train its own man-power. This has led to the institution of *pre-military schools* for those trades where protracted training is required. Typical examples are:
1. The technical school of the airforce to which pupils are admitted after 10 years of studies for two years specialization in electronics, and after 8 years – for a two years' course in aircraft maintenance.
2. The technical boarding school of the armoured corps where elementary school graduates are trained for one year in mechanics and motor electricity.
3. The boarding school of the navy, where elementary school graduates specialize for two years in wireless operation, signalling, radar and navigation.[4]

b. Elementary education

Israeli men are recruited into the army on a compulsory basis, with hardly any selection, the sole criterion being their date of birth. The only exceptions are those who fail to attain a certain physical or psychotechnical standard, criminals or maladjusted personalities, and students of religious seminars (*yeshivot*). Since Israel is a country of immigration, also youngsters who have not had the compulsory eight years of schooling are inducted, including recent newcomers with a scanty knowledge of Hebrew.

Over the years the Hebrew and elementary education program offered by the army passed through several phases. It reached full institutionalization only in 1962 with the issue of a general staff regulation to the effect that 'every serviceman on compulsory duty who has not finished elementary school shall, within the period of his service, complete his studies under an elementary education program conferring a recognized diploma upon examination.'[5]

The number of men who attend Hebrew or elementary education courses during their military service is considerable. The Chief Education Officer's staff estimates that some 5 000 soldiers a year learned Hebrew in the period of extensive immigration, nor has the number fallen off appreciably in the past few years. In 1968 there were about 4 000.[6]

Most of the men attending the elementary education courses are the sons of immigrants from Islamic countries – mainly from North Africa – or are themselves natives of these countries. The vast majority live in development towns or immigrant villages. Hence in Israel under-education is not merely an attribute of certain socio-economically backward strata but is directly related to ethnic origin. The army's educational facilities thus offer a singular opportunity to decrease the social disparity between the various ethnic groups.

In parallel with the courses for enlisted men the army also runs similar courses for its regular staff, mainly for the ranks of sergeant and sergeant major. The number of non-commissioned officers participating in such courses is, however, steadily decreasing. By now these are mainly men who joined the regular army before the general staff regulation requiring every soldier on compulsory service without full elementary schooling to participate in the army elementary education program came into force.

Many of the publications of the Chief Education Officer's Department, which we shall examine further on, are designed for the army's education courses, especially the general ones. This special instruction material became necessary because the army embarked on its large scale adult education program quite some time before the Ministry of Education had devised and implemented appropriate techniques for that purpose. Over the years the army's education department has thus developed special syllabi for its elementary education courses and published several

330

textbooks and teaching manuals. Many of the techniques first introduced by the army were later on adopted also by the civilian agencies.

c. *High school education*

Several years ago the army decided to offer a partial high school program on a voluntary basis. The army's original intention was to raise the standards of its regular staff that had not had the advantages of a full high school education.

Since the end of the fifties the army has also provided facilities for enlisted men on *compulsory service* to study for their matriculation examinations, in evening classes held at a special school.

d. *Pre-academic courses*

The army also helps interested candidates to be admitted to institutions of higher learning. The army's assistance is two-fold:
1. Special allowances are made for soldiers who take correspondence courses and they receive half of the tuition fees from the army.
2. Courses are held in the army by teachers of the academic reserve corps assigned to this duty as part of their compulsory service.

So much for the programs helping soldiers before their release from compulsory service to gain admittance to institutions of higher learning. Apart from that, the army also has the problem of its own regular officers, whom it is only too willing to allow to attend university, for several reasons:

First, to prevent junior officers from leaving the army in order to pursue their studies.

Second, to raise the standards of professional officers both in specific areas (engineering, chemistry, oriental studies) and in the field of general education.

Third, to equip officers before their retirement with a civilian career. The following priorities have accordingly been laid down:
1. Young officers up to the age of 30 whom the army is interested to keep on its rosters. They are given fully paid leave for their university studies in practically any field they like, against an undertaking to serve a given number of years for every year they spend at the university.
2. Senior officers from lieutenant-colonel upwards. Here the army pays for their studies which are intended to set them up in a civilian career. A considerable proportion go abroad to study business administration or similar subjects.

e. Pre-release vocational programs

The army is also engaged in vocational training activities of a different nature – programs designed to train ex-soldiers for a useful civilian life. The initiative in this field was taken by the Ministry of Defence which several years ago set up a vocational guidance department for ex-servicemen.

f. Assistance to the civilian education system

During the first few years after the establishment of the State of Israel, the education system expanded to twice its size and the shortage of qualified teaching staff was extremely acute. The army was called upon to fill the gap, among other things by training girl soldiers at its own teachers' college.

After their basic military training the graduates served as teachers in immigrant settlements for the rest of their compulsory service. The rate at which girls are called up to serve as teachers in development settlements depends on the requirements of these settlements. At periods when the number of college graduates was not enough to meet the demand, high school graduates were given a month's crash course after their basic training and so equipped were sent out to the settlements to teach. When conditions changed so that there was a surplus of teachers some of them were taken off their teaching posts to carry out other educational functions, especially to work in the adult education projects, youth clubs or in the national literacy campaign.

g. The advancement of marginal juvenile groups

The army's approach for many years has been that it is also called upon to fulfil educational functions even if they are clearly extra-military. This attitude found its main expression in the enlistment of sub-standard elements. Several years ago the General Staff decided twice a year to call up groups of youngsters who belong to one or more of these sub-standard categories, in order to look after their personal advancement rather than for regular military duties. The idea was to give them basic training and then send them for three months to the army school, whereupon they would be attached to *Nahal* groups in military-agricultural strongholds and *kibbutzim* where they would benefit from the influence of what is considered to be the élite of the army. This project was considered all the more essential as the majority of army rejects are members of the more backward social strata, composed of various Asian-African origin groups. The project thus has not only a general educational aspect but also serves one of the supreme collective goals of Israeli society – paring down the differences between the various ethnic groups.[7]

h. The Gadna (Youth Corps)

The youth corps is another socializing agent of the army operated in conjunction with the Ministry of Education and Culture. The scheme functions within two settings, one voluntary and one compulsory. Within the compulsory setting are the various post-elementary schools (high schools, agricultural and various vocational schools). The voluntary setting is designed for youngsters who are not continuing their formal studies, and comprises ordinary and pre-military youth clubs where they are given very rudimentary technical and mostly theoretical military training. *Gadna* trainees can also choose their own field of specialization: aviation[8] in the youth air corps, seamanship in the marine youth corps, etc. It should be stressed that most of the activities bear a social rather than a military character, and are very much like youth movement meetings. The military aspect is largely overlaid by the social aspect. Hence also the stress laid on activities of a general national or educational character: afforesetation drives, participation in archaeological digs and work in border settlements.

i. The Nahal – the agricultural-military corps

In this section of the armed forces, particular emphasis is placed on social education and vocational training, since the army regards the period of service of its *Nahal* soldiers not purely from the military angle but views it as a training period for new core groups that will ultimately found new settlements or join existing *kibbutzim* so as to supplement their numbers. Accordingly *Nahal* soldiers spend only part of their service in training and military jobs, while about half their time is devoted, if security conditions permit, to agricultural training in one of the older collective settlements. During this period the entire social group or core, including the girls, remains together. The educational-social element of *Nahal* service is given prominence right from the start, and already during the basic training period there are special group meetings and other social activities that do not exist in other army corps.

The youth and *Nahal* division of the Ministry of Defence estimates that the *kibbutz* movement by now has some 9 000 members who are ex-Nahal people. Most of them received their basic agricultural training

333

in that corps. The contribution of the *Nahal* to the agricultural sector is seen to be still more striking if one bears in mind that since 1949 it has set up 45 military-agricultural strongholds of which 20 have in the meantime become permanent settlements. In addition the *Nahal* has directly set up 15 *kibbutzim*, reestablished some 10 and provided manpower reinforcement to about 50. Altogether about 100 *kibbutzim* have been put back on their feet through Nahal manpower infusions, many of them in border areas or in remote development districts. Several *moshav*-type villages were also set up by ex-*Nahal* members who received their training in this corps.

j. The publishing services of the Chief Education Officer

The educational work of the army finds its reflection in the wide variety of publications issued by the Chief Army Education Officer. In addition to the publications intended exclusively for army personnel, there also are others directed at the public at large and some of them designed exclusively for the civilian population.

The Chief Education Officer together with the Defence Ministry's publications service also issues many books intended mainly for a civilian audience, though dealing mainly with military or allied subjects. Another type of publication consists of a series of pamphlets on local geography, wildlife, flora, fauna and archaeology. The Chief Education Officer also publishes series of pictures to be exhibited in schools and similar settings, as well as posters, films and slides, the latter mainly for youth clubs.

SUMMARY AND DISCUSSION

The wide range of educational activities of which we cited only some of the most salient examples – and this too in the briefest of outlines – can be schematically summed up as follows: The Israeli Army as a military organization naturally invests most of its resources in the training of its men, so as to turn them into good and efficient soldiers, and in the improvement of the professional standards of its regular forces. One of the means to this end is a ramified network of army courses. A goodly part of the knowledge and skill acquired in these courses can be put to good use in civilian life. Nevertheless, this type of program comes under the *first category* of professional facilities provided by the military exclusively for soldiers to enhance their mastery of the art of war.

334

The preliminary training of the *Gadna* corps may be classified as belonging to *category B* which includes military training given by the army to civilian sectors of the population. Some of the samples cited of the army's elementary, high school and education programs as well as its extensive information and entertainment services belong to the *third category* – general education projects and teaching programs in non-military disciplines. Most of the activities described, however, belong to the *fourth category* of purely educational programs which although partly provided within a military setting are primarily designed for the advancement of backward elements within the civilian sector, in aid and support of the civilian education network.

This simultaneous activity in the field of vocational training, education and culture is a specific characteristic of the Israeli Army which distinguishes it from many other military forces both in the developed democracies and in democratic and non-democratic developing societies. This, of course, is not due to sheer accident, but is a direct result of the magnitude and simultaneity of the problems with which the State of Israel has been confronted from its very inception: the intake of hundreds of thousands of immigrants, many of them from backward countries, and their adequate integration; the need for economic development and for the consolidation of the country's defences against immediate physical threats; and the preservation of the political-cultural values evolved by the Jewish community in mandatory times – democratic fair play, political tolerance and the principles of a modern welfare state. The educational policy-makers of the army, aware of the unusual expansion of the army's educational activities, have tried to formulate a set of principles and guidelines to provide the necessary legitimation for their programs. Their basic argumentation was that in a highly developed country that has considerable economic and human resources available to it, the civilian agencies are able to cope with any weak spots in its educational and cultural makeup. Not so in developing countries where the army has to assume many non-military tasks. Israel, although already from the beginning it constituted a modern society in most respects, still contained some underdeveloped enclaves, mainly as a result of the large influx of immigrants from Islamic countries. The economic and human resources at the disposal of the civilian authorities were extremely limited so that every extra assistance was welcome. Nevertheless the invasion of the army into the civilian sphere, however vital, was not always welcomed. Indirect evidence of this is furnished by an editorial which appeared in *Bamachane*, the main army paper, written in response to doubts that had arisen in connection with the army's activities on behalf of the new immigrant camps. It was suspected that new immigrants, who are not used to democratic procedures come to look upon the army as an all-powerful means for solving all social problems. 'The use of the army for executive, not strictly military tasks, is not somebody's brain-wave or the result of any abstract theory. It does not stem from a search for originality but from the hard facts of Israeli life, with all the conditions and circumstances that force us to maintain a pioneering army which is not restricted to routine military functions but also fills additional roles within the state and its undertakings. A country that consists of a hotch-potch of immigrants from different countries needs an army that can weld these disparate sections together, although the integration of immigrants is not included in the functional definition of any other army in the world. That is why the army has also been charged with providing pioneering and agricultural educational facilities. That is why it virtually acts as a general school of the nation and the state for the masses of new immigrants who acquire their first knowledge of Hebrew as well as their first concepts of Israeli civics.'[9] The same idea was restated by the previous Chief Education Officer in saying that there is full justification for the army to go beyond its routine functions insofar as the human factor is concerned. 'Since the scatter of the population along the modernization curve is very wide, the army from the human aspect serves as primary developing and promoting agent especially for the more backward sectors of the population.'[10] The award of the Israel prize – the most coveted distinction – to the Israeli Army for its educational work may be regarded as the symbolic acknowledgement of the justice of this claim by the country's body politic.

The great potential of the army as 'a developing and promoting agency' derives, according to leaders of its educational programs, from several advantages inherent in the Israeli Army. The most important of these are:

1. Its equalitarian elements. The equalitarianism of the army, despite its hierarchic structure, is reflected in a minimum of social distance. 'People used to social inferiority as a result of class affiliation soon discover that the army is different in this respect and derive deep satisfaction and new self-confidence from the sense of equality they get in its ranks.'[11]
2. The considerable emphasis placed on social mobility. Education encourages the aspiration to mobility and higher achievements. 'For young people even the slightest promotion might be a revolutionary factor in their lives in that it breaks up the classical vicious circle of the inability to make progress.'[12]

336

3. The vocational training many soldiers receive in the army which is applicable or convertible to civilian uses. This serves as a sound foundation for social and economic status after their release.
4. For young new immigrants, army service implies acceptance into 'the order of the Israelis.'[13]

These potential advantages have been utilized by the army for the reinforcement of character traits, the enhancement of social education and the development of the national identity. The army's educational activity has however not been equally successful in all spheres.[14] It is still undergoing considerable modifications. There is much experimentation going on and nothing is static. Thus the fourth category of programs and their relative standing compared with the remaining categories has been substantially modified as a result of the following three factors:

Firstly, the shrinkage of the underdeveloped enclaves, the educationally, culturally and socially backward elements having been reduced in size and their standards having been raised.

Secondly, the consolidation and growth of civilian educational agencies which are able to deal more effectively with these enclaves and make long-range educational plans.

Thirdly, the expansion of the army's security functions after the June 1967 war which led to a realignment of the Chief Education Officer's command. Thus in view of the deployment of the army's forces over more extensive territories and of budgetary limitations, entertainment and information services to civilians have been curtailed.

To obtain a proper perspective, it must be mentioned that the military has not expanded its role only in the sphere of education and culture. The army, or more precisely the Ministry of Defence, is also engaged in extensive economic and scientific activities, largely for the same reasons. On the other hand the dominance of the civilian political leadership in all central decision-making processes has been carefully preserved. This was possible first of all because Israel's political leadership has always enjoyed wide legitimation and been founded on basic consensus. Secondly, Israeli society has managed to institutionalize adequate agencies, settings and procedures to deal with the fundamental national issues. Hence the possibilities for manipulation and pressures by administrative and executive agencies which are not under direct parliamentary control are fairly small. Thirdly, retired senior army officers have extensive economic, social and political opportunities open to them in the civilian sector.

In addition to these general attributes of Israeli society some of the characteristics of the Israel Army as a social system also work in this direction. Here mention must be made of the constant periodic rotation of the high command. Secondly, in spite of the constant state of war and siege, there is no disproportionate glorification of the army as an institution and of its commanders as individuals. The fact that the security burden is spread over most of the adult population through the reserve system helps to strike a proper balance in this field. Thirdly, the popular character of the army makes for the optimal dispersion of social allegiances within the officer class which represents a highly varied range of social sub-groups and more or less reflects the pluralistic character of Israeli society.

This social constellation is an essential, if not always a sufficient, condition for preventing the growth of military cliques which claim a monopoly over political power either out of personal interests or out of a desire for political and ideological reform and revision of the civilian leadership policies. The constellation described together with other factors that have not been mentioned, has generally characterized the State of Israel since its establishment.

1. This development has elsewhere been defined as 'role expansion' of the military establishment. See M. LISSAK, 'Modernization and Role Expansion of the Military in Developing Countries: A Comparative Analysis.' *Comparative Studies in Society and History:* vol. IX, No. 3, April 1967, pp. 233–255.
2. Typical examples are described also in G. B. GLICK, 'The Non-military use of the Latin-American Military,' in N. A. BAILEY (ed.), *Latin America: Politics, Economics and Hemisphere Security.* F. A. Praeger, 1965, pp. 187–188. E. D. GLICK, *Peaceful Conflict: The Non-Military Use of the Military,* Stackpole Books, 1967, p. 114. H. HANNING, *The peaceful Uses of Military Forces,* F. A. Praeger, 1967. M. LISSAK, 'The Military in Burma: Innovations and Frustrations', *Asian and African Studies,* Vol. 5, 1969, pp. 150–161.
3. On the history of the Israeli Army and its place in the political and social life of the country see, A. PERLMUTTER, *Military and Politics in Israel,* London, Frank Cass, 1969.
4. Graduates from the military boarding high school are not commissioned automatically. The only way to be commissioned is to attend a special officers training school.
5. General staff regulation 37.0102.
6. See Israel Defence Forces, The Chief Education Officer, *Education in Israel Defence Forces,* (n.d.), p. 5 (in Hebrew).
7. Col. M. BAR-ON, *Education Processes in the Israel Defence Forces,* Tel-Aviv, December 1966, pp. 68–70.
8. Israel Ministry of Defence, *Air Gadna,* Tel-Aviv, 1963.
9. *Bamachane,* 18.1.1951.
10. Col. M. BAR-ON, *Processes of Assimilation of Ethnic Groups in the Israel Defence Forces,* Published by the Chief Education Officer (n.d.), p. 3.
11. *Ibid.,* p. 6.
12. *Ibid.*
13. *Ibid.,* p. 16.
14. It is important to emphasize that this paper deals with the description and analysis of the educational activities within the army and not with evaluation of its impact on the civilian sector. The latter issue deserves a detailed study which is still to be made.

Structured Strain in a United Nations Constabulary Force

C. C. MOSKOS JR.*

* Department of Sociology, Northwestern University, Evanston, Ill., USA.

On March 4, 1964, the United Nations Security Council unanimously adopted a resolution which recommended the establishment of an international force to keep the peace in Cyprus. The eastern Mediterranean island-republic was in a state of virtual civil war as fighting broke out between its Greek and Turkish communities. The first units of the United Nations Force in Cyprus – UNFICYP – arrived on the island three weeks later. A new episode in the checkered history of international peacekeeping forces was about to begin.

The mission of UNFICYP defined by the 1964 Security Council resolution was '... to use its best efforts to prevent a recurrence of fighting and, as necessary, to contribute to the maintenance and restoration of law and order and a return to normal conditions.' Subsequent semi-annual resolutions passed by the Security Council have kept the United Nations Force in Cyprus in being through the time of this writing (summer, 1970). Although the basic dispute between Greeks and Turks on Cyprus has remained unresolved, UNFICYP has made positive progress in its primary task of pacifying the Cypriot inter-communal war. UNFICYP, moreover, has also made substantial contribution in restoring Cyprus to conditions of normal order and stability. In at least these respects, the United Nations Force in Cyprus contrasted favorably with other U.N. peace-keeping forces in the Congo and Middle East. The Secretary General has thus been able with accuracy to term UNFICYP a 'successful' peace-keeping operation.

THE ORGANIZATION OF UNFICYP

UNFICYP had a total strength in 1970 of approximately 3 700 persons: 3 500 military personnel, and 200 civilian staff. The civilian side consisted of an official staff of about ten persons: the Special Representative to the Secretary General, political and legal advisors, an administrative section, and a public information office. These U.N. civilian officials were serving indeterminate tours in Cyprus. About another 20 or so persons on routine U.N. field service tours acted as secretaries or drivers to the civilian staff. Another civilian component of the U.N. presence in Cyprus were the 175 police officers who made up the United Nations Civilian Police (UNCIVPOL). Drawn in almost equal numbers from Australia, Austria, Denmark, and Sweden, UNCIVPOL performed liaison functions between the police forces of the Greek Cypriot and Turkish Cypriot communities.

It was the military side, however, which was by far and away the numerically dominant component of UNFICYP and which gave the United

Nations presence in Cyprus its distinguishing quality. The bulk of the military personnel were found in six national contingents, each consisting of approximately 500 officers and men. These national contingents were drawn from Canada, Denmark, Finland, Great Britain, Ireland, and Sweden: respectively referred to as Cancon, Dancon, Fincon, Britcon, Ircon, and Swedcon. Each of the national contingents was charged with responsibility for a specific region of Cyprus. Depending on the locale of their deployment, the national contingents performed duties such as: guarding 'Green Lines' (i.e. *de facto* borders between Greek and Turkish communities within cities); manning outposts – 'O.P.'s' – on the edge of Turkish enclaves in the countryside; patroling both Greek and Turkish Cypriot areas to monitor military movements and buildups, and supervising daily automobile convoys of Greek civilians through Turkish-controlled areas.

Each of the six national contingents were all similar in their being organized along the lines of reduced infantry battalions. They also shared in common a six-month tour of duty in Cyprus. There were, however, major differences between the national contingents in their recruitment and formation. Britcon and Cancon were ongoing integral military units composed entirely of regular career soldiers. Such units as the 'Pompadours' of Great Britain and the 'Black Watch' of Canada were made up of men who had soldiered together before coming to Cyprus and would presumably continue to do so afterwards. Dancon, Fincon, and Swedcon, on the other hand, were formed specifically for UNFICYP duty and were demobilized after their tour (to be replaced by another *ad hoc* unit). Moreover, the Scandinavian contingents consisted – except for senior officers – of reservists who had taken a temporary break in their civilian pursuits to volunteer for UNFICYP duty. The Irish contingent followed yet another pattern. Like the other English-speaking contingents, Ircon consisted of career regular soldiers, but like the Scandinavian contingents, it was an *ad hoc* volunteer unit formed specifically for a six-month tour in Cyprus.

A seventh national force, though not of contingent size, was the Austrian Field Hospital (AFH). The AFH was a 50-man military unit, including nine erstwhile civilian medical doctors and dentists fulfilling their Austrian military obligations. The AFH had the responsibility of treating UNFICYP soldiers whose ailments (or wounds in the event of combat) could not be handled by national contingent medical officers. The AFH also offered free dental care, a service of which great advantage was taken by UNFICYP personnel. Like the national contingents, the AFH personnel also served a six-month tour of duty in Cyprus.

344

In addition to the nationally homogeneous six contingents and Austrian Field Hospital, there were two multi-national military units in UNFICYP. One was the small 60-man Military Police Company consisting of soldiers drawn from each of the six national contingents. 'M. P. Coy' had jurisdiction over UNFICYP soldiers outside the camps of their respective national contingents. The UNFICYP Military Police, however, had no powers of punishment; violators were returned to their national contingents for disciplinary action.

With the exception of the Military Police Company, only Headquarters UNFICYP existed as a multi-national unit. With its approximately 500-man complement (about 50 officers and 450 other ranks), Headquarters was composed of representatives from each of the seven nations contributing to the United Nations military force in Cyprus. Both at the Headquarters offices and the Headquarters Officers Mess there was a genuine intermingling of disparate nationalities. Even at Headquarters, however, the multi-national representation was largely limited to staff officers; all seconded to UNFICYP from their home military establishments to serve minimum one-year tours in Cyprus. The supporting infrastructure and lower ranks of Headquarters UNFICYP was almost entirely a British affair. UNFICYP's logistics, ordnance, workshops, air support, reconnaissance squadron, and transportation corps were closely allied with the British Sovereign Base Areas. These 'SBA's' were themselves a vast complex of preexisting British military installations on Cyprus.

COLLECTION OF DATA

From October 1969 to May 1970, I was in Cyprus doing full time research on UNFICYP. Owing to my credentials as an accredited correspondent and the cooperation of the U.N. Press Office, I was granted the status of 'temporary official assignment' with UNFICYP. This allowed for my virtual complete access to all levels and ranks of UNFICYP military personnel. During the time of the field research, extended periods were spent with each of the national contingents, the Field Hospital, the Military Police Company, and Headquarters. In addition to formal interviews with 100 military officers (close to one-third of the entire UNFICYP officer complement), my findings are based on participant-observations in a variety of contexts: tactical situations, formal social affairs, informal gatherings, and perusal of UNFICYP documents and records. The openness of UNFICYP to the probings of a visitor allowed for a wide ranging opportunity to examine the social organization of a peacekeeping force. Perhaps, in some ways, this researcher was able to get a more complete picture of the social dynamics of UNFICYP than many of its formal members.

SOURCES OF CONFLICT

The variety of theoretical schemes available to the analyst of formal organizations are legion. Yet when all is said and done, there are probably only two major conceptual approaches to the examination of concrete social organizations. One approach is to ascertain what are the stated goals of the organization and then examine how much success or failure the organization has had in achieving these goals. The second perspective is to ascertain what are the kinds of differentiation within an organization and then examine the amount and types of conflict deriving from these internal cleavages. In this paper I have adopted the latter frame of reference.

There is the premise that the conflict approach can serve as an especially appropriate analytical framework to describe *all* social organizations. It does not imply that UNFICYP was a notably conflict ridden organization, but it does mean that UNFICYP like any social organization had its own internal and external sources of social strain. It is by this elemental comprehension of the inherent conflict in a social structure that researchers can begin to determine the essential sociological makeup of the organization under analysis. What follows then is in no sense an *exposé* of UNFICYP, but rather the application of a general form of social analyses to one particular formal organization.

Conflict between UNFICYP *and the United Nations Organization.* Strain between the UNFICYP organization in Cyprus and the United Nations Organization (UNO) in New York was apparent on several counts. One major source of dissatisfaction with UNO revolved around the lack of funds appropriated to UNFICYP military expenditures.

A Headquarters staff officer: 'This is the biggest penny pinching outfit you can imagine. The U.N. wastes millions on foolishness, and we can't even buy a wide-angle camera. Can you imagine! For a few pennies they will jeopardize the success of the whole operation.'

Another source of contention with UNO was the restrictions placed on the UNFICYP military in the performances of its mission.

A Canadian officer: 'We're sent here with our hands tied behind our backs. We're like traffic cops, we can only wave our hands. The politicians won't let us have any authority. If we could use a little muscle, this whole mess would be over in two weeks.'

346

Conflict between UNFICYP *and the home military establishments of contributing nations.* Because of the nature of the recruiting system – men seconded and units temporarily assigned to Cyprus from their home armies – UNFICYP often found itself at odds with the military establishments of contributing nations. Most of this strain centered around assignment of military personnel to the Headquarters UNFICYP staff. Whether or not an officer's tour would be extended depended ultimately on decisions made back in his home country's defence ministry.

There was also the general question as to what effect assignment to Cyprus had on the military careers of UNFICYP's serving officers. On this issue there were mixed views. Some believed U.N. duty offered an opportunity to demonstrate personal capabilities in an operational force, while others felt that absence from the mainstream of military advancement at home was detrimental to their military futures. The latter possibility, of course, could be a serious source of organizational strain. In either event, the elemental fact was that UNFICYP was an anomalous military structure: an officer served in a centrally commanded international force, but the power of permanent assignment and promotion rested in his home military organization. This meant that no matter what an officer's personal commitment toward a U.N. peacekeeping force might be, he knew that in both the short and long run his career advancement depended entirely on how he was evaluated within his own national army.

Conflict between Headquarters UNFICYP *and national contingents.* Much of the conflict between Headquarters UNFICYP and the national contingents was similar to that usually found between headquarters and line units in any military organization. There were criticisms by the national contingents that Headquarters was over-staffed and overly bureaucratic, or that it failed to take the contingents into account when policies were changed. For example, when the national contingents were redeployed in the spring of 1970 (in anticipation of a forthcoming reduction in UNFICYP strength), there was contingent resentment at the need to move out of established areas and be relocated in new surroundings.

A Danish officer: 'It will be disastrous to move the contingents around. It takes years to get to know the local situation and who is who in both Greek and Turk sides. If Headquarters is thinking about cutting back, the first place to start should be at Headquarters. The men in the contingents are working full-time seven days a week, at Headquarters they work half-days five days a week.'

Another vantage point illustrates a different kind of conflict between a Headquarters unit and the national contingents.

An officer in the Military Police Company: 'We have a hell of a problem trying to get cooperation from the contingents. The Irish and the British try to keep

control over their own M.P.'s even though they are assigned to M.P. Coy.
Another case. Just after I arrived, I had to send a Finn M.P. back to Fincon because
he couldn't do the job. I mean he was lazy, mean, and dumb. To make matters
worse he couldn't even say hello in English. Six months later Fincon is supposed to
send us another man. They send back the same guy, only this time he's a sergeant.
Now we're stuck with an absolute fuck-all who outranks my good men.'

Conflict between national contingents within UNFICYP. One would expect
differences between the national contingents would be a major source of
conflict within UNFICYP. In fact there was such conflict, but the bulk of the
inter-contingent strain derived from organizational features peculiar to
UNFICYP rather than hostilities between nationalities *per se*. One such
organizational tension was over the division of labor within UNFICYP.

A Swedish officer: 'We can pull our maintenance on our vehicles, but we must
send them to Dhekelia [in the SBA's]. This means the work is done slower and
not as well as we could do it. But, of course, this is to give the Brits at Dhekelia a
job. They have to find something for them to do. The Brits are using the U.N. for
their own purposes.'

An Austrian officer: 'The report [of the 1969 Economic Committee on
UNFICYP] was unfair in the way it computed costs. This made the Field Hospital
look bad compared to the British base hospitals. The report did not mention
the work the Field Hospital is doing on dental treatment, outpatient care,
and taking care of UNCIVPOL. The Chief Medical Officer at Headquarters was a
Brit and he fixed the report to make us look bad and the SBA's good.
The Brits are trying to get UNFICYP to use the British hospitals and close down
the Field Hospital.'

Another organizational strain centered on the quite real differences in
the pay scales of the various contingents. On this score the British in
particular had cause for resentment. Alone of the national contingents,
Britcon received no special U.N. pay allowances. Although most pronounced in Britcon, the differential in U.N. allowances was a source of
resentment for other nationalities as well. These allowances – paid for
from United Nations funds were in addition to base salaries paid for by
home military establishments – were highest for the Swedes and Danes:
approximately $330 U.S. monthly for officers, and $100 U.S. monthly for
other ranks.

A British officer: 'How do you think my men feel? A British soldier makes £10
a week and a Swede two miles down the road makes £30 a week for doing exactly
the same thing. How do I explain to my men about making the world safe for
peacekeeping? They want to know why they're not getting paid what that Swede
is getting paid. And I don't know what to tell him myself.'

A British officer: 'We had a British captain at Headquarters who found that
his Danish driver was earning twice as much as he was. We feel like poor
relations here. Even when we go to Cancon they do the treating because they know
we don't have any money.'

Although often in a humorous vein, there was also some inter-contingent

348

asperity of a more chauvinistic nature reflected in negative stereotypes acquired in Cyprus.

An Irish sergeant: 'Sure we can speak English with the Canadians, but my god, they're a rowdy bunch. Nobody likes a drink and a good time more than an Irishman, but those Canadians are something else again. They get loud too early, if you get what I mean.'

A Danish officer: 'When we took over Xeros from the Irish, you couldn't believe the filth there was. These Irish aren't civilized. The first thing we did was kill millions of cockroaches. Millions and millions of them. We made mountains out of them and burned them. They even spoke Irish. The Irish were with those cockroaches for four years and lived together like one big family.'

Genuine hostility between nationalities, however, was rare. And in those cases where it was present, the animosity had origins long preceding UNFICYP assignment; most notably, that of many Irish toward the British, and a few British toward the Austrians.

An Irish officer: 'We just don't talk politics with the English. It's better that way, because a lot of us couldn't control ourselves once we start talking and thinking about the old days and what's going on up North right now. It's a miracle there hasn't been a good punch-up between us yet.'

A British officer: 'Don't forget all the top Austrian officers were Nazis. They run the Field Hospital just like a stalag. One of their officers can get damn obnoxious once he gets a few drinks in him. That's when he starts complaining "why can't I wear my [German] medals. I won them in honor." It's hard enough to forget the War without him always reminding us.'

By far, however, the most frequent point of disputation between the national contingents involved invidious comparisons of their respective military prowess and organizational effectiveness.

A Danish officer: 'The British have an army to solve their unemployment problem. The Black Watch aren't soldiers, they're lumberjacks and timbermen from Canada. These are men who can't make a living at home and bring their troubles into the Army.'

A Swedish officer: 'Our men are not collected from the slums of their countries. They are volunteers who have been carefully picked. They are the cream of the crop and a much higher grade of men than you would find in a regular group of soldiers. Just compare their intelligence and manners with the Brits and the Irish and the Canadians.'

A Canadian officer: 'The Canadians and British are the only real soldiers here. The Irish are a sloppy army. The Danes and Finns are really civilians in uniform here for a vacation in the sun. The Swedes with their beards and necklaces are a hippy army.'

A British officer: 'How can you seriously compare a unit like the Pompadours with the others except the Black Watch. We and the Canadians are an army. The others are a mixed batch of civilian tourists, half-soldiers, and a few professionals who never fought a war'.

Conflict between different components within the same nationalities. In some ways conflict within the national groups represented in UNFICYP was more

349

noticeable than that between nationalities. Common to all contingents was a tension point introduced by the shortness of the six-month rotation cycle. Due to the brevity of a contingent's tour, there was a tendency to let matters – especially housekeeping and maintenance standards – slide. Advance detachments of about-to-arrive contingents were thus often placed in the position of having to receipt property which was not always fully accounted for or in proper condition. The conflict between departing and newly arriving units was manifest in the latter's complaint that little had been done previously to beautify the compound area or establish adequate standard operating procedures. Each unit tended to see itself as 'really the first to get things in shape.' There were repeated remarks in all contingents along the lines of: 'You can't imagine how bad things were here before we came over.'

Another source of intra-contingent tension was applicable only to the Scandinavian units. The contingents from Denmark, Finland, and Sweden had officer complements consisting of both reservists and career professionals. The reservists on temporary active duty were on 'contract' for a specific UNFICYP tour. There pay was equal to that of career officers of the same rank. Many of the professional officers viewed their reservist counterparts as being in Cyprus sheerly for a paid vacation. For their part, the reservists often saw the career officers as overly concerned with military formality and picayune discipline.

A Danish career officer: 'The reserve officer comes here on contract to make some easy money and have a good time. He cares nothing about making the army run a little better because he is not part of it. You tell me what kind of army pays its amateurs more than professionals.'

A Swedish reserve officer: 'You can write a whole book on what's wrong with the Swedish Army. It is rigid and authoritarian. Men who would be failures in civilian life are on the top. It is only the reserve officer who brings initiative and common sense into a fossil system.'

Three of the nations contributing military units to UNFICYP – Austria, Denmark, Sweden – also contributed civilian policement to UNCIVPOL. The relationships between the UNCIVPOL policemen with their fellow nationals on the military side of UNFICYP was a curious blend of cordiality and calculation. Natural ties of common nationality in a foreign society were sometimes strained by questions of seniority. On more than one occasion seemingly petty issues of protocol and precedence could lead to uncomfortable social situations.

The special situation of the British with their large military bases on Cyprus made for another kind of resentment. Although relations between British serving in UNFICYP and the British military in the SBA's was not

350

one of conflict, the Britcon soldier was hard pressed not to contrast his position unfavorably with that of British servicemen in the SBA's. The latter enjoyed more lenient pass privileges, more modern living accommodations, and a much greater array of post facilities. Thus the Britcon soldier suffered a sense of relative deprivation not only in comparison to his higher-paid UNFICYP counterparts but as well to his more privileged fellow nationals serving in Cyprus outside the United Nations.

A British sergeant: 'Kitchener lived in this very camp in the 1880's.
And it hasn't changed since, except that it's more run down. Yet a few miles down the road are the most comfortable British barracks in the whole road [in the SBA's]. Britcon is neither fish nor fowl. The British government cuts us off because we are part of UNFICYP. The United Nations cuts us off because we are part of the British Army in Cyprus.'

Conflict between military personnel and civilian staff within UNFICYP. Without doubt, the most structured conflict in UNFICYP was not between or within its constituent national forces, nor between different levels in the military hierarchy. Rather, the most evident strain was between UNFICYP military officers and the U.N. civilian staff in Cyprus. In one sense this was a restatement of the prevalent belief on the part of UNFICYP officers that the civilian staff – in Cyprus along with UNO in New York – was letting erroneous political considerations stand in the way of military effectiveness.

A Danish officer: 'In 1967 the Dancon commander went down to an O.P. on the Green Line where a Danish soldier had been disarmed by some Turkish fighters. He went down there with an automatic weapon and waved it at the Turks. He threatened to shoot the whole bunch right there on the spot. It worked. But it got the commander into a lot of trouble with the civilians back at Headquarters. They were out of their minds. But that is the kind of officer I would want to serve under. An officer's first responsibility is to look after the safety of his men. How can you bring peace if your men don't respect you? This is what the civilian mind will never understand.'
An Irish officer: 'A little while back there was a Finn soldier who was shot at from a Greek village. The Finns drove up their armored cars and threatened to shoot the whole village right then and there if there was another shooting. This was the only correct thing to do. Otherwise the Cyps think you're free game. You have to protect your men above all else. But the Fincon commander was in serious trouble after that. The Headquarters civilians really took after him. "No, no, no. You can't touch a hair on a Cypriot." But I'd do the same thing.'

But beyond the almost *pro forma* complaints of the inadequacy of the civilian support given military commanders, there were numerous other tensions between military personnel and civilian staff within UNFICYP. These tensions derived from differences in social background, organizational authority, and socio-political attitudes. Indeed, the differentiation between the two groups made UNFICYP a kind of microcosm of the civil-

351

military conflict long noted in independent state systems. Perhaps most apparent was the pervasive resentment of the UNFICYP officer corps toward the privileges and life styles of the U.N. civilian staff.

A Finnish officer: 'The civilian staff are the aristocrats of Cyprus.
They live like diplomats while soldiers do all the dirty work and live in old buildings and tents. I used to believe in the United Nations and give donations to it.
But not after coming here. They should give money to those soldiers on
the Green Line and the O.P.'s who deserve it. Not to the high living U.N. civilians.'

Compounding the military's displeasure with the particular life styles of the civilian staff in Cyprus, there was a generalized resentment of what was thought to be a deepseated civilian arrogance and condescension toward military personnel. On the part of some UNFICYP serving officers, there was even an ultimate questioning of the very morality of the civilian staff in their peacekeeping role.

A Swedish officer: 'Ralph Bunche – we call him "bunk" – detests soldiers.
This is true of almost all U.N. administrative staff including that in Cyprus.
It starts from the very top. We soldiers are a different breed to them.
The big problem in the U.N. is racism. Not the usual kind, but civilian racism against the military. But we soldiers are like women. The U.N. can't live with us, but can't do without us.'

A Canadian officer: 'You must remember that while we change every six months, the civilians stay on and on and on. This gives them a chance to dig in.
They have their lives invested in this operation. If peace comes what would they do?
You know the U.N. types, good at languages and not much anything else. Smooth and glib, but with no place to go home to. Men between countries. They live like ambassadors. The easiest way to save money for the U.N. is to take away the limousines and big apartments of the U.N. officials here. What's keeping us here is the civilians wanting to keep this thing going and milk it for all its worth.'

The underlying resentment of many UNFICYP military officers toward the U.N. civilian staff took one notable form in the rather frequent, and always favorable, mentions of Major General Carl von Horn. A Swedish career officer, von Horn had an impressive background in various peace-keeping activities, including command of the U.N. forces in the Congo. Von Horn had subsequently written a book scathingly critical of the U.N. civilian leadership. By a coincidental circumstance von Horn was living in retirement in Cyprus at the time of my field research. Although he was *persona non grata* in U.N. official circles – in and out of Cyprus – there were circumspect, if not subterraneous, informal contacts between von Horn and some UNFICYP military officers. But the comments given below were typical of many UNFICYP officers who had never personally met von Horn.

A Finnish officer: 'Soldiers are always looked upon by the civilian staff as an inevitable evil. The military is something dirty for U.N. officials.
This is what von Horn told so well in his book. If you see him, tell him he has many secret admirers in UNFICYP. He knows how soldiers are made to feel like

second-class citizens by U.N. officials. We have three enemies in Cyprus, you know: the Greeks, the Turks, and the U.N. civilians.'

A British officer: 'Von Horn wrote what a lot of us feel. Only we can't so publically. But somebody had to blow the whistle on what these U.N. civilians are doing to the military. Von Horn is a sort of underground hero to a lot of officers who've been in the U.N.'

ORGANIZATIONAL CONFLICT:
U.N. PEACEKEEPING VIS-À-VIS NATIONAL MILITARY FORCES

A more complete assessment of the sources of conflict found in UNFICYP requires that they be evaluated in terms of whether they are unique to United Nations peacekeeping forces (as typified by UNFICYP), or whether they are general to military organizations in the main (as represented by mono-national military establishments). This is done in the comparisons given in Chart 1. The structured strains noted in UNFICYP – both civil military and intra-military – are categorized as to whether they are: (a) applicable to most or all military organizations, (b) characteristic of most or all military organizations, but especially evident in U.N. peacekeeping forces, and (c) characteristically found only in U.N. peacekeeping forces.

One set of conflicts was that seemingly generic to military organization, inclusive of UNFICYP. Thus in civil-military relationships there was the dissatisfaction of UNFICYP military personnel with the amount of funds and kinds of facilities allotted for military purposes by civilian authorities. On this score certainly, neither its multi-national membership nor its peacekeeping mission excluded UNFICYP from one endemic source of complaint on the part of armed forces establishments.

Within the military organization of UNFICYP itself, there were the tensions between staff and line units, between reserve officers and career officers, and between officers and lower ranks. Again these kinds of UNFICYP strains were organizationally akin to virtually all national armies.

On a second level, there were the conflicts characteristic of all or most military organizations, but especially evident in UNFICYP. The political restrictions placed by civilian authorities on field commanders in their use of force have often been a source of contention in civil-military relationships. However, the novel nature of the peacekeeping mission – the very *raison d'être* of UNFICYP – placed especially heavy strains on the traditionally trained United Nations military personnel in Cyprus. Similarly, civil-military relations in national military establishments are often characterized by the military's resentment of the higher living standards of civilian officials. Such resentment is aggravated by the military's perception of civilian arrogance and condescension toward military personnel. These frequent sore points in standard civil-military relationships were exasperated in UNFICYP due to the smallness of the force and the resultant close interaction and observation between its military officers and civilian staff. Moreover, in most cases, the living and working conditions (but *not*

Chart 1. Levels of Conflict in military organizations: comparisons of U.N. peacekeeping with national military forces

| Generality of Conflict | Source of Conflict | |
	Civil-Military Relations	Intra-Military Factors
characteristic of most or all military organizations, whether national or U.N. peacekeeping forces	military resentment of lack of funds appropriated for its use	staff vs. line reserve vs. career personnel officers vs. lower ranks
characteristic of most or all military organizations, but more evident in U.N. peacekeeping forces	political restrictions on military's use of force military's perception of life styles of associated civilian officials military's perception of arrogance and condescension of associated civilian officials	division of labor invidious comparisons of military prowess by constituent units
characteristically found only in U.N. peacekeeping forces		power of assignment/ promotion residing in other than operational unit official language other than that of some units pay differences between national units negative stereotypes between national units

pay) of UNFICYP military personnel were of a lower order than was the case in their home countries.

On the same level of conflicts prevalent in most military organizations but more notable in UNFICYP were certain intra-military factors. A prime quality of much of the UNFICYP subculture centered in the invidious comparisons made between the UNFICYP contingents as to their respective military prowess, recruitment policies, and organizational merits. Although these comparisons were in fact based on real differences within UNFICYP, similar parallels can be found within mono-national armed forces; namely, conflict between services and between elite forces and regular units. The division-of-labor squabbles between certain UNFICYP units and the British bases were in one sense unique to the Cyprus operation. But in another manner these were again similar to inter-service jurisdictional rivalries within single national military establishments.

On a third level was the set of conflicts normally absent in national militaries but characteristic of U.N. peacekeeping operations as typified by UNFICYP. None of the observed civil-military conflicts fell into this category. Rather, the strains peculiar to UNFICYP lay in its internal military organization. There was the apparently unavoidable difficulties resulting from the official use of a language which placed about half of the UNFICYP military personnel at varying degrees of disadvantage. That some negative stereotypes of other national units existed – whether preexistent or acquired in Cyprus – seemed likewise unavoidable. More serious, however, than either linguistic hurdles or unfavorable national images were the pay discrepancies between constituent national components. Whether due to initially higher base salaries received from home military establishments or the system of U.N. allowances for Cyprus duty, the resentment of the lower toward the higher remunerated was a pervasive source of tension within UNFICYP.

Another conflict unique to U.N. peacekeeping forces was found in the relationship between UNFICYP and its contributing national military establishments. This was the structured strain resulting from the organizational separation of the power of assignment and promotion from the operational unit in which an officer served (i.e. between the officer's national army and UNFICYP). In other words, unlike service in the standard armed forces where duty and promotion/assignment are under the same chain of command, service in UNFICYP offered no permanent assignment nor any sort of advancement through United Nations channels.

As is probably apparent, the organizational conflicts unique to U.N. peacekeeping forces do not necessarily derive from their peacekeeping mission *per se*. The strains resulting from differences in language, inter-unit national stereotyping, discrepant pay scales, and the intermesh of career paths alternating between international and home military assignments are also those similarly inherent in other multi-national commands. At the same time, the distinctive tensions emanating from the multi-national aspects of UNFICYP overlay other more basic conflicts typically found in mono-national military organizations. Thus, UNFICYP, along with its being the first major 'success' in U.N. peacekeeping operations, displayed organizational qualities with ample precedent in conventional military structures.

We conclude then by reiterating a cardinal point made earlier in this essay. The use of a conflict framework as an interpretive variable does not stigmatize UNFICYP as especially rent by strife. Indeed, the emphasis on conflict given in the description of UNFICYP has purposefully distorted reality by obscuring the countervailing tendencies toward consensus also existing in UNFICYP. But it is to say that like all organizations UNFICYP was no exception in possessing external and internal sources of conflict; and it is in the comprehension of these conflicts that much of the underlying structure of UNFICYP is revealed. Moreover, the conflicts of UNFICYP were in the main common to all military organizations with the added strains peculiar to multi-national forces. Finally, and perhaps most important, if and when the United Nations is employed as a peacekeeping force in other locales and crises, the sources of organizational conflict found in the UNFICYP case will almost certainly be recapitulated.

Appendix 1. ORGANIZATION CHART OF UNFICYP

Key:

MPIO: Mil. Public Info. Officer
COO: Chief Operations Officer
CSO: Chief Signals Officer
CPO: Chief Personnel Officer
CMO: Chief Medical Officer
FE: Force Engineer
CLO: Chief Logistics Officer
EME: Electrical Mech. Engineers
UNCIVPOL: United Nations Civilian Police

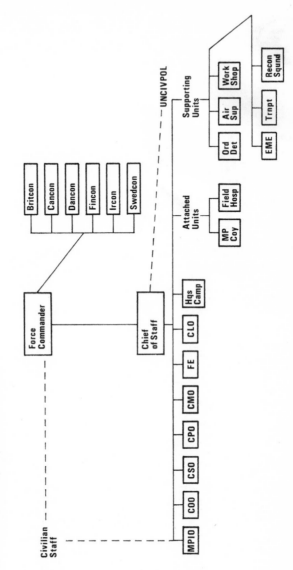

The Assessment of the Military Mind: a Critical Comment on Methodology

H. W. TROMP*

* Polemological institute, University of Groningen, The Netherlands.

'Colonel Bantry, like nearly all retired military men, is really abnormally
sensitive. He reacts very quickly to public opinion'.
(Agatha CHRISTIE: *The Body in the Library*, London, 1942)

INTRODUCTION

It is interesting to note how and where all kinds of opinions are found
about the existence of a so-called 'military mind.' This often seems to be a
General Common Denominator for anything that goes wrong: rising
arms budgets, decreasing security, wrong priorities in decisionmaking,
endless arms races, and finally, war. On the other hand, it is often stressed
how the army was and is the 'Erziehungsschule der Nation' and how
generally highly accepted values such as loyalty, sense of duty, obedience,
responsibility, service of the country, and patriotism are learned by
serving in the armed forces. On a more abstract level of scientific sophistication, the 'military mind' is often identified as a somewhat peculiar
branch of the so-called 'authoritarianism' complex, if not the ideal type
of the state of mind of the 'Authoritarian Personality.' Conservatism and
chauvinism seem to be its prominent features, along with rigidity of
thought, opposition to social change, closedmindedness to societal
developments.

However, *Gene Lyons* (1963) points out, that the notion of a military
mind is no more sinister than the notion of a scientific mind or a legal
mind or any collection of habits and attitudes that are the product of
well-developed professional training and mores. 'There is a military
mind', he states, 'and all military men, to one degree or another, possess
it. It is a mind that is used to order and predictability, that insists on
decisions being made, that cannot tolerate procrastination, that is comfortable in the manageable world of a military post and often uncon-
sciously makes over any other setting – the home, the office, even the
presidency of the United States – with the same characteristics of punctu-
ality, rank and simplicity. (...) The military mind is largely a product of
the military system, the repetitive training, the requirements of obedience, the instilling of assured responses to known stimuli, and the development of trust through respect for position and hierarchy. The system,
in turn, is essentially determined by the demands of combat.'

Sapin and *Snyder* (1954) summarized some criticisms of the military
mind as follows: 'alleged tendencies toward a rigidity in thought and
problem analysis... inadequate weighing of non-military factors in
military problems... an authoritarian approach to most social issues and

361

situations... insulation from nonmilitary knowledge... judgement of policy goals and techniques primarily in terms of military force and military strategy.'

Janowitz (1960) stated six years later, that this kind of military mind has been seriously challenged by the technological and social developments, and that, in fact, a new kind of 'military manager' comes into existence. The new values are initiative and continuous innovation; internationalism instead of ethnocentrism, and no more 'disciplinarianism': 'The new doctrine seeks to deal with human factors in combat and large scale organizations in a manner conforming to temporary thought on human relations'.

There are quite a number of scholars who have occupied themselves with theory-building about alleged or ascribed characteristics of the military mind. Generally speaking, their theories are not convincing. Often they seem plausible, but what fails are data from empirical research. The research done, is limited in scope and deficient in method. Perhaps one of the main reasons why social scientists have not been able to analyze and describe empirically the military subculture sufficiently, is that it is an often found characteristic of the military to refuse to regard themselves as a subculture with its own norms, values, ways of thinking and traditions. If they consent to research, it seems to be mostly on irrelevant matters. If they become enthusiastic at all about research, it seems to be mostly about research concerning the faults on the 'other side.' Even fundamental problems confronting the military, which arise from the widening gap between the attitudes of the younger generation and those of the professional military often seem to be solved by simply ignoring them, and in case of open conflict, by taking the way of the hardest legally permitted punishment.

Nevertheless, to the social scientist the military mind poses a challenge for investigation. If the complex of attitudes held by the military could be analysed and if the structure and content of this attitude complex could be differentiated from that of other strata of the population in society, it might become possible to make predictions about their behavior on matters of general importance.

'Militarism,' states *Murray Thomson* (1968), 'is an ideology as old as history, with deeply-based social and psychological roots. An ideology is a set of interrelated attitudes. Each attitude – each tendency to act in a certain way – is based on certain strongly-held opinions. Opinions which comprise militarist attitudes include: "Man is evil by nature; consequently wars are inevitable. There is nothing one man can do to prevent them.

362

It is man's duty to defend his country and way of life, by violence if necessary, against those who threaten them. It is idealistic to believe in love and nonviolence, for in the last analysis people cannot be trusted. Walk softly, but carry a big stick. Praise the Lord and pass the ammunition".'

According to this view it should be possible to analyse the military 'ideology' using attitude scales as a tool of research and in the final analysis one could try to find out whether there exists a significant difference between the 'state of mind' of the members of a military institution, and the non-members.

In fact, there is no reason to assume that these basic hypotheses are wrong. All evidence suggests that indeed such a thing as a military mind exists. For example, in our own research we tried to define the basic characteristics of the military mind, and we used Rokeach's Dogmatism scale (1960) on the basis of the hypothesis that a high level of military professionalism should yield a high score on the D-scale. This turned out to be exactly what the data indicated (one complicating factor was the level of education, which proved to be an important intervening variable: the level of education correlated negatively with the D-score). In this study the scores of 364 assorted young military personnel were compared with those obtained from 376 (on the basic variables almost identical) nonmilitary young people. Using an at random sampled item pool of 90 items (including the D-scale) we found meanwhile a group of six items, that discriminated the whole of the group of military and civilians very clearly. These six items could be described as a kind of 'militarism' scale in itself, as the professional military made the highest scores, followed by the conscripts, and finally, with very low scores, came the civilian group. In a further analysis we factoranalysed the whole item pool, and found a slight but unmistakable difference in the structuring of the selected items, again between the military and the civilian group. But as there was already ample evidence in other literature for the existence of a 'military mind,' the question arises what is the predictive power of such 'attitudes measuring.' This question became very intriguing, and as we conducted at about the same time experiments with internation simulation models, we tried to measure the effect of participation, using attitude-items, and in the process found that cadets of the Royal Military Academy of the Netherlands scored high on Dogmatism items, and again on the six 'militarism' items mentioned above and in general showed a somewhat 'hawkish' attitude towards international politics and international decisionmaking. But their verbal behavior in scoring on attitude scales did not in the least correlate positively – at face value – with their political behavior in the internation simulation. They showed a considerable 'dovishness' often almost ignoring incentives from the other side in raising the arms budget. Of course this can be explained as being due to other intervening variables, but was nevertheless unexpected in view of the attitude scores. The behavior of the students of the 'Academy of Dramatic Art' was equally different, compared to their attitude scores, which showed a considerably more 'pacifistic' orientation than that of the cadets. But in the simulation their behavior was not in the least consistent with these scores, either.

These observations, simultaneously made, raised serious doubts about the usefulness of attitude-scoring in general. The purpose of this paper therefore is twofold: First, to give an operational definition of the military mind in terms of attitude measuring, and secondly, to discuss the relevance of such measures in view of their prediction value.

ATTITUDES

Measuring attitudes is done by requiring subjects to indicate their agreement or disagreement with a set of statements (items) about the attitude object. The typical attitude scale measures the acceptance of evaluative statements about the attitude object. One of the weaknesses of this method is that the evaluations of the persons involved in scale construction correspond to those of the individuals whose attitudes are being measured. It is mostly assumed that for a set of statements a possible difference of opinion should lead to a non-significant error. The usefulness of an attitude scale depends upon its properties. A scale must be *reliable*, i.e. it must give consistent results; and it must be *valid* (measure what it is purported to measure). There are still more things to be mentioned relating to attitude scaling, but they are mainly technical points and they are not important for the focus of interest in this paper.

Measuring attitudes has become fashionable. Attitudes scales have been developed for almost forty years, ranging from, for example, anti-negro scales to aesthetic-values scales, and from very general constructs such as the Dogmatism (*Rokeach*, 1960) or Authoritarianism (*Adorno et al.*, 1950) scales to specific ones such as the 'sense of political futility' scale (*McClosky*, 1964).

Problems arise when one starts to compare the definitions of 'attitudes' as well as their operationalisations. *Shaw* and *Wright* (1967) state that

'...despite the variation in the definition of the term, the existing definitions agree upon one common characteristic: Attitude entails an existing predisposition to respond to social objects which, in interaction with situational and other dispositional variables, *guides and directs overt behavior of the individual.*' They mention three kinds of variance in attitude definitions. The first one concerns the difference in specificity versus generality in the determination of behavior.

The second source of variation results from the tendency to generalize the construct to include all predispositions to respond, social or non-social. In the third place there is a difference in the theoretical conception of the composition of the attitude: some writers conceptualize attitude as consisting of three components, an *affective* component, a *cognitive* component and a behavioral one (for example *Krech* and *Crutchfield*, 1962); but *Triandis* (1964) suggested that the term attitude subsumes evaluations, behavioral intentions and opinions. *Shaw* and *Wright* chose their own brand of conceptualisation here: 'we prefer to limit the theoretical construct of attitude to an affective component which is based upon cognitive processes and is an antecedent of behavior, i.e. we consider an attitude to be an evaluative reaction based upon evaluative concepts which are closely related to other cognitions and to overt behavior.' They finally define the term attitude as follows: 'A relatively enduring system of evaluative, affective reactions based upon and reflecting the evaluative concepts or beliefs which have been learned about the characteristics of a social object or class of social objects.' They summarize the general characteristics of attitudes as follows:
1. Attitudes are based upon evaluative concepts regarding characteristics of the referent object and give rise to motivated behavior;
2. Attitudes are construed as varying in quality and intensity (or strength) on a continuum from positive through neutral to negative;
3. Attitudes are learned, rather than being innate or a result of constitutional development and maturation;
4. Attitudes have specific social referents, or specific classes thereof;
5. Attitudes possess varying degrees of interrelatedness to one another;
6. Attitudes are relatively stable and enduring.

They conclude, 'that attitude is best viewed as a set of affective reactions towards the attitude object, derived from the concepts or beliefs that the individual has concerning the object, and *predisposing the individual to behave in a certain manner toward the attitude object.*'

It is the last part of this sentence that seems particularly interesting:

365

'...predisposing the individual to behave in a certain manner.' It is not for the first time that this remark is found in attitude literature, and, as *Wicker* (1970) states, 'one possible reason for the popularity of the attitude concept is that social psychologists have assumed that attitudes have something to do with behavior.' *Cohen* (1964) puts it very short and very clear: ... 'Thus attitudes are always seen as precursors of behavior, as determinants of how a person will actually behave in his daily affairs.'

Nevertheless, after an extensive review of the literature, in particular of the studies where some empirical relation between attitudes and actions was the focus of interest, *Wicker* comes to the conclusion that there is... 'little evidence to support the postulated existence of stable, underlying attitudes within the individual which influence both his verbal expressions and his actions.'

In a way, critique like this was foreseen, for example by *Shaw* and *Wright*, when they wrote: 'Behavior is determined by a complex set of forces, so that the effect of any determinant is contingent upon the number and strength of other determinants operating at any given time. Therefore, it is possible that two persons holding opposite attitudes toward a given object will behave in identical ways (outwardly, at least) toward that object.' It seems to be one of the major points of critique on the attitude-scaling procedures in general, that so little is said or investigated about its relevance: the theoretical or scientific relevance, and particularly the relevance for society. Attitude scaling seems to have become a very sophisticated technique, but little is validated about what is measured exactly, and furthermore what one can do with the results of attitude scaling remains unclear.

CRITICAL COMMENTS ON ATTITUDE SCALING

One can wonder about the relevance of verbal responses given in an interview situation on stimuli that are also verbal and have neither anything to do with the actual situation in which the respondent is interviewed, nor with the situation to which the statement refers. When one asks to respond to a statement with 'agree/not agree' (for example 'I am completely opposed to allowing negrous into white neighbour-hoods') there are references possible to three kinds of social situations. The respondent can at the moment of answering the question identify himself with a reference group outside the interview situation (and the interviewer can only guess at which one); he can answer the question depending on his relationship with the interviewer, i.e. referring to the interview situation; and he can refer to the actual content of the question and identify with the social situation as described in the statement.

Perhaps this remark can be put in another way: attitude scaling presumably starts from the assumption that the sociological dimension is not relevant at all, and does not make any difference to the actual scoring. But it is possible too, to assume that attitudes are a function of the individual's participation in a group, subculture or institution, and to regard attitude scores as an affirmation of the ideology of the group to which the individual refers at the moment he gives responses to the attitude statements. Perhaps it is exactly of this possibility that *Rokeach* was thinking, when he wrote at the end of his study 'The open and the closed mind': ... 'The structural properties that define the organization of belief-disbelief systems may be merely the cognitive representation of parallel structural properties existing in social organizations.' Does an attitude score say something about a personality variable, or does it reflect the social situation (the group, its values, its norms) to which the individual refers or identifies with at the moment of answering the items of the scale? It should be noted that each individual belongs to more than one group, and that his behavior can often be explained by looking for his reference groups. And there is no reason to assume that only his behavior and not his attitudes are influenced by these reference groups.

A second point of criticism comes to the surface, when an explicit distinction is made between *verbal* and *behavioral* affirmation of an ideology, which is presented in the condensed form of attitude statements. A remark of *Scheflen* (1968) illustrates this point clearly. 'Personality,' he says, 'could be defined as an integration of all the parts an individual characteristically plays in programs and how he performs them. Culture (...) could be defined as a program of programs including all the statements about programs and about roles that are handed down with them (...). When one is learning a program, the commentary may be learned with it and henceforth repeated with the formats without knowing why. In this way, linguistic accompaniments that do not represent understanding or insight into the activities may be transmitted from generation to generation. It can be asserted that, in some cases at least, people not only learn how they are to refer to, think of, feel about programs. This last point has a number of implications for psychological theory. We have traditionally assumed that feelings and thoughts precede and cause behavior; this view opens the possibility that behavior may precede feelings and thoughts, or all may occur simultaneously.' *Van der Dennen* (1970) concludes: '... subjects cannot adequately report what they are doing; what they can report are cultural or idiosyncratic myths about

367

behavior. (...) When requested to give motives, they give sanctioned motivations.'

The main point of this criticism has to do with the tacit assumption that man is a 'homo rationalis,' that his behavior is directed by his thoughts: in other words, that the mind is the independent variable and the behavior the dependent one. But there is no evidence for such an assumption. People act according to, or at least in response to expectations of the groups to which they belong. Their behavior, as far as it is not ritualized (as mostly seems to be the case) does not depend primarily on rational thinking. Most of it is already prescribed by indoctrinated 'programs' (*Scheflen*) which form the content of their culture; and if they use their brains, it is perhaps more to rationalize their behavior afterwards, than to direct it.

In the same way ritualized behavior can be described as a scenario or a program, ideology might be described as ritualized thinking and statements about behavior. But the idea that there is a relationship between ideology (defined as a complex of more or less consistent attitudes towards social objects) and behavior is an intuitive, not a scientific notion. *Van der Dennen* states in accordance with this, that 'it is more adequate to speak of the manifestations of an ideological infrastructure with situationally codable aspects' and he gives an example of what happened with the concept 'punitivity.' In marital relations, it will be called 'paternalism', to dissidents in the 'ingroup' the term 'authoritarian aggression' (as defined by *Adorno* c.s.) seems appropriate, and in connection with outgroups in general the notion of 'xenophobia' or 'ethnocentrism' will be used. To specific outgroups or coloured minorities 'racism' or 'anti-semitism' are often found labels. To the ideological antagonist on nationstate level 'belligerence,' 'militarism,' 'nationalism,' 'anti-communism' or 'pacifism' seem to be the appropriate terms; 'punitivity' to everybody in general is distinguished from the other notions by calling it 'misanthropy' or 'intolerance,' and when it has to do with attitudes about certain behaviors or verbalisations on a more religious level it will be mentioned as 'religious orthodoxy.' You can add 'fundamental distrust' to the concept of punitivity in general, and then you will have an appropriate description of paranoia.

There are still quite a number of other vulnerabilities of the attitude concept, and its operationalisations. But the question of the relevance of attitude measuring and in particular, the prediction value of attitude scores in predicting behavior remains the most important one.

Clearly, the attitude concept received so much attention, because it worked so well. It appeared that people could indeed be measured on

368

scales, that their scores proved to remain consistent over a period of time, and in the end the operationalisation and the refining of attitude measurement has become one of the finer intellectual exercises in the social sciences. It will not be the first time, that in the course of things a few basic questions do not get the attention they deserve, or even seem to have been forgotten altogether.

BEHAVIOR

In predicting overt behavior, additional factors beside attitudes need to be taken into account. But what factors? *Weissberg* (1965) wrote: ...'An attitude, not matter how conceived, is simply one of the terms in the complex regression equation we use to predict behavior; none cannot expect it to do too much. I think we must take seriously Lewin's formula, $B = f(P, E)$ (Behavior = a function of (Personality, Environment)). If the latent variable (attitude) is conceived inside P...one still needs to know the specific nature of the environment, the form of the function relating P and E, and the other predispositions and their interactions with the one under consideration, before one can accurately predict behavior. The embarrassing thing is that we have not systematically investigated these other sources of influence on overt behavior, and not that we are unable to predict the overt behavior solely from the predisposition.'

Nevertheless, other factors have been mentioned. *Wicker* (1970) summarizes a number of them; they are proposed as explanations for attitude-behavior inconsistencies. They are roughly divided in *personal* and *situational* factors. The personal factors are other attitudes held by the individual, competing motives, verbal, intellectual and social skills, and activity levels. As situational factors, which seem to be of far greater importance in predicting behavior, he mentions actual or considered presence of certain people, normative prescriptions of proper behavior, alternative behaviors available, specificity of attitude objects, unforeseen extraneous events, and expected and/or actual consequences of various acts. *Fishbein* (1967) attempted to combine several factors into a systematic formulation. *Wicker* summarized this as follows: 'Rather than viewing attitude toward a stimulus as a major determinant of behavior with respect to that object, the theory identifies three kinds of variables that function as the basic determinants of behavior: (1) attitudes toward the behavior; (2) normative beliefs both personal and social; and (3) motivation to comply with the norms. The first component, attitudes toward behavior, depends upon (*a*) the individual's beliefs about the consequences of performing a particular behavior (in a given situation) and (b) his evaluation of these consequences. The second component may be broken down into two categories of normative beliefs: (1) the individual's beliefs about what he personally feels he should do and (2) the individual's belief about what "society" "says" he should do.' *Fishbein* states that the relative importance of attitudes towards the behavior of an individual, personal normative beliefs and motivation, and social normative beliefs and motivation must be empirically determined, and he suggests that the weights may vary from behavior to behavior, and from person to person.

All of it comes down to the simple statement, that attitudes can indeed influence behavior, but that it is not known under what conditions and to what extent; and it is not even known how much of the variance in behavior depends on the attitudes held by the individual. Perhaps it is only a marginal factor, perhaps even as a factor it is not important at all.

Roghmann (1966) in the process of revising the authoritarianism and dogmatism theories, proposes to define 'personality' as the totality of individual dispositions, skills, accumulated knowledge, social and cultural norms, values and attitudes, social roles and social status; personality in this sense can be interpreted as a vector with a number of components $(P = p-, p-, p- \dots p-\dots p-)$. These components are more or less latent factors, which become manifest in different compositions in each social situation. Secondly, Roghmann assumes that there will be a feedback process between latent components/factors influencing behavior, in the direction of acquiescence. This model has two advantages: first, the social situation is introduced as a factor, on the same level as the structure and the content of the individual's beliefs; and secondly, the organization of the individual's personality is not contemplated as relatively rigid, but it is implicitly assumed that it can be changed in the course of time.

Figure 1. Feedback pattern between three main factors

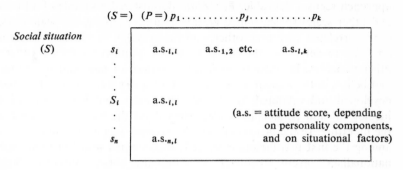

Personality (P)

$(S =)$ $(P =) p_1 \ldots \ldots \ldots \ldots p_j \ldots \ldots \ldots \ldots p_k$

Social situation
(S) s_l a.s.$_{l,l}$ a.s.$_{1,2}$ etc.   a.s.$_{l,k}$

S_i a.s.$_{i,l}$

(a.s. = attitude score, depending on personality components, and on situational factors)

s_n a.s.$_{n,l}$

Figure 2

The implications of this model are clear. Attitude scores deal with only a part of the total number of components/factors – that part of them that can be measured with a number of stimuli called items. Behavior cannot be predicted, because too many components are not known. On the other hand, changes in the attitude scores can be expected if the social situation strongly varies. (This could be operationalized by comparing the scores of the same individuals on the same scales, token in very differing roles, for example at one time in the role of military man, at a second time, as a member of a church or of a political party.)

THE ASSESSMENT OF THE MILITARY MIND

In assessing the military mind, attitudes *and* behavior should be taken into account.

On the 'attitudinal' level of analysis, the explorative studies of *Eckhardt* (*et al.*, 1970) seem to be of importance, and a short summary should be given here. He factoranalyzed scores of sets of attitude items purported to measure a military mind. In one of his first approaches (1967) a review was made of the literature about empirical attitude studies around the topic of 'militarism.' Militarism, defined as the belief in the effectiveness of military deterrence, or the reliance on military strength to defend one's nation and its values, or aggressive foreign policy in general, has been found to be positively correlated with authoritarianism (Adorno's F-scale), conservatism, religiosity, lack of peace responsibility, and even 'neuroticism,' according to Eckhardt.

But in these studies, militarism has been correlated with only one

371

other variable in practically all of the studies as a general rule. A second approach seemed desirable. *Eckhardt* administered a sample of all these and other scales to one single group of subjects. Next, the scale scores were correlated with each other, and the correlation matrix was factor-analysed to determine the extent to which militarism coheres with the other variables, in order to look for a pattern of interrelated attitudes and beliefs in the human mind. At least 59 scales were used (all of them developed and validated by others). The scales contained a variety of ideological and personality scales selected on the basis of a review of the literature. In the factoranalysis, the primary factor of militarism was among the first two factors extracted; it contained scales of militarism, nationalism, severe treatment of criminals, anti-Communism, anti-internationalism, conservatism, anti-democratic attitudes, authoritari-anism, anti-Semitism. The items of these scales were characterized by a readiness to use or threaten to use force and punishment to control behavior of those believed to be deviating from the values of Western adult society (including the Communist 'enemy,' children, Jews, Negroes, foreigners, lowerclass people, sexual deviates, and mental patients). The factor of militarism was correlated with ideological factors of conserva-tism, nationalism, religiosity, lack of internationalism, lack of knowledge of foreign affairs and political cynicism, and with the personality factors of extraversion, misanthropy, faulty childhood disciplines, lack of social responsibility and neuroticism. *Eckhardt* concludes that these scales together can be placed on a basic dimension called 'compulsion-com-passion.' 'Compulsion' is characterized by a general tendency to influence human behavior by restriction and punishment. He himself defines compulsion 'as the readiness to use the force or threat of punishment as a preferred means of controlling human behavior and resolving human conflicts.' Compassion is defined 'as the opposite and pole of this dimen-sion (...) as the readiness to use reason or persuasion as a preferred means of guiding behavior and resolving human conflicts.' He describes the operationalisation of these two concepts as follows: ... 'four major aspects of this dimension have been analyzed: affective, behavioral, cognitive, and ideological. Affectively, compulsion has been operationally defined by higher scores on scales of extraversion, misanthropy (lack of faith in human nature), lack of empathy, neuroticism (lack of selfcon-fidence), family discord, and faulty childhood disciplines (anxious, directive, hypocritical, inconsistent and punitive). Ideologically, com-pulsion has been operationally defined by higher scores on scales of militarism, nationalism, lack of internationalism, religiosity, conservatism, political cynicism and a sense of political inefficacy. Cognitively (...) by higher scores on scales of rigidity and uncertainty of responses, and by lower scores on scales of general curiosity, general information and knowledge of foreign affairs. Behaviorally, compulsion has been operationally defined by known groups of mental patients and normal controls (which have validated most of the affective scales); known groups of reserve officers and ROTC students vs. peace church, peace group and peace research supporters (validating the ideological scales of militarism and nationalism vs. internationalism); known groups of Conservative Party vs. New Democratic (labor, socialist) Party supporters (validating the ideological scales of conservatism); known groups of orthodox church members vs. Quakers, Unitarians, Jews, agnostics and atheists (validating the ideological scales of religiosity); and lower education (validating the cognitive scales of greater uncertainty, lower curiosity, lower information in general, less knowledge of foreign affairs and less flexibility).'

These studies suggest, that it is after all possible to come to generalizations about attitude dimensions that have an empirical base. But then, the same questions arise. What about the validation of all these attitude scales? According to the factor analyses, 60-70 scales used on the same group, fall apart on the dimension compulsion-compassion: and this can be interpreted as a basic distinction of which all other scales are differently labelled variations. Perhaps it is only a question of what label to attach. Clearly such general theories as *Adorno*'s 'Authoritarian Personality' or *Rokeach*'s 'Open vs. Closed Mind,' are distinguished by different labels but in fact, high scores on *Rokeach*'s Dogmatism scale correlate positively with high scores on Authoritarianism, and often *Rokeach*'s D-scale is used as a better version of the older F-scale. In fact, they present perhaps different measures for the same attitude dimension. And what is more, *Eckhardt*'s compulsion-compassion dimension clearly fits into the authoritarianism pattern: it comes in its description close to the definition and operationalisation of the authoritarian personality.

According to *Eckhardt*'s research, it could be assumed that the compulsion-compassion dimension is a basic distinction of which other dimensions are variations. A 'military mind' could be operationally defined as one with a high score on the compulsion side of the scale, and which significantly differs from the scores of the average total population.

Assuming that a significant difference between military and civilian people on a compulsion-compassion dimension as well as on more specific scales exists, this difference should be further investigated on the behavioral level, by comparing it with behavioral output. Behavior too

373

can be observed, analysed and measured; but one remembers what *LaPiere* already wrote in 1934: ... 'The questionnaire is cheap, easy and mechanical. The study of human behavior is time consuming, intellectually fatiguing, and depends for its success upon the ability of the investigator. The former method gives quantitative results, the latter mainly qualitative. Quantitative measurements are quantitatively accurate; qualitative evaluations are always subject to errors of human judgment. Yet it would seem far more worthwhile to make a shrewd guess regarding that which is essential than to accurately measure that which is likely to prove quite irrelevant.'

Two operationalisations of the problem are possible. The first one could be to compare the attitudes with behavior in an experimental set-up, abstracting from all other interfering variables. The second one is to measure the attitude, and to measure the behavior, and to compare them – without abstracting possible interferences from intervening variables, and thereby taking the risk of finding no relation at all. In fact, the choice that is to be made here is one of the main problems for social scientists, for example when they are trying to do relevant research about reality with simulation models.

The data-output of simulations is almost as confusing as that of the real world, the only difference being that in principle, the researcher has access to all these data in the simulated world. But then there are too many relationships, too many intervening variables, and in a way the whole system functions as a kind of blackbox. The input is known, and the output can be analysed; what happened in between seems not accessible to rigid scientific research. Perhaps that is the main reason why researchers often try to abstract from all intervening variables, merely studying the relationship between two isolated factors – but the level of abstraction is possibly negatively correlated with the level of reality. *Rapoport*'s 'Prisoners Dilemma' (1965) gives an example of a study on a high level of abstraction; *Richardson*'s (1960) models of the arms races, on the other hand, can be mentioned as an example of the other extreme, presenting in very simple equations an explanation of a real-world process, with all factors included.

Some kind of 'middle range theories' between the sweeping generalizations on the one hand and the microscopic detail studies on the other, should be developed. If, for example, there is no doubt about the relevance of analysing the military mind and the behavior that corresponds to it, attitudinal studies have to be taken into account – and in my opinion, perhaps the best way to do this is according to the methods developed by *Eckhardt*. But then, the researcher should investigate behavioral data too, and the first thing to do seems to be to develop appropriate measuring techniques. Otherwise, the concept of the 'military mind' stays what it is now: an elegantly formulated folk belief, which describes scientifically what common sense already knows, and which has perhaps no relevance at all for the prediction of the actual behavior.

SUMMARY

The content of this paper can be summarized as follows:
1. The concept of the 'military mind' has been found frequently in the literature, and it seems relevant to investigate its real meaning and relevance by means of empirical validation.
2. On face value, the concept seems already satisfactorily validated, and it is generally accepted that 'the military mind' exists. Difficulties arise when one starts to operationalise the term, and in particular when one asks questions about its implications on the behavioral level. A very common procedure is to operationalize the supposed content of the military mind in the form of statements in an attitude scale, and to compute the scores of military men versus those of civilians; usually, a significant difference is found. But this says nothing about the subsequent behavior (particularly the overt behavior, not the verbal behavior).
3. A brief survey on the theory and research with the attitude concept raises serious doubts about its relevance in general, in particular when one tries to come to grips with the factors that influence behavior. On the other hand, there can be no doubt that the attitude concept is valuable, but one of the main problems is still that of validation. The analyses and theories of *Adorno et al.*, of *Rokeach* and in particular *Eckhardt* seem to indicate that most of the attitude scales measure in fact the same thing, although it may be labelled differently (hard/soft, rigid/flexible, more authoritarian/less authoritarian, more dogmatic/less dogmatic, toughminded/tenderminded, compulsion/compassion, etc.).
4. Therefore ordinary attitude scaling alone is not the appropriate tool in measuring the 'military mind' (or any other mind). Behavioral data should be analysed too. Before one can try to do any relevant research, one should perhaps focus one's attention again on methodological questions, and try to determine and make measurable all of the factors that influence behavior.

REFERENCES

ADORNO, T. W., FRENKEL-BRUNSWIK, E., LEVINSON, D. J., and SANFORD, R. N., *The Authoritarian Personality*. New York, 1950.

BONJEAN, Ch., HILL, R., and McLEMORE, D., *Sociological Measurement*. San Francisco, 1967.

BOSKMA, P., and TROMP, H. W., *A Report on explorative experiments with simulation models of international relations, and the effects of participation.* Paper presented on the IIIrd Conference of the International Peace Research Association (IPRA) at Karlovy Vary, Sept. 1969, to be published in the *Proceedings of IPRA*, Groningen, 1970.

COHEN, A. R., *Attitude Change and Social Influence.* New York, 1964.

DENNEN, J. M. G. VAN DER, *The Rationale of Attitude Measurement*. Mimeographed. Polemological Institute, Groningen, 1970.

ECKHARDT, W., 'The factor of militarism'. *Journal of Peace Research* (Oslo), 1969, 2, 123–133.

ECKHARDT, W., 'Peace Research communication', *Peace Research*, Vol. 1, n. 2, December 1969.

ECKHARDT, W., 'Cross Cultural Conservatism', *Peace Research*, Vol. 2, n. 5, May 1970.

ECKHARDT, W., 'Cross Cultural Militarism', *Peace Research*, Vol. 2, n. 6, June 1970. (*Peace Research, a monthly journal of original research on the problem of war*; a publication of the Canadian Peace Research Institute.)

FISHBEIN, M., 'Attitude and the prediction of behavior'. In M. FISHBEIN (Ed.), *Readings in attitude theory and measurement*. New York, 1967.

FISHBEIN, M., 'The relationship between beliefs, attitudes and behavior'. In S. FELDMAN (Ed.), *Cognitive Consistency*. New York, 1966.

LAPIERE, R. T., Attitudes versus Actions. *Social Forces*, 1934, 13.

LEWIN, K., 'Behavior and development as a function of the total situation'. In: *Field theory in Social Science* (1964).

MILLER, D., *Handbook of Research Design and Social Measurement*. New York, 1964.

HARTMAN, I., *Dogmatism and the Military Mind.* Unpublished Research Report. Polemological Institute, Groningen, 1969.

HÖHN, R., *Die Armee als Erziehungsschule der Nation*. Bad Harzburg, 1963.

JANOWITZ, M., *The professional soldier*. New York, 1960.

KRECH, D., CRUTCHFIELD, R., and BALLACHY, E., *Individual in Society*. McGraw-Hill, 1962.

LYONS, G. M., 'The military mind'. *The Bulletin of the Atomic Scientists*, 1963, 9, 19–22.

McCLOSKY, H., Consensus and Ideology in American Politics. *American Political Science Review*, 1964, 58, 361–382.

MEULEN, E. VAN DER, *The military versus society. A factoranalytical study on differences in the structure of thinking*. Unpublished research report, Polemological Institute, Groningen, 1970.

PET, J., *Effects of simulations on political attitudes of the participants.* Unpublished research report, Polemological Institute, Groningen, 1970.

RAPOPORT, A., and CHAMMAH, A. M., *Prisoners Dilemma, A study in conflict and cooperation*. Ann Arbor, 1965.

RICHARDSON, L. F., *Arms and Insecurity*. Pittsburgh, 1960.

RICHARDSON, L. F., *Statistics of deadly quarrels*. London, 1960.

ROBINSON, J. P., RUSK, J. G., and HEAD, K. B., *Measures of Political Attitudes*. University of Michigan, 1969.

ROGHMANN, K., *Dogmatismus und Autoritarismus*. Meisenheim and Glas, 1966.

ROKEACH, M., *The Open and the Closed Mind.* New York, 1960.

SAPIN, B. M., and SNYDER, R. C., *The Role of the Military in American Foreign Policy.* Garden City, 1954.

SCHEFLEN, A. E., Human Interaction: Behavioral programs and their integration in interaction. *Behavioral Science,* Vol. 13, 1968, 44–54.

SHAW, M. E., and WRIGHT, J., *Scales for the Measurement of Attitudes.* New York, 1967.

THOMSON, M., Militarism 1969, a survey of world trends. *Peace Research Reviews,* Vol. II, 5, 1968.

TRIANDIS, H. C., Exploratory factor analyses of the behavioral component of social attitudes. *Journal of abnormal social psychology,* 1964, 68, 420–430.

WEISSBERG, N. C., On DeFleur and Westie's Attitude as a scientific concept. *Social Forces,* 1965, 43, 422–425.

WICKER, A. W., Attitudes versus Actions: The Relationship of Verbal and Overt Behavioral Responses to Attitude Objects. *Journal of Social Issues,* 1969, XXV, 4, 41–78.

Armed Forces and Ideology

R. NAUTA*

* University of Groningen, department of industrial and social psychology, The Netherlands. At the time of this research affiliated with the Royal Naval College, The Netherlands.

1. INTRODUCTION

'Johnson – murderer' is a slogan that several people consider to be tinged with ideology.

For those who use this characterization it is mostly far from simple to indicate what exactly is specifically 'ideologic' about a certain statement. The use of the term 'ideological' mostly suggests a feeling of uneasiness, originating from a perceptible difference between the representation of a certain state of affairs expressed in a pronouncement and one's own perception of reality.

The discrepancy in the apprehension of reality we mentioned, we do not consider accidental. We suppose – and this is indicated by the use of the word 'ideological' – that the distortion of reality, with which one is confronted, is one-sided and illegitimate: either to the benefit of him, who thinks 'ideologically' or to the detriment of him, who does not agree with the vision embodied in the statement. To him, who does not believe in it, an ideology is menacing and alarming.

The use of the word 'ideological' has a polarizing effect, it tends to a division of the political and social arena into two camps: those, who have got hold of the truth and those who have not.

Now if certain opinions are being characterized as 'ideological,' in many cases a plea in defence of such a definition is a reciprocal charge of the same import. Not I, but he who thinks that I think ideologically, thinks ideologically.

The debate about truth, which in itself does have theological implications, has now reached the level of religious persecution. The vicious circle – within which one is no longer able nor willing to talk sense together – is closed. The two parties mutually accuse one another of presenting a distorted image of reality.

Every accusation addressed to the other is resting on their own (mis)-perception, while they are setting aside the question of what that reality is actually like.

The special field where these problems abound is that of the armed forces. In this article we intend to give an explanation and an adstruction of the dualism, that the soldier acts and thinks ideologically and – on the other hand – the view of the soldier himself, that he is ever more trying to rid himself of ideological clusters and in his behaviour, is ever more guided by pragmatic considerations.

2. IDEOLOGY IN THE ARMED FORCES

Many of those, who have made the Armed Forces the object of their study, call the occupation of a regular officer a profession. This means that one of the characteristics of the occupation is its professional ethics. These ethics govern the relations among the members of the occupational group themselves and the relation between them and the outside world. In the more traditional professions, such as that of officers, professional ethics largely govern the principles of their conduct.

These ethics form a whole complex of norms and rules, both formal and informal, affecting the behaviour of an officer, and with which an officer should comply, if he is to be considered a loyal member of the occupational group.

One part of this complex whole of rules and regulations comprises the political opinions considered characteristic of an officer. It is to this part of professional ethics that Janowitz declares the concept 'ideology' applicable.

With great lucidity the development of a military ideology is described by Morris Janowitz in his book 'The professional soldier.' When Janowitz uses the term 'ideology,' he refers especially to those explicated political views that live within the military establishment.

The changes in the view on organizational authority that occurred during the last 50 years, demand that an officer – both with regard to himself and with respect to others – should be able to answer the question: 'Why do we fight?' An answer to this question presupposes an explicit exposition of the political proposition put forward. Instead of referring to a concept as 'military honour' – an end in itself to which the military exploit, as a matter of course, was a means – some warrant had to be found now, for the views underlying the military exploit. If a concept like 'military honour' does emerge during the argumentation, it is no longer an end, but it merely functions as a means to reach the objective aimed at in the political ideology. The character of the concept 'ideology' as it is being used in this paper, is of a neutral, descriptive nature. It is not the substantial but the formal content, which makes this part of professional ethics conceptually an ideology.

Now when, however, with regard to the military establishment, the concept 'ideology' is used in an evaluative sense, this will not be founded on the structural definition Janowitz gives of the concept, but it will be based on the assumption prevailing about the substantial content of the ideology.

This will particularly be based on a certain view concerning the relation between means and ends within the framework of the military ideology. The typification 'ideological' will be used when identity is assumed between the military means and the politically defined ends. To make this quite clear, we shall once more consider the concept 'military honour.' Military honour traditionally used to be the intrinsic value, characterizing an officer. It used to be an end in itself and military exploit was instrumental in attaining this end. Because of the evolution which – due to an increased interaction between society and armed forces – took place in the soldier's way of thinking, the concept 'military honour' lost its final character, and became a means to attain political ends of a higher order. If, however, the soldier is blamed for thinking and acting ideologically, it is being assumed – for instance in all sorts of definitions of the concept 'military mind' – that the traditional values, which an officer used to uphold, were in themselves maintained as ultimate goals: a view, which the soldier himself – may be, in some cases, from sheer necessity – has discarded. He has come to realize that, in the last resort, it is not up to him to define the political ends of a military action.

The only freedom of action, which – as part of his function, from a political point of view – is left to the military, is to indicate the range of means and any priorities within that range, desirable if the objective is to be attained. Now it is here that within the military establishment there is some divergence. The 'absolutists' know but one means and one end: war and victory; the 'pragmatists,' however, realize that the relation between the means chosen and the ends to be attained is more complicated. Among them, there is the realization that the military means are not only instrumental to the attainment of any given end, but at the same time they may dictate what ends are to be attained.

It is this development towards an increasing degree of pragmatism that is characteristic of the modern armed forces. Within the armed forces the concept 'ideology' is handled as a neutral category, within that structural framework, however, there is a divergence between doctrines, varying according to their content.

The reproach that the armed forces should think and act ideologically, introduces a distinction without a difference; the reproach that in a special way – characterized according to their content – they should behave in a doctrinaire way, opens up possibilities for a significant debate.

3. AN ALTERNATIVE DEFINITION OF THE CONCEPT 'IDEOLOGY'

In his article 'Ideology as a Cultural System' Clifford Geertz defines the function of an ideology as the satisfaction of a need for authoritative concepts, 'which render meaningful the otherwise incomprehensible social situation.' It is the literary style as a vehicle of ideology, which gives an ideology its ideology characteristics. The literary style has the capacity to grasp, formulate and communicate social realities that elude the tempered language of science. It is the use of words and sentences in a specific way which gives these words, otherwise neutral, their ideological colour.

This style is, for instance, characterized by the use of the metaphor: 'it asserts one thing that is something else. And worse even, it tends to be most effective when it is most wrong. The power of a metaphor – and also of other phenomena – derives precisely from the interplay between the discordant meanings it symbolically coerces into a unitary framework and from the degree to which the coercion is successful in overcoming the psychic resistance such semantic tension inevitably generates in anyone in a position to perceive it. When it works a metaphor transforms a false knowledge into an apt analogy; when it misfires it is mere extravagance.'

Characteristic of the ideologic style is the appeal made to the listener to accept authority. In some cases, rejection of this appeal will only be possible by appealing to an other, possibly an opposing authority. Herewith a start is made with an explanation of the vicious circle, where discussions are characterized by criminations and recriminations of taking up ideologic positions: it is the contrast between two equally strong but antagonistic demands for authority.

In this connection it should be remarked that the word 'ideology' itself fits into the category of authoritative concepts, which is characteristic of the ideologic idiom.

After further analysis, the accusatory character of the word ideology, when used in connection with the armed forces, appears to be related to the relation between the demand for authority and ideology, described earlier in this paragraph.

The evaluative aspects of the word ideology seem to be based on the supposed authoritative manner – using authoritative concepts – in which the military establishment justifies the place of the armed forces in the larger unit of society. A negative appreciation of this justification then leads to the accusation that the soldier handles certain views in an ideological way.

4. AN ADSTRUCTION OF THE PROBLEMS

In order to be able to give a more quantitative indication besides a qualitative consideration of the problems, we looked for a possibility for

384

the operationalisation of the concept 'ideology.' Sartori assumes that ideology (or ideologism, if one stresses the functional aspects of the ideology) is related to the symbolic orientation by which individuals orient themselves and navigate in the political and social field. Ideology says something about the way how one believes – it is related to the structure of the belief-system. Ideologism is linked with the degree to which one relies on authority for information; especially to the way these authorities are selected and how the instructions emanating from these authorities are assessed.

Likewise it may be said that the use of the term ideology necessarily implies that there is a falsifiable definition of the term, because only then is there a notion of ideology that is of explanatory value. Therefore, according to Sartori, we should distinguish between ideology and pragmatism. Both terms act as opposite poles on a continuum ranging between absolute and conditional acceptance of authority.

This also links up with an other pair of concepts belonging to social psychology: the open and the closed mind. Rokeach also uses the dependence on authority as one of his measures to differentiate an open and closed cognitive system. A more operational description of the contrast between ideology and pragmatism can now be found with the help of the dogmatism scale.

The central question during the more field-directed research was the one after the accuracy of the statement that the soldiers think and act ideologically. Or better formulated: to find out wether soldiers think ideologically to a greater extent than any other group of civilians. This, irrespective of possible suppositions with regard to the reason of that ideologic thinking, by using the concepts 'ideologism' and 'pragmatism' as operationalized by us. By introducing the concept 'pragmatism,' we can also give a positive answer concerning the view of the soldier himself that the structure of his thinking and his method of problem-solving is to an ever higher degree pragmatically orientated.

Two groups of students took part in the research: naval cadets from the Royal Naval College at Den Helder and pupils of a Teachers' Training College of the same town. With respect to various aspects, the comparability of the two groups could be ascertained:

a) *Age*, b) *kind of training:* both groups consisted of pupils of an advanced vocational training college, c) *kind of occupation:* both professions are, by nature – either intentionally or unintentionally – comparatively authoritarian, d) *identification with their future career:* with regard to the members of both groups applies that, owing to changes in their training and their probable careers, role-identification with the present holders of office

385

in the profession is less uniform and clear. The difference between the two groups lies in the culture and content of their respective training, in the different nature of the future profession of their members and the scope this offers.

The groups were being compared with respect to their answers to various attitude-scales. The attitude-scales used, were scales to measure dogmatism as a structural variable; and to measure bureaucracy, social orientation, political conservatism, militarism and preference for a certain social constellation – the so-called order-scale – as content variables. All the scales except the one that tries to measure preference for a certain social order, were found in the available literature. The fairly wide selection-criterion for the choice of the scales was the possible connection with the usual descriptions of the attitude-system, characterizing the soldier. Besides these scales, some items from a research by Hartman were included, which pretended to be an operationalization of Huntington's description of the concept 'military mind.' In Hartman's research, these items showed a difference in answering between military and non-military groups.

Concerning the so-called 'order'-scale, we assumed that the concept 'order' would form the core of all other attitudes.

All items were scored on a six-point-scale, running from 6 = agree most emphatically to 1 = disagree most emphatically. A high score means: dogmatic, bureaucratic, negative view of human nature, conservative, pro status quo in the social order. A higher score on the Huntington-items signifies cordial agreement with the values incorporated in the 'military mind.'

The expectation was that the group of naval cadets should score higher on both the structural variable (the dogmatism-scale) and on the content variables.

The results of the research are printed below.

Average group totals

	Dogmatism	Content	Social Order	Military Mind
Naval Cadets	73.0	165.4	44.5	23.1
Pupil-Teachers	75.4	124.9	39.5	13.7
Naval Cadets	$n = 40$	Dogmatism-scale	n items = 24	
Pupil-Teachers	$n = 33$	Content scales	n items = 43	
		Social order-scale	n items = 10	
		Military mind	n items = 6	

Between the two groups there is no difference in ideological style. Both are equally ideologic.

There is no reason to suppose that the military group is more pragmatically or ideologically biassed, compared with the civilian group. It should be remarked here, that this is a relative pronouncement; to be able to account for a development towards a less ideologic position, we should have made a comparison between various military groups in various stages of training and career, or we should have followed up this research by conducting a longitudinal research among this group of naval cadets. The difference between the two groups lies in the more substantial part of the belief system. There is a marked difference, both for all the content variables together and for these variables separately, between the military group and the group of teachers. The military group is more conservative, has a negative view of human nature, is more militaristic, more bureaucratic, but is not orientated more ideologically or pragmatically than the group of teachers. It is also striking that the group of naval cadets and the group of pupil-teachers should differ in their acceptances of the status quo, albeit that the scores of the two groups point in the same direction on the continuum of acceptance versus rejection.

If one were to name the difference between the two groups, the term 'ideologic' is – to say the least – unfortunate. It would be better to call the differences one finds after the nature of the object, that is to say: more conservative, more pessimistic, more bureaucratic etc., without, however, following them up with the immediate conclusion that the opinions, because they are more conservative etc., will also be more tinged with ideology. On the contrary – from the above results we may simply infer that the pupil-teachers are as ideologic as the group of naval-cadets, albeit that the content of their views is contradictory. The discussion between the two groups – or, to put it in a more general way: between the two positions – is not hampered by substantial differences, but is hampered because they both refer to a different authority. On the ground of this different orientation, a material difference is regarded as an attack on the authority towards which one had directed oneself, and consequently as an attack on the entire belief-system connected with it. When we look at the military variables, the contrast between the two groups increases even more, and referring to the contrast between the views of 'armers' and 'disarmers,' which Niezing indicates, it becomes possible to sketch a similar conflict: 'the ideologies at both ends render any debate useless.'

The problems concerning the impossible discussion were clearly shown during an evaluation at the end of an inter-nation simulation at the Royal Naval College. Participants in this simulation were naval officers and

387

naval cadets and some members of the above-mentioned group of pupil-teachers. During the evaluation one of the pupil-teachers remarked that the results of the simulation corresponded with his originally negative expectations concerning the behaviour of the soldiers, because the soldiers – by declaring war – showed a warlike instead of a peaceable spirit; a remark that caused general hilarity among the group of soldiers. They too were convinced by this remark, of the accuracy of their original expectations with regard to the views of this category of pupil-teachers: the remark as such did not, therefore, require any further serious comment.

When we consider the military sub-groups separately, we arrive at the following results:

Average group totals by branch

	Dogmatism	Content	Social Order	Military Mind
Nautical Branch	71.5	166.2	44.7	24.2
Technical Branch	72.3	153.0	41.5	18.6
Electrotechnical Branch	76.5	167.3	45.7	22.8
Administrative Branch	74.1	168.1	44.1	24.0
	74.1	162.2	43.6	25.4

Nautical Branch	$n = 19$
Technical Branch	$n = 8$
Electrotechnical Branch	$n = 6$
Administrative Branch	$n = 7$
$T+E+A$	$n = 21$

From a historical point of view, the most tradition orientated branch of service is the nautical branch of service. The technical, electrotechnical and administrative branches of service are being more and more affected by external professional models, on account of which their military loyalty gets a conditional character. Is there among these variously orientated branches of service – one might be apt to wonder – a marked discrepancy with respect to the values relevant to the military profession? It appears that in relation to the externally orientated branches of service, the nautical branch of service is least dogmatically – consequently most pragmatically orientated.

As far as the more substantial attitudes are concerned, differences in an opposite direction occur: here it is the nautical branch of service that is most conservative, most pro status quo, representing most clearly the military values – albeit that the differences observed are slight. Remarkable is the not very stable position of the technically orientated branches of service. On the one hand, the technical branch of service is the most progressive, on the other hand the electrotechnical branch of service is more conservative and most dogmatic (i.e. more ideologically orientated). The difference between the technical and electrotechnical branch of service resembles the controversy about the role of the technical officer, analyzed by Kolkowicz. It seems that his pronouncement, that the technical officer is more progressive and more pragmatic, is not altogether borne out by the results of our research. Remarks by Russian officers about the phenomenon that the technical officer should exactly be dogmatic and narrowminded, do not seem to be exclusively relevant to the situation in the USSR: On the one hand, the officer with a technical profession is more progressive than his more purely military orientated colleagues. On the other hand, this more technically orientated officer wants to be accepted by the so-called 'traditionalists' in the army, whose values and virtues he has come (or: been compelled) to appreciate. In order to reduce the conflict between the two orientations, some of these officers become 'plus royaliste que le roi' (more loyal than the king) and they embrace the traditional values in a more rigid and ideological way. Regarding our original expectations that preference for a certain way of social order should form the core of the belief-system, a cluster-analysis showed that this expectation could only be confirmed by the group of pupil-teachers. In the military group, the concept 'social order' was found in one cluster with the concept 'authority' from the dogmatism-scale, so that we may take it that for the soldier, his views concerning the desired social order have an ideologic character and function rather as a structural variable than as a substantially modified variable.

The results of the research described above, served to indicate the problems arising when the word 'ideologic' is being used in a nonchalant, nay in an 'ideological' way. The additional theory served to create a framework, within which the use of the word 'ideologic' may be better understood. It might be said that a study of the word 'ideologic' implies an analysis of the meta-ideology of ideology. An attempt hereto has been made. However, concluding with one of Alfred Adler's favourite maxims: 'Alles kann auch anders sein' (But after all, everything may just as well be quite different).

REFERENCES

GEERTZ, C., 'Ideology as a cultural system,' in D. E. APTER (ed.), *Ideology and Discontent*, The Free Press. New York, 1964, pp. 47–76.

HARTMAN, J., *Dogmatisme en 'Military Mind,'* Rijksuniversiteit Groningen, 1969.

HOOGERWERF, A., 'Depolitisering en ontideologisering: een theoretische analyse,' *Acta Politica*, 1965, pp. 21–35.

JANOWITZ, M., *The Professional Soldier*, The Free Press, New York, 1960.

KOLKOWICZ, R., *The impact of modern technology on the Soviet officer corps*, Paper 6th World Congress of Sociology, 1966.

LA PALANBARA, I., 'Decline of ideology,' a dissent and an interpretation, *The American Political Science Review*, 1966, LX, 1, pp. 1–16.

MERELMAN, R. M. 'The development of political socialisation,' *The American Political Science Review*, 1969, LXIII, 3, pp. 750–767.

NIEZING, J., 'Armers and disarmers, a false dichotomy reconsidered,' in J. NIEZING, *Sociology, War and Disarmament*, Universitaire Pers Rotterdam, 1970, pp. 15–27.

OSGOOD, Ch. E., 'Conservative words and radical sentences in the semantics of international politics,' in R. JUNGK and J. GALTUNG (eds.), *Mankind 2000*, London, 1969, pp. 54–65.

ROKEACH, M., *The Open and Closed Mind*, Basic Books Inc., New York, 1960.

SARTORI, G., 'Politics, ideology and belief system,' *The American Political Science Review*, 1969, LXIII, 2, pp. 1–40.